The **Redesigned SAT** & PSAT Course Book

Reading, Writing & Language
and Essay

SUMMIT
EDUCATIONAL
GROUP

Focusing on the Individual Student

Copyright Statement

The Redesigned SAT & PSAT Course Book, along with all Summit Educational Group Course Materials, is protected by copyright. Under no circumstances may any Summit materials be reproduced, distributed, published, or licensed by any means.

Summit Educational Group reserves the right to refuse to sell materials to any individual, school, district, or organization that fails to comply with our copyright policies.

Third party materials used to supplement Summit Course Materials are subject to copyright protection vested in their respective publishers. These materials are likewise not reproducible under any circumstances.

Ownership of Trademarks

Summit Educational Group is the owner of the trademarks "Summit Educational Group" and the pictured Summit logo, as well as other marks that the Company may seek to use and protect from time to time in the ordinary course of business.

SAT is a trademark of the College Board.
PSAT is a trademark jointly owned by the College Board and the National Merit Scholarship.

All other trademarks referenced are the property of their respective owners.

CONTENTS

WRITING AND LANGUAGE OVERVIEW

WRITING AND LANGUAGE

ESSAY

Preface

Since 1988, when two Yale University graduates started Summit Educational Group, tens of thousands of students have benefited from Summit's innovative, comprehensive, and highly effective test preparation. You will, too.

Successful test-takers not only possess the necessary academic skills but also understand how to take the SAT. Through your SAT program, you'll learn both. You'll review and develop the academic skills you need, and you'll learn practical, powerful and up-to-date test-taking strategies.

The *Summit Redesigned SAT & PSAT Course Book* provides the skills, strategies, and practice necessary for success on the SAT. The result of much research and revision, this book is the most effective, innovative, and comprehensive preparation tool available.

This book's first chapter – Test-Taking Fundamentals – and the overview chapters give students a solid foundation of SAT information and general test-taking strategies. The following chapters cover the verbal content strands of the SAT – Reading, Writing and Language, and the Essay. Each chapter is divided into manageable topic modules. Modules consist of the skills, strategies, and common question types for particular topics, *Try It Out* questions, and *Put It Together* questions. At the end of each chapter, homework questions provide additional practice.

We are confident that you will not find a more complete or effective SAT program anywhere.

We value your feedback and are always striving to improve our materials. Please write to us with comments, questions, or suggestions for future editions at:

> edits@mytutor.com

Your program will give you the skills, knowledge, and confidence you need to score your best.

Good luck, and have fun!

Chapter Summaries

We've reproduced the Chapter Summaries below to give you a preview of what you'll be covering. The Summaries are meant to serve as quick, condensed reference guides to the most important concepts. Obviously, you can't bring them into the test with you, but from now up until the night before the test, use them to preview and review the material covered in this book. Of course, Chapter Summaries also reside at the end of each chapter.

General Test-Taking Summary

❑ Don't read the questions before you read the passage.

❑ Don't skim the passage.

❑ Use the Two-Pass Approach for each passage.

❑ Focus on one question at a time.

Reading Summary

Reading the Passages

☐ As you are reading and analyzing a passage, acknowledge the role of the writer. Try to determine the writer's opinion on the passage's topic. Ask yourself: Why did the writer choose to write the passage as he or she did?

☐ **Stay engaged**. Do not read passively, waiting for the passage to reveal information to you. Instead, interact directly with the passage and think about what the author is saying or trying to convey.

☐ **Map the Passage**. Develop an organized understanding of a Reading passage by finding the main idea of each paragraph.

☐ Treat paired passages as two separate passages.

1. Read the first passage and answer the questions for it.

2. Read the second passage and answer the questions for it.

3. Answer the questions that concern both passages.

Answering the Questions

☐ Ask questions while you read.

☐ Understand the question before you look at the answer choices.

☐ Make sure that you've found the **best** answer, not just a good one. Reading questions, especially difficult ones, will usually contain at least one or two choices that are "almost right."

Writing and Language Summary

Pronouns

- ❑ **Pronoun Agreement** – A pronoun must agree with the noun it refers to in number, gender, and person. Similarly, nouns that relate to the same thing must agree in number.

- ❑ **Ambiguous Pronouns** – A pronoun must clearly refer back to the noun or nouns it represents. If there is no antecedent or more than one possible antecedent, the pronoun is ambiguous.

- ❑ **Compound Phrase** – To check for the proper form in a compound phrase, remove the rest of the group.

- ❑ **Pronoun Case** – In order to determine whether a pronoun is a subject or object, try plugging in an easier pronoun (such as "he/him") and see which works best.

    A pronoun that follows a preposition requires the objective case and not the subjective case. The pronoun "who" always refers to the subject. The pronoun "whom" always refers to an object.

- ❑ **Relative Pronouns** - Don't use *that* or *which* when referring to people. People are always *who* or *whom*.

- ❑ **Its vs It's** – "It's" is always a contraction of "it is." Likewise, "its" is always a possessive pronoun. Similarly, "they're" is a contraction of "they are," and "their" is a possessive pronoun. "You're" is a contraction of "you are," and "your" is a possessive pronoun.

- ❑ **One and You** – Pronouns *one* and *you* are not interchangeable. Whichever of these pronouns is being used must be carried throughout the sentence.

Subject-Verb Agreement

- ❑ Singular subjects require singular verbs, and plural subjects require plural verbs.

- ❑ **Ignore the Extras** – To simplify sentences, remove all extra information between the subject and the verb. Then, make sure the subject and verb agree.

- ❑ **Compound Subjects** – Subjects grouped by "and" are plural, even if the "and" joins two singular words.

- ❑ **Delayed Subject** – When the subject follows the verb, flip the sentence to put the subject first.

- ❑ **Indefinite Pronouns** – Pronouns containing "one," "body," or "thing" are singular.

Comparisons

❑ Make sure that comparisons are logical and parallel. The same types of ideas should be compared to each other.

❑ When comparing someone (or something) to a group that she is a part of, you can't just compare her to the whole group. Remember to use "other," comparing her to the rest of the group, not to herself.

❑ Use the comparative form of an adjective to compare two things. Comparative forms add either "-er" or are preceded by "more." (e.g., quicker, more courageous)
Use the superlative form of an adjective to compare three or more things. Superlative forms add either "-est" or are preceded by "most." (e.g., quickest, most courageous)

Idioms

❑ The idiom questions on the SAT will often involve prepositions. Make sure the correct preposition is being used.

Diction

❑ Diction is the choice of words used. Many English words are commonly misused in casual conversation, so make sure you understand the proper ways to use them.

Fragments

❑ **Where's the Verb?** – A verb ending in *ing* is not a complete verb. An *ing* verb creates a fragment if the sentence does not include another, complete verb.

❑ **Relative Pronouns** – Be careful with relative pronouns, such as *who, which,* and *that.* They may create incomplete ideas by changing how the action of the sentence relates to the subject.

Run-ons

❑ Run-on sentences result when multiple independent clauses are improperly joined. You can correct run-ons in a variety of ways, including the three below:
1. Add a period and create two sentences.
2. Add a comma and a conjunction.
3. Use a semicolon.

❑ **Comma Splice** – When two independent clauses are joined with a comma but without a conjunction, this mistake is called a comma splice. Fix a comma splice by adding a semicolon, a period, or a comma and a conjunction.

❑ **Relative Pronouns** – Some run-on sentences are best fixed with the addition of relative pronouns, such as *who, which,* and *that.*

Conjunctions

- ❑ **Coordinating Conjunctions** – The most common conjunctions can be remembered with the acronym FANBOYS: *for, and, nor, but, or, yet,* and *so.*

- ❑ **Subordinating Conjunctions** – Certain conjunctions can be used at the beginning of dependent clauses. These include *although, because, before, since, unless, until, whereas, whether, which,* and *while.*

- ❑ **Paired Conjunctions** – Certain conjunctions are used to connect two paired ideas. Use proper phrasing with paired conjunctions.

Parallelism

- ❑ Sentence elements and ideas that are alike in function should also be the same in grammatical form so that they are "parallel."

- ❑ **Lists** – Use parallel structure with elements in a list or in a series.

- ❑ **Paired Conjunctions** – Conjunctions used in pairs (e.g., not only... but also, both... and, either... or, neither... nor) require that the words following each conjunction be parallel.

- ❑ **Comparisons** – Use parallel structure with elements being compared.

Modifiers

- ❑ **Faulty Modification** – Modifiers should be placed next to what they modify. Misplaced modifiers create ambiguity or cause a change in meaning.

- ❑ **Dangling Modifier** – Check for modifying phrases that appear at the beginning of a sentence and ask who or what is being modified. The subject that directly follows the modifier should be what the modifier describes.

Verb Tense

- ❑ Verb tenses should remain consistent unless the sentence indicates a change in time.

- ❑ **Has or Had** – The most challenging verb tense questions typically require an understanding of the difference between past, past perfect, and present perfect tenses.

Semicolons

❑ Semicolons, like periods, are used to link two independent clauses. A semicolon indicates that two ideas are related. Semicolons and periods are usually interchangeable.

❑ **Run-Ons** – Use semicolons to fix comma splices and other run-on errors.

❑ **Misused Semicolons** – Be on the lookout for semicolons that are used with conjunctions or where commas or colons should be used.

Colons

❑ **Before the Colon** – Colons should be used only at the end of a complete sentence.

❑ **After the Colon** – Colons are most commonly used to introduce lists, but they may also be used to present information that clarifies or elaborates on the independent clause.

Commas

❑ **Scene Setters** – If a sentence begins with a phrase that sets time, place, or purpose, then the phrase should be followed by a comma.

❑ **Independent Clauses and Conjunctions** – When two independent clauses are joined by a conjunction, there should be a comma placed before the conjunction.

❑ **Nonrestrictive Clauses** – Clauses that provide nonessential information about a subject are offset by commas. Nonessential clauses can also be offset by parentheses or dashes.

When a name is paired with an identifier, carefully consider whether the name or the identifier provides information essential to understanding the reference.

❑ **Series** – Commas separate items in a list.

Apostrophes

❑ **Singular Possessive** – When the possessor is a singular noun, possession can be indicated by adding '*s*.

❑ **Plural Possessive** – When the possessor is a plural noun ending in *s*, possession can be indicated by adding an apostrophe. Plural nouns that do not end in *s* can be made possessive by adding '*s*.

❑ **Pronouns** – Pronouns do not require apostrophes to indicate possession. Rather, pronouns have their own possessive forms.
There is one exception to this rule: the possessive form of the indefinite pronoun *one* requires an apostrophe.

Main Idea

❑ **Stay on Point** - Every portion of a passage should contribute to the main idea. Do not choose to include a detail just because it is related to the general topic of the passage.

Addition

❑ **The Right Place** – Added sentences must logically connect to the sentences around them.

❑ **Relevance** – Added sentences must be relevant to the focus of passage and should support and strengthen the passage's ideas.

Deletion

❑ **Cut the Excess** – Sentences should be deleted if they are not relevant to the focus of the passage or do not support and strengthen the passage's ideas.

Organization

❑ **Get in Order** – When organized properly, an essay's ideas should build upon each other and transition naturally.

Transitions

❑ Transitions show whether one idea contrasts, supports, or causes another.

❑ **Connect Ideas** – Pay attention to the ideas that come before and after a transition.

Wordiness

❑ **Avoid redundancy** – Eliminate details that are unnecessarily repeated. Look out for synonyms that do not add new information.

❑ **Get to the Point** – Eliminate stalling or unnecessary phrases.

Style

❑ **Word Choice** – When choosing between synonyms, carefully consider the exact meaning of each word in the context of the passage. You will often need to know the main idea of the passage in order to understand the writer's intended meaning of a word.

❑ **Tone** – Make sure the language of passages is consistent in tone. Avoid language that is too complex or too informal.

Data Graphics

❑ **Accuracy** – Information in the passage must accurately reflect the data in the graphic.

❑ **Relevance** – Information in the passage must be relevant to the main idea.

Essay Summary

- ❑ **Do not attempt to start writing before you read the article**. A skilled response to the SAT essay assignment depends on a thorough understanding of the source text, so you must read the article before you attempt to write an essay about it.

- ❑ During your second reading of the article, you're looking for *how* the author makes the argument.

- ❑ Once you have assessed the effectiveness of the author's arguments, write a thesis based on your judgment, and expand it to create an outline.

  Your central claim should not be your opinion on the issue, but your judgment of the author's overall persuasiveness throughout the source text.

- ❑ Using your outline as a guide, spend at least half of the allotted time to write a response to the source text. Refer back to your notes on the article early and often.

- ❑ Give yourself a couple minutes to clean up spelling and punctuation errors. Don't erase! It takes too much time. Cross out mistakes and rewrite as necessary.

Assessment and Objectives Worksheet

Complete this worksheet after the first session and refer back to it often. Amend it as necessary. It should act as a guide for how you and your tutor approach the program as a whole and how your sessions are structured.

The assessment will come from information that you and your parent(s) provide and from your initial diagnostic test. Keep in mind that you know yourself better than anyone else. Please be honest and open when answering the questions.

Student's Self-Assessment and Parent Assessment

- How do you feel about taking standardized tests? Consider your confidence and anxiety levels.

- Work through Table of Contents. Are there particular areas that stand out as areas for development?

- Other Concerns

Diagnostic Test Assessment

- Pacing

  o Did you run out of time on any or all sections? Did you feel rushed? Look for skipped questions or wrong answers toward the end of sections.

  o How will the concept of Setting Your Goal help you?

- Carelessness

  o Do you feel that carelessness is an issue? Look for wrong answers on easy questions.

  o Why do you think you make careless mistakes? Rushing? Not checking? Not reading the question carefully? Knowing "why" will allow you to attack the problem.

- Are certain areas for development evident from the diagnostic? Work through the questions you got wrong to further identify areas that might require attention.

Initial Score Goals

Note that score goals should be adjusted as necessary through the program.

Overall Goal: _____   Reading and Writing Goal: _____

Math Goal: _____   Essay Goal: _____

Program Objectives

Consider your assessment, and define your objectives. Make your objectives concrete and achievable.

Objective*	How to Achieve the Objective

*Sample Objectives

Objective	How to Achieve the Objective
Reduce carelessness by 75%.	Before starting to work on a question, repeat exactly what the question is asking.
Use Active Reading skills to avoid losing focus while reading passages.	Practice reading skills every day. Read novels or magazines at an appropriate reading level. Ask questions and engage the text while you read.
Reduce test anxiety.	Build confidence and create a detailed testing plan. Start with easier questions to build confidence and slowly build toward more challenging questions. Take pride in successes and continue to reach for goals. Try to relax.
Learn how to fully develop an essay example with specific details.	Show models of well-developed sample paragraphs. Develop paragraphs with tutor. Learn effective language for analyzing arguments.
Get excited about the test prep.	Stay positive. Know that score goals can be achieved. Learn tricks to beat the test. Make the test like a game. Focus on progress.

SUMMIT
EDUCATIONAL
GROUP

Test-Taking Fundamentals

- ❑ About the SAT
- ❑ Your SAT Program
- ❑ Your Commitment
- ❑ PSAT and SAT Test Structure

Introduction

Welcome! You are about to embark on a course that will empower you to reach your highest potential on the SAT.

About the SAT

What does the SAT measure? According to the College Board, it is a test of how well you've mastered important knowledge and skills in three key areas: reading, writing, and math. The College Board also says that an SAT score predicts how well you are likely to do in college and career. We feel that, to some extent, the SAT is a measure of how good you are at taking standardized tests. Either way, the SAT is an important element in the college admissions process.

Your SAT Program

Over the course of this program, you are going to learn to master the SAT by developing your test-taking abilities, working on fundamental SAT skills, and practicing with real SAT questions.

❏ Develop test-taking strategies.

Your instructor will emphasize both general test-taking strategies and problem-specific strategies. You will practice these techniques in session, during homework, and on practice tests. Our strategies make the SAT less intimidating and more like a challenging game.

❏ Build a strong foundation of skills.

You might need to review and practice skills in one or more topics that appear on the test. You might just be rusty, or the topic might be unfamiliar to you. Your diagnostic test, along with ongoing assessment, will uncover your areas for development. Over the course of your program, you and your tutor will work to strengthen these areas.

❏ Learn to recognize SAT question types.

While the SAT doesn't repeat exact questions from one test to another, it does repeat question types. After all, it's a <u>standardized</u> test. To help you become familiar with SAT question types and topics, you will work almost entirely with SAT-style questions. The ability to recognize question types allows you to be a proactive, rather than reactive, test-taker. You'll learn to see a question, recognize the topic and type, and immediately know what techniques and strategies to apply in order to solve it.

❑ Take practice tests under timed, real conditions.

Much like a scrimmage or a dress rehearsal, taking practice tests under realistic conditions removes the mystery of the test, helps reduce test anxiety, and increases your confidence. The experience of taking a practice test, combined with a thorough analysis and review of the test, forms the core of any successful test preparation program. We strongly recommend that you take 2 to 4 proctored practice tests during the course of your test prep program. Your tutor can help you schedule these.

❑ Review and rework the questions you get wrong, repeatedly.

This is the most powerful and simple tip for improving your SAT score. After a test is scored or a homework set is graded, it's natural to focus on the result and allow that score to dictate how you feel about yourself. Change this tendency, and instead view the test for what it is – feedback. What can I learn from this test? How can I use this test to improve? Dive into the test and focus on the questions you got wrong. For each question, note the question topic and type and work on the question until you can solve it. Don't just look at it and say, "Oh yeah, I know how to do that." Write out the solution. You'll learn it better.

But once is not enough! Review and rework these same questions again and again until you've mastered them. Make it part of every homework assignment. This process ensures that you're constantly reviewing and learning those topics and question types that are giving you trouble – a surefire path to a higher score.

Additionally, keep a notebook of techniques, rules, and formulas that are tripping you up. Review this list regularly.

Your Commitment

Your commitment to the program will determine how much you get out of it. Your instructor has made a commitment to your success on the SAT, and you need to make a commitment to helping yourself.

❑ Attend all sessions.

❑ Pay attention during sessions.

❑ Ask questions when you don't understand something.

❑ Complete all homework assignments.

❑ Take full-length, proctored practice tests.

PSAT and SAT Test Structure

The SAT is made up of four tests: Reading, Writing and Language, Math, and the Essay (which is optional). The Math Test is divided into two sections, one that allows a calculator and one that doesn't.

	PSAT	SAT

Format	4 Sections
	• 1 Reading
	• 1 Writing and Language
	• 2 Math
	  - 1 No-Calculator Section
	  - 1 Calculator Section
		5 Sections (with essay)
		• 1 Reading
		• 1 Writing and Language
		• 2 Math
		  - 1 No-Calculator Section
		  - 1 Calculator Section
		• 1 Essay (optional)

Reading	60 minutes, 47 questions 5 passages Content: • Information and Ideas • Rhetoric • Synthesis	65 minutes, 52 questions 5 passages Content: • Information and Ideas • Rhetoric • Synthesis
Writing and Language	35 minutes, 44 questions 4 passages Content: • Expression of Ideas • Standard English Conventions	35 minutes, 44 questions 4 passages Content: • Expression of Ideas • Standard English Conventions
Math	70 minutes, 48 questions Content: • Problem-Solving & Data Analysis • Heart of Algebra • Passport to Advanced Math • Additional Topics in Math	80 minutes, 58 questions Content: • Problem-Solving & Data Analysis • Heart of Algebra • Passport to Advanced Math • Additional Topics in Math
Essay	No Essay	50 minutes, 1 prompt
Scoring	Evidence-Based Reading and Writing: 160-760 Math: 160-760	Evidence-Based Reading and Writing: 200-800 Math: 200-800 Essay: 6-24
Time	2 hours, 45 minutes	3 hours, 50 minutes (with essay)

Reading Overview

- ❑ The SAT Reading Test

- ❑ The PSAT Reading Test

- ❑ Test Structure

- ❑ Scoring and Scaling

- ❑ Setting Your Goal

- ❑ The Instructions

- ❑ Working Through the Reading Test

The SAT Reading Test

❑ The SAT Reading Test measures your skills in reading, comprehending, and analyzing 500-750-word passages. You've likely been practicing most of these skills on school assignments for years.

Format	52 questions 5 passages multiple-choice
Content	Information and Ideas Rhetoric Synthesis
Scoring	Evidence-Based Reading and Writing score: 200-800 　　　Reading Test score: 10-40
Time	65 minutes

❑ Reading Test questions divide into three content areas:

Content Area	Sample Topics
Information and Ideas	reading closely, citing textual evidence, determining central ideas and themes, summarizing, understanding relationships, and interpreting words and phrases in context
Rhetoric	analyzing word choice, text structure, point of view, purpose, and arguments
Synthesis	analyzing multiple texts and quantitative information

The PSAT Reading Test

❑ The PSAT Reading Test contains 5 passages with a total of 47 questions.

Format	47 questions 5 passages multiple-choice
Content	Information and Ideas Rhetoric Synthesis
Scoring	Evidence-Based Reading and Writing score: 160-760 Reading Test score: 8-38
Time	60 minutes

❑ The PSAT and SAT are scored on vertically aligned scales. This means, for instance, that a student scoring 550 on the PSAT is demonstrating the same level of achievement as a student scoring 550 on the SAT. It does <u>not</u> mean that the same student is predicted to score a 550 on the SAT. The PSAT is reported on a slightly lower scale (160-760), reflecting the fact that the exams test the same body of skills, but at age-appropriate levels.

Test Structure

☐ Questions generally follow the order of the passage, but do not progress from easy to difficult.

65 Minutes

MULTIPLE-CHOICE																				
Passage 1										Passage 2										
1	2	3	4	5	6	7	8	9	10	11	12	13	14	15	16	17	18	19	20	21
NOT IN ORDER OF DIFFICULTY																				

MULTIPLE-CHOICE																				
Passage 3											Passage 4									
22	23	24	25	26	27	28	29	30	31	32	33	34	35	36	37	38	39	40	41	42
NOT IN ORDER OF DIFFICULTY																				

MULTIPLE-CHOICE										
Passage 5										
43	44	45	46	47	48	49	50	51	52	
NOT IN ORDER OF DIFFICULTY										

> **The number of questions for each Reading passage varies from 10-11.**

☐ The Reading Test contains 5 passages with 10-11 questions each. You have an average of 13 minutes to spend on each passage – about 5 minutes to read the passage and 45 seconds to answer each question.

The passages range in complexity from grades 9-10 to college-level.

☐ Each test includes passages in the following content areas:

• 1 U.S. and World Literature passage per test.

These passages are selected from classic and contemporary literary works.

• 2 History/Social Studies passages per test.

These passages are selected from portions of United States founding documents and "Great Global Conversation" texts (historically important texts on civic and political life).

• 2 Science passages per test.

These passages are selected from accounts of historical discoveries and summaries of recent developments in Earth science, chemistry, physics, and biology.

Scoring and Scaling

You'll receive an Evidence-Based Reading & Writing section score from 200-800, a Reading Test score from 10-40, and subscores in Words in Context and Command of Evidence. The subscores will be reported on a 1-15 scale. Some of the questions will also count toward one of the two cross-test subscores called Analysis in Science and Analysis in History/Social Studies. College admissions offices will care most about the Evidence-Based Reading & Writing section score.

1 Total Score (400-1600 scale)	SAT		
2 Section Scores (200-800 scale)	Evidence-Based Reading & Writing		Math
3 Test Scores (10-40 scale)	Reading	Writing & Language	Math
2 Cross-Test Scores (10-40 scale)	Analysis in Science		
	Analysis in History / Social Studies		
7 Subscores (1-15 Scale)	Words in Context		Heart of Algebra
	Command of Evidence		Passport to Advanced Mathematics
		Expression of Ideas	Problem Solving & Data Analysis
		Standard English Conventions	

❑ **How Your Score is Calculated** – You receive 1 raw point for a correct answer. You lose nothing for incorrect answers. Your **raw score** is calculated by adding up raw points. Your raw score is then converted to a scaled Reading **test** score from 10-40 (8-38 for PSAT). This test score is combined with your Writing and Language Test score to generate an overall Evidence-Based Reading and Writing **section** score from 200-800 (160-760 for PSAT).

❑ **Never leave a question blank**. Since there is no penalty for wrong answers, you should answer every single question on the SAT.

Setting Your Goal

Set a goal. Envision where you want to be when you've finished your SAT preparation. Using your diagnostic results and previous test scores, work with your instructor to set a realistic score goal.

❑ Set your targets in the table below.

My Targets

My overall SAT Goal: _____

My Evidence-Based Reading and Writing Goal: _____

My Reading Test Goal: _____

How many questions do I need to answer correctly (raw score)? _____

The Instructions

☐ The instructions are the same on every SAT. Familiarize yourself with the instructions before you take the test. At test time, you can skip the instructions and focus on the problems.

DIRECTIONS

Each passage or pair of passages below is followed by a number of questions. After reading each passage or pair, choose the best answer to each question based on what is stated or implied in the passage or passages and in any accompanying graphics (such as a table or graph).

Note that the College Board advises you to answer questions <u>after</u> reading the passage. This approach is the best way to work through the Reading Test. Do not try to answer questions before reading through the passage.

Working Through the Reading Test

❑ **Don't read the questions before you read the passage.**

In order to move quickly through the Reading Test, you must efficiently answer the questions, which take up most of your time. You will only be able to solve these questions with speed and confidence if you have actively read the passage first. Resist the urge to rush ahead; the time spent reading the passages will pay off in the end!

❑ **Don't skim the passage. Read actively.**

The Reading questions require a strong understanding of the passage as well as an understanding of the author's role and perspectives. A brief look at the passage won't be enough to solve the questions with accuracy and speed.

It is useful to skim the passage only if you are previewing the passage before thoroughly reading it or if you are very limited on time.

❑ **Focus on one passage at a time**.

Answer all of the questions to a passage before you move onto the next passage.

❑ Within each passage, maximize your score by focusing on the easier questions first. Each question is worth 1 raw point. Regardless of its difficulty, every question counts the same.

Would you rather earn $20 working for 1 hour or earn $20 working for 10 minutes? The answer is easy, right? Similarly, on the Reading Test, you should spend your time earning points as efficiently as you can. Put your time and energy into the questions within your capabilities, starting with the easiest and finishing with the hardest.

❑ **Focus on one question at a time**.

The SAT is timed, so it's normal to feel pressure to rush. Resist the temptation to think about the 10 questions ahead of you or the question you did a minute ago. Relax and focus on one question at a time. **Patience** on the SAT is what allows you to work more quickly and accurately.

❑ **Use the Two-Pass Approach for <u>each passage</u>.**

Step 1: On your first pass through a Reading passage, answer all of the questions you can, but don't get bogged down on an individual question. If you're stuck, mark it and move on. Remember: Each question is worth the same amount – 1 raw point.

Step 2: Make a second pass.

If you skipped and/or marked any, go back and work on these questions – it shouldn't be more than 1-3 per passage. Focus first on the ones you think you have the best chance of answering correctly. For some, you'll find the right answer fairly easily. For the others, aggressively eliminate answer choices and make educated guesses.

By answering simpler questions, you may have gained a stronger understanding of the passage, which can help you answer the questions that seemed too challenging at first.

Step 3: Don't leave any answers blank.

At this point, you shouldn't have any questions unanswered, but if you do, guess on any remaining questions before you move on to the next passage. Even if you feel like you really don't know the answer, it will be easier to guess while you're still thinking about the passage.

❑ There is no penalty for guessing, so make sure you answer every question. With about 30 seconds remaining for the test, you should answer any remaining questions.

❑ **Use Process of Elimination (POE).** Even if you can't find the correct answer, you'll almost always be able to eliminate one or two incorrect answers. The more answer choices you can eliminate, the greater the likelihood you'll get the right answer.

IMPORTANT: Once you have eliminated an answer, cross if out in the test booklet. Crossing out answers prevents you from wasting time looking at eliminated answers over and over again.

SUMMIT
EDUCATIONAL
G R O U P

Reading

❏ Reading at a Higher Level

❏ Active Reading

❏ Answering the Questions

❏ Anticipating the Answer

❏ Process of Elimination (POE)

❏ Question Types
  o Detail Questions
  o Main Idea Questions
  o Words in Context Questions
  o Inference Questions
  o Analogous Reading Questions
  o Evidence Questions
  o Point of View Questions
  o Purpose Questions
  o Structure Questions
  o Word Choice Questions
  o Data Graphics Questions

❏ Paired Passages

Reading at a Higher Level

In order to score well on the SAT Reading Test, you must be able to read for more than basic details. Although answering some of the most straightforward SAT Reading questions may only require you to understand basic details from the passage, the majority of the questions will require more analysis and a deeper understanding of the text.

❏ As you are reading and analyzing a passage, acknowledge the role of the writer. Try to determine the writer's opinion on the passage's topic. Ask yourself: why did the writer choose to write the passage as he or she did?

❏ To perform your best on the Reading Test, you will have to use the following skills:

- Understand key details.

- Summarize ideas as you read.

- Identify how each piece of a passage works. Pay attention to how each part of a passage relates to the parts around it.

- Consider the author. How does he or she feel about the topic?

PUT IT TOGETHER

The following passage was adapted from an article about a style of architecture known as "Greek Revival," which was popular in America during the first half of the nineteenth century.

The American Revolution brought a cultural as well as a political liberation. In the years after the war, Americans turned away from British influence in architecture. Political leaders wanted more vital
5   influences to take its place, influences more appropriate for the buildings erected by a new democracy.

In the years between 1820 and 1860, the young nation had gained its feet and was striding forward
10 with conscious vigor and confidence. The population, increasing rapidly, pressed relentlessly to the West, converting successive frontiers into settled territories. Economic expansion was proceeding at a fabulous rate: the seemingly limitless natural resources were
15 being developed (and also exploited), and the industrial power which later carried the nation to greatness was being established.

This success brought a new independence, as the young country no longer needed to rely on others.
20 With this independence came a desire for a new identity, one distinct from the nation's European roots. There was a conscious separation from Europe and a fierce will to be American. America had become a society whose way of life required unique
25 and adequate forms of cultural expression. In search of an artistic symbol of American values, the nation turned to the classical world of Greece and Rome.

Thus began a period in architectural history known as the "Greek Revival." American architects
30 copied their forms from Greek and Roman ruins – pediments, colonnades, Ionic and Corinthian columns. This style penetrated almost all sections of the country. Greek Revival moved westward with the advancing frontier and could be seen in surprising
35 refinement and beauty in areas which were wilderness but a few years before. The designers of this period seemed to possess an innate talent for adapting the new architectural fashion to the requirements of any region, preserving traditional
40 usages, accepting local building materials, and adapting to differences in the climate.

The word "Revival" is an unfortunate misnomer. This style was not simply a copy of classic Greek details. More than a revival, it was a unique
45 reimagining. The result was quite original and distinctively American. Never before had architecture in America been under less influence from England or France.

DETAIL

In paragraph two (lines 8-17), the author characterizes the period from 1820 to 1860 as a time of

A) struggle for Americans, whereas European nations were enjoying prosperity.
B) innovation in artistic techniques and styles.
C) growing appreciation for classical art.
D) American growth and economic success.

MAIN IDEA

Which choice best summarizes the claims made in the third paragraph (lines 18-27)?

A) Economic growth resulted in the materialistic values of 19th-century America.
B) America's new independence led to the desire for artistic individuality.
C) Cultural differences brought tense rivalries between 19th-century Western nations.
D) Characteristics of classical Greek art were used by Americans in various artistic fields.

PURPOSE

The main purpose of the fourth paragraph (lines 28-41) is to

A) analyze an unusual tradition.
B) criticize a particular culture.
C) describe the progression of a trend.
D) illustrate the differences between traditional and modern styles.

POINT OF VIEW

Based on the passage, the author refers to the use of the term "Revival" as unfortunate (line 42) because he believes that

A) American architects were unoriginal.
B) the term undermines the creativity of the American style.
C) imitation of our ancestors is disrespectful.
D) American architects did not borrow influences from any European cultures.

Active Reading

❑ We do not recommend speed-reading, nor do we recommend reading the questions first. It is difficult enough to understand an SAT passage without trying to keep all the questions in your head as you read! The Reading Test gives you enough time to read each passage thoroughly.

❑ **Stay engaged**. Do not read passively, waiting for the passage to reveal information to you. Instead, interact directly with the passage and think about what the author is saying or trying to convey.

Never expect a passage to interest or entertain you. It's your job to get involved.

❑ **Map the Passage**. Develop an organized understanding of a Reading passage by finding the main idea of each paragraph.

Each paragraph generally develops a thought, example, detail, or point. By noting the main idea in each paragraph, you can create an organized map of how the passage works and how the overall main idea is developed.

In addition to helping you organize the information of the passage, Mapping also ensures that you do not lose focus or read through the whole passage without understanding it.

❑ **Read with your pencil**. Make notes that help you understand the reading. You can underline important words and phrases, mark where there are contrasting ideas, note where you have questions or confusion, and jot down your ideas.

❑ Use a question mark to identify any part of the passage you don't understand. Often, when you read further, you will find additional information that clarifies the parts that had confused you before.

❑ Ask questions while you read:

- What is the main point of each paragraph? Underline it, or make a note in the margin.

- How does each paragraph fit into the development of the passage? What does each paragraph accomplish?

- What is the main idea of the passage as a whole?

- What is the author's purpose in writing this passage?

- What is the author's tone/attitude? Look for strong verbs and adjectives.

TRY IT OUT

The following passage was adapted from an article about the use of radar image data in the study of bat activity.

The hundreds of millions of bats in the U.S. are in serious trouble, threatened by such hazards as wind turbines and a fungal infection called white-nose syndrome, all while facing the uncertainty of a
5   changing climate. Most bats hide in caves during the day and venture out only at night, making them notoriously difficult to study. But if scientists are going to help them, they need to be able to track them. To that end, biologists Winifred Frick of the
10   University of California at Santa Cruz and Tom Kunz of Boston University have teamed up with some unexpected allies: weather researchers Phillip Chilson, an atmospheric physicist at the University of Oklahoma, and radar scientist Ken Howard of the
15   U.S. National Severe Storms Laboratory.
The U.S. National Weather Service's 156 Nexrad Doppler radar stations gather tremendous amounts of data. They scan the country in 5- to 10- minute intervals, 24 hours a day, from 0.5 degrees to
20   19.5 degrees above the horizon. In doing so, the radar stations detect much more than weather. Anything in the air—insects, birds, wind turbines, low-flying planes, forest-fire smoke, falling meteors, debris from NASA disasters, and bats—bounces a signal back.
25   Radar scientists call the signal from flying animals "bioclutter." "From a meteorological standpoint, it's noise," Howard says. "It contaminates all our algorithms. It misleads people. We have examples that look like severe storms, but it's actually bats
30   coming out of the ground."
The weather-radar images shown on TV broadcasts have mostly been scrubbed of such clutter. But unscrubbed maps are far more complex. Clear, cloudless nights are filled with flocks of animals on
35   the wing, which appear on radar maps as a thick cloud of fuzzy green dots, similar to raindrops. If a cloud of bat-size objects appears at dusk at the location of a known bat cave, they're probably bats, which means that the Weather Service's 20-year-old,
40   1.2-petabyte raw radar archive is also an archive of two decades of bats in flight.
Radar scientists are working to make the archive more useful for researchers. One of their goals is to produce animal-only maps and animal counts, much
45   as they produce weather maps and rainfall counts today. In order to accurately screen for various life-forms, though, the scientists need to know more about how individual animals appear on radar.

1 What is the main idea of the first paragraph?

2 What is the main idea of the second paragraph?

3 What is the main idea of the third paragraph?

4 What is the main idea of the last paragraph?

5 What is the main idea of the whole passage?

Answering the Questions

❑ Questions do not follow the order of the passage, nor do they progress from easy to difficult. Use your knowledge of question types and your sense of which questions are more challenging to work strategically through questions.

❑ Tackle each passage's questions using the following three steps:

1. Attack the easy and medium questions first.

   After you've finished actively reading the passage, work through the set of questions, answering all of the questions that seem to be easy and medium.

   Remember: you get one raw point for each question, whether it is simple or challenging, and whether it takes you 10 seconds or 3 minutes. Don't sink too much time into a question you cannot solve.

2. Make a second pass through the questions to work on the problems you skipped and marked. Focus on the questions you understand the best.

   Do as many of these as you can. You might be able to find the right answer to some of them. For others, you might be able to eliminate answer choices and make an educated guess.

   As you answer the other questions for the passage, you'll gather information that will likely help you to answer the difficult questions you've skipped.

3. Guess on the remaining questions.

   Before you move on to the next passage, guess on any remaining questions. Even if you feel like you really don't know the answer, it will be easier to guess while you're still thinking about the passage.

❑ When a question refers to specific line numbers, read a few lines before and after the given lines to get the full context. Refer to the notes you made while Mapping the Passage.

   Line numbers point you to the general area where the correct answer is found. You will almost always need the context around those lines to get the correct answer.

Anticipating the Answer

❑ Understand the question before you look at the answer choices. Jumping too quickly into the answer choices is like relying on an inaccurate map to give you directions.

With practice, you'll learn to trust yourself and to not be misled by wrong answers.

If necessary, practice by covering up the answer choices with your hand and answering the question without looking at the answer choices first.

❑ Many of the questions in the SAT Reading Test have more than one answer choice that could technically be true. However, each question has only one answer choice that is best.

If you try to solve Reading questions by testing which answer choices could be true, you will likely get stuck on several answer choices that all seem to work. This method is not only frustrating, but also time-consuming. You will be able to work with more speed and confidence if you anticipate the answer before looking at the answer choices.

> Although viruses share some of the distinctive properties of living organisms, they are not technically alive. They are unable to grow or reproduce in the same way that living creatures do. Instead, they act like parasites in order to reproduce. After locating and making contact with the right kind of cell, a virus injects its genetic material. It then uses the host cell, which is unable to distinguish the virus's genes from its own, to replicate. This process kills the cell, creating a new virus organism.
>
> As it is used in context, the phrase "they are not technically alive" means that viruses:
>
> Before you look at the answer choices, try to come up with your own answer for the question, based on the information in the passage.
>
> Answer: _____
>
> Look at the answer choices provided. Which is most similar to your own answer? _____
>
> A) are unable to reproduce on their own.
> B) use other cells to create life.
> C) attack living cells.
> D) only exist in theory.

TRY IT OUT

Actively read the following passage. Answer the questions that follow, using your own words.

The following passage is adapted from an essay about ant colonies.

We are apt to think of Japan as a densely populated country, with its 120 million inhabitants occupying 377,708 square kilometers. But if we read that along the Ishigari coast of the northern Japanese
5 island of Hokkaido there is a super-colony of ants which contains 306 million workers and 1,080,000 queens, occupying a mere 2.7 square kilometers, we suddenly become aware that in sheer numbers Japan belongs predominantly to the ants, not to the
10 Japanese.

Ants are a hundred-million-year success story. Their physical attributes are impressive; if humans had the relative speed and strength of ants, they would be able to run as fast as a racehorse and lift
15 cars. After so many years of evolution, there are now over 8,000 known species of ants, each specialized to be successful in its particular habitat. Ants and termites compose one-third of all living matter in the tropical rain forests of the Brazilian Amazon. One
20 eminent biologist has ascribed their worldwide ecological dominance (they are only absent from the tops of the highest mountains, and from Antarctica, Iceland, Greenland, and Polynesia east of Tonga) to their close connection with the ground. In
25 evolutionary history, they are the first group of social insects that lived and foraged primarily in the soil. Their ground dwellings provide protection and structure, which help ants survive and thrive.

But most important to ants' success is their
30 social organization, a rare evolutionary achievement which gives them an advantage over solitary insects. This organization depends on the division of labor. An ant has about a million cells in its brain, compared with twelve billion in a human's, but
35 owing to the division of labor (into about fifty categories), the colony can work to perfection.

The ant colony is an exclusively matriarchal society whose activity pivots on the welfare of the queen. Each ant colony has at least one or more
40 queens, whose job is to lay the eggs for the nest. But further evolutionary potential for life depends on the sterile worker. Its altruism supports and defends the community. The examples of the workers' self-denying behavior are astounding: for foraging
45 workers, the level of sacrifice approaches suicide—15 percent of those engaged in dangerous searches for food outside the colony perish—and the aging workers that engage in defense of the colony suffer

high death rates and weight losses of 40 percent for
50 those who survive.

Ants' ability to divide the tasks that need to be done depends on their ability to communicate. Our lives are governed principally by sight and sound, whereas the lives of ants are dominated by a world of
55 chemical communication, primarily of taste and smell. Pheromones—glandular secretions released as signals by one ant and received by another of the same species—play the central role in ant society. Ants use fifty categories of chemical signals, and
60 pheromonal communication includes trail-laying, alarm signals, attraction, recruitment, recognition of nest mates and particular castes, nest markers, and sexual communication. These signals are essential to the ant's persistence and prosperity.

65 Many scientists believe that the future of biology lies in the study of groups rather than of individual organisms. Because of their abundance and the ease with which their lifestyle can be studied, ants are the ideal subjects for the study of community ecology.
70 The eight thousand described species of ants—there are probably just as many as yet undiscovered—and the various systems around which their societies are organized bring home to us most vividly that the laws of biology are written in the language of diversity.

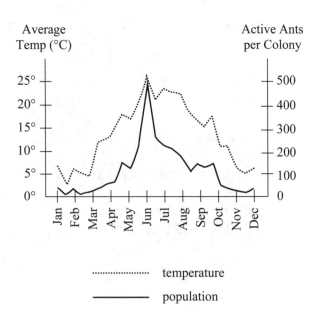

.... temperature

———— population

1

The author is primarily interested in explaining…

_____

_____

2

Which choice provides the best evidence for the answer to the previous question?

_____

_____

3

In line 48, "suffer" most nearly means….

_____

_____

4

The author describes worker ants (lines 40-50) in order to illustrate that they….

_____

_____

5

The author lists all of the following reasons for the success of ants EXCEPT for their….

_____

_____

6

The overall tone of the passage is one of….

_____

_____

7

Which choice provides the best evidence for the answer to the previous question?

_____

_____

8

According to lines 19-24, an eminent biologist has attributed ants' continuing success to their:

_____

_____

9

The term _matriarchal society_, as it is used in line 37-38, means which of the following?

_____

_____

10

When the author states, "the future of biology lies in the study of groups," (lines 65-66) it can be reasonably inferred that it is referencing which of the following facts?

_____

_____

11

The graph following the passage offers evidence that the population of an ant colony increases with

_____

_____

> **Can you anticipate the answer to #5?**
>
> **What is the best way to solve this type of question?**

PUT IT TOGETHER

Actively read the following passage. Answer the questions that follow.

The following passage is adapted from an essay about ant colonies.

We are apt to think of Japan as a densely populated country, with its 120 million inhabitants occupying 377,708 square kilometers. But if we read that along the Ishigari coast of the northern Japanese
5 island of Hokkaido there is a super-colony of ants which contains 306 million workers and 1,080,000 queens, occupying a mere 2.7 square kilometers, we suddenly become aware that in sheer numbers Japan belongs predominantly to the ants, not to the
10 Japanese.

Ants are a hundred-million-year success story. Their physical attributes are impressive; if humans had the relative speed and strength of ants, they would be able to run as fast as a racehorse and lift
15 cars. After so many years of evolution, there are now over 8,000 known species of ants, each specialized to be successful in its particular habitat. Ants and termites compose one-third of all living matter in the tropical rain forests of the Brazilian Amazon. One
20 eminent biologist has ascribed their worldwide ecological dominance (they are only absent from the tops of the highest mountains, and from Antarctica, Iceland, Greenland, and Polynesia east of Tonga) to their close connection with the ground. In
25 evolutionary history, they are the first group of social insects that lived and foraged primarily in the soil. Their ground dwellings provide protection and structure, which help ants survive and thrive.

But most important to ants' success is their
30 social organization, a rare evolutionary achievement which gives them an advantage over solitary insects. This organization depends on the division of labor. An ant has about a million cells in its brain, compared with twelve billion in a human's, but
35 owing to the division of labor (into about fifty categories), the colony can work to perfection.

The ant colony is an exclusively matriarchal society whose activity pivots on the welfare of the queen. Each ant colony has at least one or more
40 queens, whose job is to lay the eggs for the nest. But further evolutionary potential for life depends on the sterile worker. Its altruism supports and defends the community. The examples of the workers' self-denying behavior are astounding: for foraging
45 workers, the level of sacrifice approaches suicide— 15 percent of those engaged in dangerous searches for food outside the colony perish—and the aging workers that engage in defense of the colony suffer

high death rates and weight losses of 40 percent for
50 those who survive.

Ants' ability to divide the tasks that need to be done depends on their ability to communicate. Our lives are governed principally by sight and sound, whereas the lives of ants are dominated by a world of
55 chemical communication, primarily of taste and smell. Pheromones—glandular secretions released as signals by one ant and received by another of the same species—play the central role in ant society. Ants use fifty categories of chemical signals, and
60 pheromonal communication includes trail-laying, alarm signals, attraction, recruitment, recognition of nest mates and particular castes, nest markers, and sexual communication. These signals are essential to the ant's persistence and prosperity.

65 Many scientists believe that the future of biology lies in the study of groups rather than of individual organisms. Because of their abundance and the ease with which their lifestyle can be studied, ants are the ideal subjects for the study of community ecology.
70 The eight thousand described species of ants—there are probably just as many as yet undiscovered—and the various systems around which their societies are organized bring home to us most vividly that the laws of biology are written in the language of diversity.

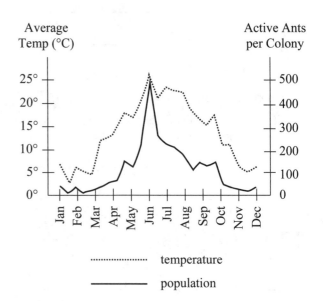

temperature

population

1

The author is primarily interested in explaining

A) why some areas of the world do not have ants.
B) why ants continue to flourish as a species.
C) when biologists began to study ants.
D) how the life cycle of the ant works.

2

Which choice provides the best evidence for the answer to the previous question?

A) lines 29-31 ("But… insects")
B) line 32 ("This… labor")
C) lines 37-39 ("The ant… queen")
D) lines 39-40 ("Each… nest")

3

In line 48, "suffer" most nearly means

A) agonize over.
B) experience.
C) deteriorate.
D) participate in.

4

The author describes worker ants (lines 40-50) in order to illustrate that they

A) heed only the orders of the queen ant.
B) encounter predators while searching for food.
C) feed themselves before feeding other ants.
D) risk their lives for the sake of their colonies.

5

The author lists all of the following reasons for the success of ants EXCEPT for their

A) number of colonies.
B) self-denying behavior.
C) system of communication.
D) specialization of job functions.

6

The overall tone of the passage is one of

A) surprised admiration.
B) whimsical puzzlement.
C) enlightened appreciation.
D) curious skepticism.

7

Which choice provides the best evidence for the answer to the previous question?

A) lines 12-15 ("Their… cars")
B) lines 15-17 ("After… habitat")
C) lines 17-19 ("Ants… Amazon")
D) lines 27-28 ("Their… thrive")

8

According to lines 19-24, an eminent biologist has attributed ants' continuing success to their:

A) determination and self-preservation.
B) hard, armor-like exoskeletons.
C) ground-based habitats.
D) ability to divide labor among many members of the community.

9

The term *matriarchal society*, as it is used in line 37-38, means which of the following?

A) A society where a mother's nurturing care is essential to the survival of her young
B) A society that revolves around the male members of a species
C) A society that revolves around the female members of a species
D) A society marked by persistent sexism

10

When the author states, "the future of biology lies in the study of groups" (lines 65-66), it can be reasonably inferred that it is referencing which of the following facts?

A) The key to ants' survival is their ability to function in a community.
B) There are over 8,000 known species of ants.
C) An ant has about a million cells in its brain.
D) The lives of ants are dominated by a world of chemical communication.

11

The graph offers evidence that the population of an ant colony increases with

A) maturity of queen ants.
B) complexity of labor organization.
C) climate temperature.
D) proximity to human settlements.

SUMMIT
EDUCATIONAL
GROUP

Process of Elimination

❑ Correct answers to Reading questions might not jump out at you; often, you will have to eliminate answer choices. Wrong answers range from clearly wrong to almost right.

❑ Make sure that you've found the **best** answer, not just a good one. Reading questions, especially difficult ones, will usually contain at least one or two choices that are "almost right."

❑ Eliminate answer choices that:

- aren't relevant or true.

- might be true but don't answer the question asked.

- might be true but are too broad.

- might be true but are too narrow.

- are exactly the opposite of what is correct.

- address the wrong part of the passage.

- use words and phrases from the passage, but do not answer the question correctly.

- are too extreme.

❑ Look for opposites.

If two answer choices are exact opposites, one of them is likely the correct answer.

❑ Look out for answer choices that are only mostly correct.

Some answer choices will be almost perfect, but will have one detail or word that does not work. Do not choose an answer choice just because parts of it sound good.

❑ Be careful of incorrect names and facts.

Some answer choices will be almost correct – the right answer, but with the wrong name plugged in, or with the names swapped.

❑ Be on the lookout for answer choices that are designed to attract your attention away from the correct answer.

> I like driving at night. It's dark and comfortable in my car. No one can see me. I'm in a safe little world, and outside in the dark, the lights of the houses and streets have turned the real world into something else – nice, dark and secure. I drive along in the dark and look at the houses with their lights on, looking in the windows, seeing living rooms, curtains and comfortable, warm houses. Late at night, I dream of living on an island with white sand and a bright blue sky – a place free of other people.
>
> The phrase "a place free of other people" indicates that the author
>
> A)   believes society is too commercially oriented.
> B)   is kept awake at night by the sound of traffic.
> C)   feels unsafe when driving during the day.
> D)   is seeking independence from others.
>
> Try to isolate the correct answer by eliminating the other answer choices. Explain how you can prove answers are incorrect.
>
> A) _____
>
> B) _____
>
> C) _____
>
> D) _____

❑ Using Process of Elimination doesn't mean you should rush through the question and immediately start reading answer choices. With each question, your first step should be to understand the question and try to answer it before reading the answer choices.

PUT IT TOGETHER

This passage is from the autobiography of a Mexican-American author who revisits her childhood home.

We piled into the station wagon and drove over to the east side of town, arriving after dawn. I hadn't seen the house in five years, and was struck by how small it was. I remembered it as sweet, and plenty big
5   enough for four, but now it seemed tiny—the whole of the original house would have fit into my mother's current living room, and the house she lives in now is by no means large. She'd told me that when the family first moved here, when I was a new baby, the
10 refrigerator was outside in the yard, because there was no room for it indoors.

The light green paint still flaked off the stucco walls of the house in long, leaden chunks. The stockade fence my father had built around the yard
15 when I was four still stood. Outside the yard, vultures still nested in the pair of soaring eucalyptus trees. The one on the right still held, in its topmost branches, the giant limb that had been felled by a storm when I was a small girl. For most of my life,
20 my father had been trying to get that limb down. He thought it would make perfect firewood that would last all winter, but he'd never been able to climb high enough to knock it loose.

The new residents had torn out the jumping cholla
25 cactus I fell into the first time I rode my bicycle without training wheels, and had hung it as a trophy on the gate where my sister and I used to swing.

It wasn't the house I cared about so much as the desert it sat in. Mesquite trees curled like beloved
30 ghosts in the sandy dirt that surrounded the little cottage. Thick underbrush filled the spaces between them, low thorny bushes interspersed with cacti. A sweet dry smell rose from the plants.

"Here!" I shouted, spotting an overgrown trail
35 into the brush.

It was harder than I remembered—the sharp ground hurt my feet, and thorns reached out to tear at my arms and hair. As a child I had run through these desert woods, built worlds in the arms of trees. I'd
40 come home at dusk, full of stories, and sit on my mother's knee. She'd comb the twigs and burrs out of my hair—my souvenirs, we called them—and I'd tell her the adventure that went with each one.

The trail took us to my secret place, a fort my
45 sister and I had built in the belly of sprawling mesquite. Big limbs arched low to the ground around a contraption of junk. Rotting tires arranged as seats, a decaying blanket draped over a discarded bathtub, by now frozen where we'd dropped it the last time
50 my sister had played the sleeping princess in our

game. A tiny plastic tea service sat half buried under the tree.

I dropped into a crouch, scooping the fine dirt and letting it run through my fingers.
55 "Here," I said, turning toward my new husband. "This is where I came from."

Tears welled in my eyes, I was so excited to be home. I held a dirty hand out to him. He stood over me, his face registering distress.
60 "I can see now why your mother worked so hard to get you out of here," he said. "She must have promised herself never to let you live like this again."

I stood up beside him and looked around. What seemed to me to be the glowing, teeming world of a
65 happy childhood was a place where strange trees towered above crumbling houses. Dust was held in place by yellowed weeds. The only body of water for miles was in the decrepit swimming pool on the ranch next door. It looked like poverty to him, like
70 filmstrips of third world villages where children need your love, expressed in American currency. To me it was the thing not foreign, the landscape of safe dreams and the touchstone of reality in a world of inauthentic cities. How could he think my mother had
75 taken us away to escape this? This place was the beloved she gave up to be near her own mother again, not the thing she fled. The inches between my dusty outstretched fingertips and his clean hand multiplied as I curled them back in toward my palm.
80 "I think we'd better go back to the car," I said. "There's nothing left here I want you to see."

1

Which of the following sentences serves as the best summary of the author's description in lines 1-23?

A) Though the scale with which I judged it had changed, the house really hadn't.
B) Seeing the house I grew up in reminded me of all of the negative experiences of my childhood.
C) My deep love of nature was fostered by the beautiful surroundings of my childhood home.
D) My childhood home had always been in poor shape, but now it has decayed even further.

2

The description of the large limb caught in the highest branches of one of the trees (lines 17-23) most clearly conveys

A) the unchanging condition of the yard since her childhood.
B) the author's fond memories of her father working around the house.
C) the fragility of life in the desert.
D) the large amount of time that has passed since her childhood.

3

Lines 39-43 ("I'd come . . . each one") depict the author's

A) childhood poverty.
B) distant relationship with her mother.
C) intrepid nature.
D) collection of souvenirs.

4

The items that the author describes in lines 47-52 ("Rotting tires . . . under the tree") are examples of

A) common childhood mementos.
B) gifts that she gave to her sister.
C) refuse littering her childhood playground.
D) artifacts of her past.

5

The primary effect of the husband's response in lines 60-62 is to

A) demonstrate the degree to which he supports the author.
B) remind the reader that the husband has been in the scene from the beginning.
C) let the author know that it is time for them to leave.
D) reveal to the author how little her husband understands her feelings about her childhood.

6

The image of the two characters' hands in lines 77-79 underscores the

A) new distance between the young couple.
B) cleanliness of the husband as opposed to the soiled hands of his wife.
C) squalor in which the narrator was raised.
D) narrator's inability to return home.

7

The author's statement in the final paragraph implies that

A) she regrets opening up her childhood to her husband.
B) she has shown her husband everything she brought him there to see.
C) she is worried about the car.
D) there is nothing left in Mexico that she cares about.

8

The overall tone of the passage is best described as

A) playful.
B) mysterious.
C) detached.
D) nostalgic.

Give reasons to eliminate incorrect answers:

A) _____

B) _____

C) _____

D) _____

Checkpoint Review

The following is an excerpt from a passage about Susan B. Anthony.

Susan B. Anthony—champion of the modern American woman—declared to the United States of America that if a woman is a person, a woman has a right to play a role in the freest democratic republic
5 in the world. What would this country have looked like if Anthony had not been so courageous? Unique among her public addresses is the following speech, which poignantly but precisely lays out her argument for the female American:

10 "Friends and fellow citizens, I stand before you tonight under indictment for the alleged crime of having voted in the last presidential election, without having a lawful right to vote. It shall be my work this evening to prove to you that in thus voting, I not only
15 committed no crime but, instead, simply exercised my citizen's rights, guaranteed to me and all United States Citizens by the National Constitution, beyond the power of any state to deny.

"The preamble of the Federal Constitution says:
20 "'We, the people of the United States, in order to form a more perfect union, establish justice, insure domestic tranquility, provide for the common defense, promote the general welfare, and secure the blessings of liberty to ourselves and our posterity, do
25 ordain and establish this Constitution for the United States of America.'

"It was we, the people; not we, the white male citizens; nor yet we, the male citizens; but we, the whole people, who formed the Union. And we
30 formed it, not to give the blessings of liberty, but to secure them; not to the half of ourselves and the half of our prosperity, but to the whole people—women as well as men. And it is a downright mockery to talk to women of their enjoyment of the blessings of
35 liberty while they are denied the use of the only means of securing them provided by this democratic-republican government—the ballot.

"For any state to make sex a qualification that must ever result in the disenfranchisement of one
40 entire half of the people is to pass a bill of attainder, or an ex-post facto law, and is therefore a violation of the supreme law of the land. By it the blessings of liberty are forever withheld from women and their female prosperity. To them this government has no
45 just powers derived from the consent of the governed. To them this government is not a democracy. It is not a republic. It is an odious aristocracy; a hateful oligarchy of sex; the most hateful aristocracy ever established on the face of the globe; an oligarchy of

50 wealth, where the rich govern the poor. An oligarchy of learning, where the educated govern the ignorant, or even an oligarchy of race, where the Saxon rules the African, might be endured; but this oligarchy of sex, which makes father, brothers, husband, sons, the
55 oligarchs over the mother and sisters, the wife and daughters, of every household—which ordains all men sovereigns, all women subjects, carries dissension, discord, and rebellion into every home of the nation.
60 "Webster, Worchester, and Bouvier all define a citizen to be a person in the United States, entitled to vote and hold office.

"The only question left to be settled now is: Are women persons? And I hardly believe any of our
65 opponents will have the hardihood to say they are not. Being persons, then, women are citizens; and no state has a right to make any law, or to enforce any old law, that shall abridge their privileges or immunities. Hence, every discrimination against
70 women in the constitutions and laws of the several states is today null and void, precisely as is every one against Negroes."

Articulately and fiercely, with force and with dignity, Susan B. Anthony defined the goal of not
75 only the modern feminist, but also the modern humanist—she placed on the backs of those in power the burden of explaining to the American people why it was that half of their population was granted a sub-human status.

1

In her speech, what crime does Anthony say that she committed?

A) Speaking at temperance rallies
B) Organizing against the government
C) Voting
D) Resisting arrest

2

It can be reasonably inferred that Anthony believed

A) the ideal of justice put forth in the Constitution was not being served.
B) the education of women was the key to their empowerment.
C) she lived in the freest nation in the world.
D) the government had no just powers.

Checkpoint Review

3

Which choice provides the best evidence for the answer to the previous question?

A) lines 14-18 ("I.. deny")
B) lines 33-37 ("And… ballot")
C) lines 44-47 ("To… republic")
D) lines 50-53 ("An… endured")

4

The passage primarily emphasizes the idea that Anthony

A) fought for the modern American woman with her sharp words.
B) broke the law in proving her point.
C) was characterized by an admirable dignity.
D) should be commended for her passion, although her words were to no avail.

5

Which choice provides the best evidence for the answer to the previous question?

A) lines 2-5 ("declared… world")
B) lines 27-29 ("It… Union")
C) lines 63-66 ("The… not")
D) lines 73-75 ("Articulately… humanist")

6

In the context of the passage, "For any state to make sex a qualification that must ever result in the disenfranchisement of one entire half of the people is to pass a bill of attainder, or an ex-post facto law," (lines 38-41) suggests that

A) making sex a factor in one's ability to vote in a democracy should be voted into effect by the public.
B) not allowing women to vote is disregarding the Constitution in a way that would normally demand legal process.
C) a bill of attainder is the only way to grant women the right to vote.
D) the government she fought was not a democracy.

7

Anthony quotes the Constitution of the United States in order to

A) provide historical background for her argument.
B) argue against it.
C) demonstrate the skill with which it was written.
D) use it to support her argument.

8

As it is used in line 29, the word *Union* most nearly means

A) meeting.
B) organization.
C) activist group.
D) national community.

9

When Anthony asks, "Are women persons?" (lines 63-64) she is expressing a

A) deep curiosity.
B) paradoxical statement.
C) surprising hypocrisy.
D) rhetorical question.

10

As it is used in line 57, "subjects" most nearly means

A) topics.
B) issues.
C) employees.
D) servants.

Detail Questions

❑ Detail questions ask about information that is directly presented in the passage.

❑ Detail questions typically appear in the following forms:

> The author indicates that...
> According to the passage,...

❑ Watch for rewording.

The correct answers to detail questions may be hard to find because they have been reworded. Pay attention to how information can be stated differently.

PUT IT TOGETHER

This passage is adapted from Sam Stoddard, "What's the (Dark) Matter?"

The Milky Way Galaxy is spinning quickly—too quickly. In fact, matter that populates the universe spins so rapidly that it should have torn itself apart long ago. As any child who has fallen off of a merry-
5 go-round knows, as the speed of rotation increases, objects are pulled away from the center and flung outwards. Children combat this centrifugal force by clinging tightly to the handles of a merry-go-round as it spins; objects in space are able to remain in
10 position thanks to the pull of gravity. But there is not enough observable matter in galaxies like our own to have enough gravity to cancel out the tremendous stress placed on galaxies as they spin. The merry-go-rounds of the universe are moving so quickly that it
15 should be impossible for the stars and planets to stay on for the ride—and yet galaxies remain intact.

This puzzle has led researchers to infer that only a small portion of the matter that makes up our universe is observable by traditional means. There
20 must be at least five times as much gravity holding galaxies together as can be accounted for by the stars, planets, dust clouds and other objects that absorb, reflect, or emit light. Researchers hypothesize that much of the mass in the universe does not interact
25 with the electromagnetic field; this otherwise unobservable matter is known as dark matter. But what is dark matter? And how can scientists study something that they cannot see?

Deep below the Alps, scientists aren't merely
30 searching for dark matter; they are working to create it. The European Organization for Nuclear Research has constructed the largest particle accelerator in history: the Large Hadron Collider, or LHC. Beginning operation in 2008, the LHC is a 27-
35 kilometer ring that uses superconducting electro-magnets to accelerate high-energy particles to nearly the speed of light. Separate ultra-high vacuum tubes house the tiny particles as they spin in opposite directions before being merged into a single tube
40 where they collide and break apart, forming new particles and releasing energy. The collisions that take place within the LHC mimic the formative processes that characterized the early universe; scientists detect and study the particles that result in
45 order to better understand the variety of substances that inhabit our universe.

Researchers have theorized that dark matter particles can be created using the LHC; however, even if they could be produced, they would still not
50 be directly observable. Instead, scientists believe they can prove the existence of dark matter by observing its effects. Dark matter is believed to interact only very weakly with ordinary matter, so any dark matter created would likely slip past particle detectors; but
55 as it does, it would carry energy and momentum away with it. Because scientists can estimate the amount of energy produced in a given collision, the presence of any newly created dark matter could be demonstrated by comparing the measurable energy
60 produced to predicted estimates.

To date, collisions produced by the LHC between a variety of particles at different levels of kinetic energy have been unable to produce dark matter. Furthermore, even if the presence of unknown
65 particles was to be observed, scientists cannot be certain that dark matter is responsible; the hidden particles could be something else entirely. Nevertheless, simply gaining knowledge of the conditions under which such a candidate can be
70 created would give scientists a strong idea of where to look for further evidence of dark matter, bringing us one step closer to understanding the elusive form of matter that may hold our galaxy together.

1

According to the passage, some scientists hypothesize that dark matter

A) exists only in the Milky Way Galaxy.
B) is present in all galaxies in space.
C) must be created in a laboratory setting because it does not occur naturally.
D) can be found only within galaxies that contain planets capable of sustaining life.

2

The author indicates that dark matter probably cannot be observed directly because

A) there is not enough illumination in space.
B) it is too dark in color to be seen.
C) it does not interact with the electromagnetic spectrum.
D) it is obscured by large galaxies and other clusters of visible matter.

Main Idea Questions

❑ Main idea questions ask you to determine the author's focus or point in writing a particular paragraph or the passage as a whole.

Through your use of Mapping the Passage, you should be able to find the main idea of each paragraph and the whole passage.

❑ Main idea questions typically appear in the following forms:

The central claim of the passage is...
The main idea of the first paragraph is...
Which of the following statements best expresses the central idea of the passage?
The passage primarily focuses on...

❑ Do not assume that the first paragraph will contain the main idea of the passage or that the first sentence will contain the main idea of a paragraph. Although you may have learned to write essays this way, not all authors will follow these guidelines.

❑ As you read through the possible answers for a main idea question, eliminate answer choices that:

- draw a broader conclusion than the passage does.

- talk about only a portion of the passage.

- have nothing to do with the topic.

- may sound reasonable, but are not mentioned in the text.

Make sure that you focus on the correct part of the passage. Incorrect answers often seem correct when you consider a part of the passage that is different from what the question references.

PUT IT TOGETHER

This passage is adapted from Sam Stoddard, "What's the (Dark) Matter?"

The Milky Way Galaxy is spinning quickly—too quickly. In fact, matter that populates the universe spins so rapidly that it should have torn itself apart long ago. As any child who has fallen off of a merry-
5 go-round knows, as the speed of rotation increases, objects are pulled away from the center and flung outwards. Children combat this centrifugal force by clinging tightly to the handles of a merry-go-round as it spins; objects in space are able to remain in
10 position thanks to the pull of gravity. But there is not enough observable matter in galaxies like our own to have enough gravity to cancel out the tremendous stress placed on galaxies as they spin. The merry-go-rounds of the universe are moving so quickly that it
15 should be impossible for the stars and planets to stay on for the ride—and yet galaxies remain intact.

This puzzle has led researchers to infer that only a small portion of the matter that makes up our universe is observable by traditional means. There
20 must be at least five times as much gravity holding galaxies together as can be accounted for by the stars, planets, dust clouds and other objects that absorb, reflect, or emit light. Researchers hypothesize that much of the mass in the universe does not interact
25 with the electromagnetic field; this otherwise unobservable matter is known as dark matter. But what is dark matter? And how can scientists study something that they cannot see?

Deep below the Alps, scientists aren't merely
30 searching for dark matter; they are working to create it. The European Organization for Nuclear Research has constructed the largest particle accelerator in history: the Large Hadron Collider, or LHC. Beginning operation in 2008, the LHC is a 27-
35 kilometer ring that uses superconducting electro-magnets to accelerate high-energy particles to nearly the speed of light. Separate ultra-high vacuum tubes house the tiny particles as they spin in opposite directions before being merged into a single tube
40 where they collide and break apart, forming new particles and releasing energy. The collisions that take place within the LHC mimic the formative processes that characterized the early universe; scientists detect and study the particles that result in
45 order to better understand the variety of substances that inhabit our universe.

Researchers have theorized that dark matter particles can be created using the LHC; however, even if they could be produced, they would still not
50 be directly observable. Instead, scientists believe they can prove the existence of dark matter by observing its effects. Dark matter is believed to interact only very weakly with ordinary matter, so any dark matter created would likely slip past particle detectors; but
55 as it does, it would carry energy and momentum away with it. Because scientists can estimate the amount of energy produced in a given collision, the presence of any newly created dark matter could be demonstrated by comparing the measurable energy
60 produced to predicted estimates.

To date, collisions produced by the LHC between a variety of particles at different levels of kinetic energy have been unable to produce dark matter. Furthermore, even if the presence of unknown
65 particles was to be observed, scientists cannot be certain that dark matter is responsible; the hidden particles could be something else entirely. Nevertheless, simply gaining knowledge of the conditions under which such a candidate can be
70 created would give scientists a strong idea of where to look for further evidence of dark matter, bringing us one step closer to understanding the elusive form of matter that may hold our galaxy together.

1

The central claim of the passage is that

A) the dark matter that holds our galaxy together was created with the Large Hadron Collider.
B) scientists are trying to create dark matter in order to disprove the theory of gravity.
C) scientists are using the LHC to search for an explanation for an apparent lack of matter in the galaxy.
D) dark matter causes our galaxy to rotate too quickly, and so scientists are studying dark matter in the hopes of weakening its interaction with ordinary matter.

2

The main idea of the first paragraph (lines 1-16) is that

A) scientists are split between two contradictory hypotheses to explain a recognized phenomenon.
B) scientific principles often originate in childhood experiences.
C) there is an apparent contradiction in the structure of our galaxy.
D) a previously accepted theory has been disproven by recent discoveries.

Words in Context Questions

❑ Words in context questions ask you what a word or phrase means in the context of the passage.

These questions do not test your vocabulary as much as they test your ability to understand how words can have different meanings in different situations.

❑ Words in context questions typically appear in the following forms:

As it is used in lines ____, the word _____ most nearly means...
In the context of the passage, the statement in lines ____ most nearly means that...
The phrase _____ refers to the...
Which of the following words from the passage is used figuratively?
The author uses the term _____ to refer to...
In the context of the passage, the phrase _____ can most nearly be paraphrased as...
When the author says, "_____," she most nearly means...

❑ The correct answer to a words in context question may be a secondary or obscure definition of the selected term.

❑ Read the entire sentence to understand the context in which the word or phrase is used. If necessary, also read the sentences that appear before and after.

When you encounter a word you don't recognize or a sentence you don't understand, you can use the surrounding information to help you determine what it means. Even if you can't determine the exact meaning, you should be able to make an educated guess.

PUT IT TOGETHER

This passage is adapted from Sam Stoddard, "What's the (Dark) Matter?"

The Milky Way Galaxy is spinning quickly—too quickly. In fact, matter that populates the universe spins so rapidly that it should have torn itself apart long ago. As any child who has fallen off of a merry-
5 go-round knows, as the speed of rotation increases, objects are pulled away from the center and flung outwards. Children combat this centrifugal force by clinging tightly to the handles of a merry-go-round as it spins; objects in space are able to remain in
10 position thanks to the pull of gravity. But there is not enough observable matter in galaxies like our own to have enough gravity to cancel out the tremendous stress placed on galaxies as they spin. The merry-go-rounds of the universe are moving so quickly that it
15 should be impossible for the stars and planets to stay on for the ride—and yet galaxies remain intact.

This puzzle has led researchers to infer that only a small portion of the matter that makes up our universe is observable by traditional means. There
20 must be at least five times as much gravity holding galaxies together as can be accounted for by the stars, planets, dust clouds and other objects that absorb, reflect, or emit light. Researchers hypothesize that much of the mass in the universe does not interact
25 with the electromagnetic field; this otherwise unobservable matter is known as dark matter. But what is dark matter? And how can scientists study something that they cannot see?

Deep below the Alps, scientists aren't merely
30 searching for dark matter; they are working to create it. The European Organization for Nuclear Research has constructed the largest particle accelerator in history: the Large Hadron Collider, or LHC. Beginning operation in 2008, the LHC is a 27-
35 kilometer ring that uses superconducting electro-magnets to accelerate high-energy particles to nearly the speed of light. Separate ultra-high vacuum tubes house the tiny particles as they spin in opposite directions before being merged into a single tube
40 where they collide and break apart, forming new particles and releasing energy. The collisions that take place within the LHC mimic the formative processes that characterized the early universe; scientists detect and study the particles that result in
45 order to better understand the variety of substances that inhabit our universe.

Researchers have theorized that dark matter particles can be created using the LHC; however, even if they could be produced, they would still not
50 be directly observable. Instead, scientists believe they can prove the existence of dark matter by observing its effects. Dark matter is believed to interact only very weakly with ordinary matter, so any dark matter created would likely slip past particle detectors; but
55 as it does, it would carry energy and momentum away with it. Because scientists can estimate the amount of energy produced in a given collision, the presence of any newly created dark matter could be demonstrated by comparing the measurable energy
60 produced to predicted estimates.

To date, collisions produced by the LHC between a variety of particles at different levels of kinetic energy have been unable to produce dark matter. Furthermore, even if the presence of unknown
65 particles was to be observed, scientists cannot be certain that dark matter is responsible; the hidden particles could be something else entirely. Nevertheless, simply gaining knowledge of the conditions under which such a candidate can be
70 created would give scientists a strong idea of where to look for further evidence of dark matter, bringing us one step closer to understanding the elusive form of matter that may hold our galaxy together.

1

As used in line 16, "intact" most nearly means

A) inappropriate.
B) whole.
C) unsullied.
D) pristine.

2

As used in line 38, "house" most nearly means

A) defend.
B) inhabit.
C) fortify.
D) hold.

Inference Questions

❑ Inference questions ask you to draw conclusions that are not directly stated in the passage.

❑ Inference questions typically appear in the following forms:

> It can be logically inferred from the passage that…
> It is implied in the fifth paragraph that…
> A reasonable conclusion from _____ is that…
> In the context of the passage as a whole, it is most reasonable to infer that…
> What does the author suggest when he states that _____?

❑ An inference is a logical conclusion based on evidence. It is important to make sure that your inferences are based on the information in the passage and not on outside knowledge or vague possibilities.

❑ Inference questions can be very challenging, because most require a deep level of understanding of the passage.

Often, it is best to leave these questions for last. Answering the other questions may help you to understand the passage better, which will make it easier to answer difficult problems like these.

Analogous Reading Questions

❑ An analogous reading question is a challenging type of inference question that asks you to identify an idea that is parallel or analogous to an idea expressed in the passage.

❑ Analogous reading questions typically appear in the following forms:

> Which of the following most resembles the relationship described in the passage?
> Which is most analogous to the situation described in lines 14-23?

❑ Such a question requires you to understand the concept, as opposed to the specifics, of the highlighted section of the passage. Once you understand the idea in the passage, finding an analogous situation becomes much easier.

PUT IT TOGETHER

This passage is adapted from Sam Stoddard, "What's the (Dark) Matter?"

The Milky Way Galaxy is spinning quickly—too quickly. In fact, matter that populates the universe spins so rapidly that it should have torn itself apart long ago. As any child who has fallen off of a merry-
5 go-round knows, as the speed of rotation increases, objects are pulled away from the center and flung outwards. Children combat this centrifugal force by clinging tightly to the handles of a merry-go-round as it spins; objects in space are able to remain in
10 position thanks to the pull of gravity. But there is not enough observable matter in galaxies like our own to have enough gravity to cancel out the tremendous stress placed on galaxies as they spin. The merry-go-rounds of the universe are moving so quickly that it
15 should be impossible for the stars and planets to stay on for the ride—and yet galaxies remain intact.

This puzzle has led researchers to infer that only a small portion of the matter that makes up our universe is observable by traditional means. There
20 must be at least five times as much gravity holding galaxies together as can be accounted for by the stars, planets, dust clouds and other objects that absorb, reflect, or emit light. Researchers hypothesize that much of the mass in the universe does not interact
25 with the electromagnetic field; this otherwise unobservable matter is known as dark matter. But what is dark matter? And how can scientists study something that they cannot see?

Deep below the Alps, scientists aren't merely
30 searching for dark matter; they are working to create it. The European Organization for Nuclear Research has constructed the largest particle accelerator in history: the Large Hadron Collider, or LHC. Beginning operation in 2008, the LHC is a 27-
35 kilometer ring that uses superconducting electro-magnets to accelerate high-energy particles to nearly the speed of light. Separate ultra-high vacuum tubes house the tiny particles as they spin in opposite directions before being merged into a single tube
40 where they collide and break apart, forming new particles and releasing energy. The collisions that take place within the LHC mimic the formative processes that characterized the early universe; scientists detect and study the particles that result in
45 order to better understand the variety of substances that inhabit our universe.

Researchers have theorized that dark matter particles can be created using the LHC; however, even if they could be produced, they would still not
50 be directly observable. Instead, scientists believe they can prove the existence of dark matter by observing its effects. Dark matter is believed to interact only very weakly with ordinary matter, so any dark matter created would likely slip past particle detectors; but
55 as it does, it would carry energy and momentum away with it. Because scientists can estimate the amount of energy produced in a given collision, the presence of any newly created dark matter could be demonstrated by comparing the measurable energy
60 produced to predicted estimates.

To date, collisions produced by the LHC between a variety of particles at different levels of kinetic energy have been unable to produce dark matter. Furthermore, even if the presence of unknown
65 particles was to be observed, scientists cannot be certain that dark matter is responsible; the hidden particles could be something else entirely. Nevertheless, simply gaining knowledge of the conditions under which such a candidate can be
70 created would give scientists a strong idea of where to look for further evidence of dark matter, bringing us one step closer to understanding the elusive form of matter that may hold our galaxy together.

1

It can be reasonably inferred from the passage that if dark matter did not exist, galaxies and other clusters of matter in space would

A) break apart.
B) implode.
C) merge to form larger clusters of matter.
D) spin more rapidly.

2

The method scientists use to study the theory of dark matter, as described in lines (37-46), is most analogous to

A) children playing on a swing set and experiencing the pull of gravity.
B) a student researching economics by reading a selection of books on economic theory.
C) an acoustical engineer studying sound by measuring noise generated in an echo chamber.
D) a psychologist conducting interviews in order to analyze the behavioral effects of a mental disorder.

Evidence Questions

❑ Evidence questions ask you to cite portions of the passage in order to justify your answer to previous questions. These questions appear twice per passage.

Evidence questions usually appear after detail or inference questions.

❑ Evidence questions appear in the following form:

Which choice provides the best evidence for the answer to the previous question?

❑ You can use an evidence question to help solve the question that appears before it. Note where evidence questions appear and use the line numbers provided in the answer choices to help guide you as you answer the previous questions. This lets you solve two questions at once.

PUT IT TOGETHER

This passage is adapted from Sam Stoddard, "What's the (Dark) Matter?"

The Milky Way Galaxy is spinning quickly—too quickly. In fact, matter that populates the universe spins so rapidly that it should have torn itself apart long ago. As any child who has fallen off of a merry-
5 go-round knows, as the speed of rotation increases, objects are pulled away from the center and flung outwards. Children combat this centrifugal force by clinging tightly to the handles of a merry-go-round as it spins; objects in space are able to remain in
10 position thanks to the pull of gravity. But there is not enough observable matter in galaxies like our own to have enough gravity to cancel out the tremendous stress placed on galaxies as they spin. The merry-go-rounds of the universe are moving so quickly that it
15 should be impossible for the stars and planets to stay on for the ride—and yet galaxies remain intact.

This puzzle has led researchers to infer that only a small portion of the matter that makes up our universe is observable by traditional means. There
20 must be at least five times as much gravity holding galaxies together as can be accounted for by the stars, planets, dust clouds and other objects that absorb, reflect, or emit light. Researchers hypothesize that much of the mass in the universe does not interact
25 with the electromagnetic field; this otherwise unobservable matter is known as dark matter. But what is dark matter? And how can scientists study something that they cannot see?

Deep below the Alps, scientists aren't merely
30 searching for dark matter; they are working to create it. The European Organization for Nuclear Research has constructed the largest particle accelerator in history: the Large Hadron Collider, or LHC. Beginning operation in 2008, the LHC is a 27-
35 kilometer ring that uses superconducting electro-magnets to accelerate high-energy particles to nearly the speed of light. Separate ultra-high vacuum tubes house the tiny particles as they spin in opposite directions before being merged into a single tube
40 where they collide and break apart, forming new particles and releasing energy. The collisions that take place within the LHC mimic the formative processes that characterized the early universe; scientists detect and study the particles that result in
45 order to better understand the variety of substances that inhabit our universe.

Researchers have theorized that dark matter particles can be created using the LHC; however, even if they could be produced, they would still not
50 be directly observable. Instead, scientists believe they can prove the existence of dark matter by observing its effects. Dark matter is believed to interact only very weakly with ordinary matter, so any dark matter created would likely slip past particle detectors; but
55 as it does, it would carry energy and momentum away with it. Because scientists can estimate the amount of energy produced in a given collision, the presence of any newly created dark matter could be demonstrated by comparing the measurable energy
60 produced to predicted estimates.

To date, collisions produced by the LHC between a variety of particles at different levels of kinetic energy have been unable to produce dark matter. Furthermore, even if the presence of unknown
65 particles was to be observed, scientists cannot be certain that dark matter is responsible; the hidden particles could be something else entirely. Nevertheless, simply gaining knowledge of the conditions under which such a candidate can be
70 created would give scientists a strong idea of where to look for further evidence of dark matter, bringing us one step closer to understanding the elusive form of matter that may hold our galaxy together.

1

Which of the following best describes how scientists believe the Large Hadron Collider could be used to learn about dark matter?

A) Dark matter could be converted to a visible substance using superconducting electromagnets.
B) Dark matter should become more visible as it approaches the speed of light.
C) The extreme pressure under the Earth surface condenses dark matter until it becomes visible.
D) The effects of newly created dark matter could be observed, even though dark matter itself cannot be detected.

2

Which choice provides the best evidence for the answer to the previous question?

A) Lines 4-7 ("As… outwards.")
B) Lines 37-41 ("Separate… energy.")
C) Lines 41-46 ("The… universe.")
D) Lines 56-60 ("Because… estimates.")

Point of View Questions

Point of view questions ask you to consider the perspective of the author. These questions deal with tone, attitude, and opinion.

❑ Point of view questions typically appear in the following forms:

> The point of view from which the passage is told is best described as that of...
> Which of the following statements would the author most likely agree with?

These questions may seem similar to main idea questions, because both require you to understand the overall point of the passage.

❑ Avoid extremes.

When reviewing your answer choices for point of view questions, beware of answers that are too strongly worded. Ask yourself if the degree of intensity suggested by the answer corresponds with the intensity of the passage.

PUT IT TOGETHER

The following passage was adapted from a book about the origins of slavery in America.

After the American Revolution, slavery received attention as a dilemma of growing complexity and prominence. The institution of slavery conflicted with the society the new country's leaders were attempting
5 to create. However, slavery retained legal acceptance in most arenas for another hundred years. At the time of the war, an estimated 500,000 slaves resided in the colonies (out of a total population of only 2.5 million), three quarters of whom were located in the
10 south, 200,000 in Virginia alone. The Revolution did not alleviate this situation, however, and the number of slaves actually grew during the war.

Before the American Revolution, slavery was seen by many as another degree of "un-freedom" in a
15 largely un-free world, a view supported by the overall worthlessness of individual life in pre-humanitarian times. This position, however, became more difficult to support following the writing of the Declaration of Independence and state constitutions in the 1770s and
20 1780s. The assertion "that all men are created equal, that they are endowed by their Creator with certain unalienable Rights," seemed entirely incompatible with the practice of slavery. Leaders struggled to clarify the principle of equality, and many disagreed
25 regarding which people were granted the inherent right of freedom. A recent historian writes of the conflict, "Slavery was a national institution and nearly every white American directly or indirectly benefited from it. By 1776, however, nearly every
30 American leader knew that its continued existence violated everything the Revolution was about." From the modern perspective of humanitarian-era thought, the lack of action taken against slavery is problematic and difficult to understand.
35 Initially, slavery came into question because of the use of the term in political rhetoric of the day. The word "slavery" was unavoidable, demanding examination with regards to the literal institution of slavery in America, as well as its use in describing
40 America's subservience to England. The term was invoked often in the 1760s and 1770s to describe the condition of the American colonies in relation to Great Britain.

During the war, many slaves gained their
45 freedom, although often for purely tactical, rather than ethical or humanitarian, reasons. In 1775 Lord Dunmore, the Royal Governor of Virginia, offered freedom to slaves who would escape and aid the British cause. This was the largest source of
50 emancipation before the Civil War. It resulted in tens of thousands of slaves fighting for England. Slaves

joining the British cause were guaranteed a new life after the war, regardless of the outcome. In turn, Virginia and Maryland made similar counter-offers.
55 The debate over the colonies' relationship with England led to a fundamental questioning of human freedom. From this questioning, the weapons for the argument against slavery were forged.

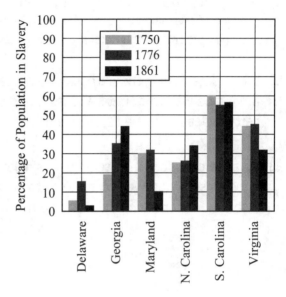

1

The author's examination of slavery in the context of the American Revolution can best be characterized as

A) an impassioned plea to stop mistreating our fellow human beings.
B) a philosophical exploration of the source of man's inhumanity to man.
C) a careful evaluation of early America's failure to abolish slavery.
D) a biased historical overview of slavery during the American Revolution.

SUMMIT
EDUCATIONAL
GROUP

Purpose Questions

❑ Purpose questions ask you to consider why the passage is constructed as it is. These questions require an acknowledgement of the author's role in writing the passage.

❑ Purpose questions typically appear in the following forms:

> The main purpose of the passage is to...
> One of the main purposes of the last paragraph is for the author to...
> The author uses the details listed in lines _____ primarily to...

❑ When determining the purpose of a passage, consider the author who wrote it. Each part of a passage was written for a reason, and the author crafted the passage to communicate certain ideas, arguments, or emotions.

❑ Purpose questions may seem very similar to main idea questions. However, main idea questions only ask you to consider the content of the passage, whereas purpose questions also ask for consideration of the author's intent.

PUT IT TOGETHER

The following passage was adapted from a book about the origins of slavery in America.

After the American Revolution, slavery received attention as a dilemma of growing complexity and prominence. The institution of slavery conflicted with the society the new country's leaders were attempting
5   to create. However, slavery retained legal acceptance in most arenas for another hundred years. At the time of the war, an estimated 500,000 slaves resided in the colonies (out of a total population of only 2.5 million), three quarters of whom were located in the
10 south, 200,000 in Virginia alone. The Revolution did not alleviate this situation, however, and the number of slaves actually grew during the war.

Before the American Revolution, slavery was seen by many as another degree of "un-freedom" in a
15 largely un-free world, a view supported by the overall worthlessness of individual life in pre-humanitarian times. This position, however, became more difficult to support following the writing of the Declaration of Independence and state constitutions in the 1770s and
20 1780s. The assertion "that all men are created equal, that they are endowed by their Creator with certain unalienable Rights," seemed entirely incompatible with the practice of slavery. Leaders struggled to clarify the principle of equality, and many disagreed
25 regarding which people were granted the inherent right of freedom. A recent historian writes of the conflict, "Slavery was a national institution and nearly every white American directly or indirectly benefited from it. By 1776, however, nearly every
30 American leader knew that its continued existence violated everything the Revolution was about." From the modern perspective of humanitarian-era thought, the lack of action taken against slavery is problematic and difficult to understand.

35 Initially, slavery came into question because of the use of the term in political rhetoric of the day. The word "slavery" was unavoidable, demanding examination with regards to the literal institution of slavery in America, as well as its use in describing
40 America's subservience to England. The term was invoked often in the 1760s and 1770s to describe the condition of the American colonies in relation to Great Britain.

During the war, many slaves gained their
45 freedom, although often for purely tactical, rather than ethical or humanitarian, reasons. In 1775 Lord Dunmore, the Royal Governor of Virginia, offered freedom to slaves who would escape and aid the British cause. This was the largest source of
50 emancipation before the Civil War. It resulted in tens of thousands of slaves fighting for England. Slaves joining the British cause were guaranteed a new life after the war, regardless of the outcome. In turn, Virginia and Maryland made similar counter-offers.

55 The debate over the colonies' relationship with England led to a fundamental questioning of human freedom. From this questioning, the weapons for the argument against slavery were forged.

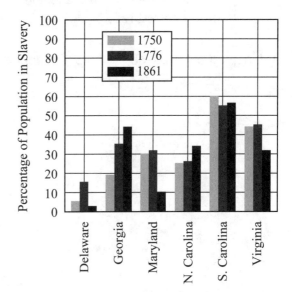

1

The main purpose of the passage is to

A) contrast opposing views on historical international wars.
B) describe the living conditions of slaves during the American Revolution.
C) emphasize the complexity of an era's political policies.
D) stress the urgency of solving a widespread issue.

2

The final paragraph primarily serves to

A) shift the focus of the passage from slavery to religion.
B) introduce a new supporting topic.
C) draw a conclusion from the ideas presented in the passage.
D) characterize the two sides of the slavery debate in terms of their arguments.

Structure Questions

❑ Structure questions ask you to summarize the organization of the passage.

❑ Structure questions typically appear in the following forms:

> Which choice best describes the developmental pattern of the passage?
> During the course of the passage, the central focus shifts from...
> Which choice best reflects the overall order of arguments in the passage?

❑ Mapping the Passage will help you understand the developmental structure of a passage.

PUT IT TOGETHER

The following passage was adapted from a book about the origins of slavery in America.

After the American Revolution, slavery received attention as a dilemma of growing complexity and prominence. The institution of slavery conflicted with the society the new country's leaders were attempting
5 to create. However, slavery retained legal acceptance in most arenas for another hundred years. At the time of the war, an estimated 500,000 slaves resided in the colonies (out of a total population of only 2.5 million), three quarters of whom were located in the
10 south, 200,000 in Virginia alone. The Revolution did not alleviate this situation, however, and the number of slaves actually grew during the war.

Before the American Revolution, slavery was seen by many as another degree of "un-freedom" in a
15 largely un-free world, a view supported by the overall worthlessness of individual life in pre-humanitarian times. This position, however, became more difficult to support following the writing of the Declaration of Independence and state constitutions in the 1770s and
20 1780s. The assertion "that all men are created equal, that they are endowed by their Creator with certain unalienable Rights," seemed entirely incompatible with the practice of slavery. Leaders struggled to clarify the principle of equality, and many disagreed
25 regarding which people were granted the inherent right of freedom. A recent historian writes of the conflict, "Slavery was a national institution and nearly every white American directly or indirectly benefited from it. By 1776, however, nearly every
30 American leader knew that its continued existence violated everything the Revolution was about." From the modern perspective of humanitarian-era thought, the lack of action taken against slavery is problematic and difficult to understand.

35 Initially, slavery came into question because of the use of the term in political rhetoric of the day. The word "slavery" was unavoidable, demanding examination with regards to the literal institution of slavery in America, as well as its use in describing
40 America's subservience to England. The term was invoked often in the 1760s and 1770s to describe the condition of the American colonies in relation to Great Britain.

During the war, many slaves gained their
45 freedom, although often for purely tactical, rather than ethical or humanitarian, reasons. In 1775 Lord Dunmore, the Royal Governor of Virginia, offered freedom to slaves who would escape and aid the British cause. This was the largest source of
50 emancipation before the Civil War. It resulted in tens of thousands of slaves fighting for England. Slaves joining the British cause were guaranteed a new life after the war, regardless of the outcome. In turn, Virginia and Maryland made similar counter-offers.

55 The debate over the colonies' relationship with England led to a fundamental questioning of human freedom. From this questioning, the weapons for the argument against slavery were forged.

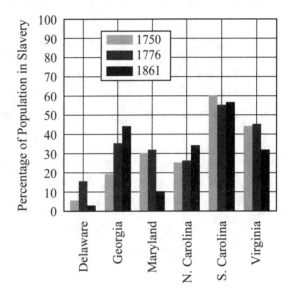

1

During the course of the second paragraph (lines 13-34), the author's focus shifts from

A) justification for a mentality to acknowledgment of a logical contradiction.
B) generalization about human morals to specific accounts from human history.
C) reflections on the mistakes of the past to identification of modern solutions.
D) analysis of a problem to evaluation of several potential solutions.

Word Choice Questions

❑ Word choice questions ask you to make observations about the effect of certain words in passages.

These questions are often similar to purpose questions, because they require you to consider why the author wrote the passage as it is. They may also relate to point of view questions, because they often involve tone.

❑ Word choice questions typically appear in the following forms:

The reference to "_____" has mainly which effect?
The author uses the word "_____" to emphasize...
How does the word "_____" help establish the tone of the passage?

❑ As you read, make note of words (particularly strong verbs and adjectives) that indicate tone. Be aware of the author's attitude toward the subject. If the author states an opinion, how does the tone of the passage support that opinion?

PUT IT TOGETHER

The following passage was adapted from a book about the origins of slavery in America.

After the American Revolution, slavery received attention as a dilemma of growing complexity and prominence. The institution of slavery conflicted with the society the new country's leaders were attempting
5 to create. However, slavery retained legal acceptance in most arenas for another hundred years. At the time of the war, an estimated 500,000 slaves resided in the colonies (out of a total population of only 2.5 million), three quarters of whom were located in the
10 south, 200,000 in Virginia alone. The Revolution did not alleviate this situation, however, and the number of slaves actually grew during the war.

Before the American Revolution, slavery was seen by many as another degree of "un-freedom" in a
15 largely un-free world, a view supported by the overall worthlessness of individual life in pre-humanitarian times. This position, however, became more difficult to support following the writing of the Declaration of Independence and state constitutions in the 1770s and
20 1780s. The assertion "that all men are created equal, that they are endowed by their Creator with certain unalienable Rights," seemed entirely incompatible with the practice of slavery. Leaders struggled to clarify the principle of equality, and many disagreed
25 regarding which people were granted the inherent right of freedom. A recent historian writes of the conflict, "Slavery was a national institution and nearly every white American directly or indirectly benefited from it. By 1776, however, nearly every
30 American leader knew that its continued existence violated everything the Revolution was about." From the modern perspective of humanitarian-era thought, the lack of action taken against slavery is problematic and difficult to understand.

35 Initially, slavery came into question because of the use of the term in political rhetoric of the day. The word "slavery" was unavoidable, demanding examination with regards to the literal institution of slavery in America, as well as its use in describing
40 America's subservience to England. The term was invoked often in the 1760s and 1770s to describe the condition of the American colonies in relation to Great Britain.

During the war, many slaves gained their
45 freedom, although often for purely tactical, rather than ethical or humanitarian, reasons. In 1775 Lord Dunmore, the Royal Governor of Virginia, offered freedom to slaves who would escape and aid the British cause. This was the largest source of
50 emancipation before the Civil War. It resulted in tens of thousands of slaves fighting for England. Slaves joining the British cause were guaranteed a new life after the war, regardless of the outcome. In turn, Virginia and Maryland made similar counter-offers.
55 The debate over the colonies' relationship with England led to a fundamental questioning of human freedom. From this questioning, the weapons for the argument against slavery were forged.

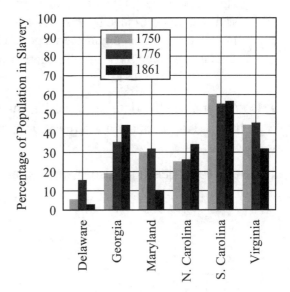

1

The author uses the term "un-free" (line 15) to describe pre-Revolutionary thought in order to

A) show that un-freedom was then considered the opposite of slavery.
B) emphasize there was no concept of freedom, but only various levels of lack of freedom.
C) indicate that everyone was enslaved to Britain before the Revolution.
D) reveal how much slavery was then accepted and practiced in the American colonies.

2

How do the words "difficult," "struggled," and "problematic" help establish the tone of the second paragraph?

A) They establish the controversial nature of an issue that the author discusses objectively.
B) They establish the illogical nature of political policies that the author criticizes.
C) They establish the frustrating nature of a riddle with which the author is irritated.
D) They establish the ingenious nature of a solution that the author praises.

Data Graphics Questions

❑ Data graphic questions ask you to make connections between information presented in charts and tables to the ideas presented in a passage.

❑ Data graphic questions typically appear in the following forms:

> The graph following the passage offers evidence that...
> Which statement made by the author is most consistent with the data in the table?
> Is the author's main argument supported by the data in the table?
> Data in the graph most strongly support which of the following statements?

❑ Do not analyze the data presented in the graphics until you get to the questions that relate to them. Use the question to guide your analysis of the data.

❑ Data graphic questions usually appear at the end of a passage's set of questions.

PUT IT TOGETHER

The following passage was adapted from a book about the origins of slavery in America.

After the American Revolution, slavery received attention as a dilemma of growing complexity and prominence. The institution of slavery conflicted with the society the new country's leaders were attempting
5 to create. However, slavery retained legal acceptance in most arenas for another hundred years. At the time of the war, an estimated 500,000 slaves resided in the colonies (out of a total population of only 2.5 million), three quarters of whom were located in the
10 south, 200,000 in Virginia alone. The Revolution did not alleviate this situation, however, and the number of slaves actually grew during the war.

Before the American Revolution, slavery was seen by many as another degree of "un-freedom" in a
15 largely un-free world, a view supported by the overall worthlessness of individual life in pre-humanitarian times. This position, however, became more difficult to support following the writing of the Declaration of Independence and state constitutions in the 1770s and
20 1780s. The assertion "that all men are created equal, that they are endowed by their Creator with certain unalienable Rights," seemed entirely incompatible with the practice of slavery. Leaders struggled to clarify the principle of equality, and many disagreed
25 regarding which people were granted the inherent right of freedom. A recent historian writes of the conflict, "Slavery was a national institution and nearly every white American directly or indirectly benefited from it. By 1776, however, nearly every
30 American leader knew that its continued existence violated everything the Revolution was about." From the modern perspective of humanitarian-era thought, the lack of action taken against slavery is problematic and difficult to understand.

35 Initially, slavery came into question because of the use of the term in political rhetoric of the day. The word "slavery" was unavoidable, demanding examination with regards to the literal institution of slavery in America, as well as its use in describing
40 America's subservience to England. The term was invoked often in the 1760s and 1770s to describe the condition of the American colonies in relation to Great Britain.

During the war, many slaves gained their
45 freedom, although often for purely tactical, rather than ethical or humanitarian, reasons. In 1775 Lord Dunmore, the Royal Governor of Virginia, offered freedom to slaves who would escape and aid the British cause. This was the largest source of
50 emancipation before the Civil War. It resulted in tens of thousands of slaves fighting for England. Slaves joining the British cause were guaranteed a new life after the war, regardless of the outcome. In turn, Virginia and Maryland made similar counter-offers.

55 The debate over the colonies' relationship with England led to a fundamental questioning of human freedom. From this questioning, the weapons for the argument against slavery were forged.

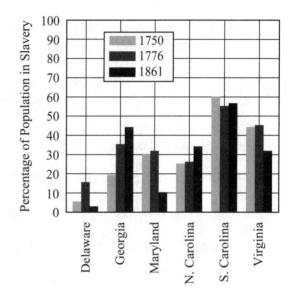

1

Data in the graph indicate that, in the years from the writing of the Declaration of Independence to the American Civil War of 1861, the greatest decline in the percentage of population in slavery occurred in which state?

A) Virginia
B) Georgia
C) Maryland
D) South Carolina

2

Which idea in the passage is best supported by the data provided in the graph?

A) Before the American Revolution, slavery was accepted as one of many injustices in the world.
B) The term "slavery" was used to describe America's relationship with Great Britain.
C) There was ongoing disagreement about equality and the right of freedom.
D) The Declaration of Independence asserted that "all men are created equal."

Paired Passages

❑ The Reading Test may contain two short passages that address the same or related topics.

The first few questions following the passages will relate to the first passage. Next will be several questions relating to the second passage. Finally, there will be several questions that address both passages.

❑ Paired passages are not longer than single passages, but they may be more complex than single passages because they require you to compare and contrast two viewpoints.

As you actively read the second passage, look for where the authors agree and disagree. This will prepare you for the later questions.

❑ Treat the paired passages as two separate passages.

1. Read the first passage and answer the questions for it.

2. Read the second passage and answer the questions for it.

3. Answer the questions that concern both passages.

PUT IT TOGETHER

Questions 1-11 are based on the following passages.

Passage 1 is adapted from an article analyzing the social perception of zoos. Passage 2 is adapted from an article about mankind's relationship to nature.

Passage 1

According to a sign on the chain-link fence where the front gate used to be, Brooklyn's Prospect Park Zoo is being converted into a "cageless natural habitat." This seems a preposterously bold claim,
5 considering that most of the world's remaining natural habitats are, in fact, caged or fenced to keep us out and the animals in. Clearly, whatever is being planned here in Brooklyn will turn out as unnatural as the previous arrangement of cages and pens; it will
10 just be rendered more naturalistically, the animals more subtly contained—better, perhaps, for the animals and certainly for us, for our consciences.

Animals aren't any happier in the new "natural" habitats. These are places we've designed to make
15 ourselves happier about our continued keeping of them. We are, in a sense, trying to eliminate zoos even as we go on designing and maintaining them. With our new habitats, we are trying to conceal from ourselves the zoo as living evidence of our
20 antagonism toward nature, the zoo as manifestation of the fact that our slow, fitful progress toward understanding the animals has always been coterminous with conquering and containing them.

People do not go to zoos to learn about the
25 imminent disappearance of species or to see habitats better viewed on nature shows on public-television. People visit zoos, I think, to engage the wild's otherworldliness; to look, on the most basic level, at ways we didn't end up being. We are, by definition,
30 such fleeting observers of evolution's slow-moving work that visiting a zoo and staring at animals can somehow stay us awhile, reinvolve us in the matter of existence.

By pitting us so closely, one-on-one with
35 displaced and incarcerated animals, the zoo confronts us with our own strange need to look at them in the first place, to sidle up to their apparent blankness and project upon it, however divergent our projections might be. Somehow, while a day at the old city zoo
40 began with our standing face to face with an animal, it always ended with our confronting some truth about ourselves.

Passage 2

We are part of nature, and yet for centuries we've acted as though nature were something apart
45 from us, apart from the specifically human condition. As exploration and industrialization increasingly brought the natural world under human control, nature itself came to seem more and more vulnerable, increasingly precious. Well, now we have lost it.
50 Human encroachment has all but engulfed it.

There is no frontier remote enough, no haven safe enough, to elude advancing human technology. The paradox is that, as we have begun to recognize nature's rightful independence from human values,
55 we have succeeded in dominating to the point that now nature cannot get along without us. It cannot survive without our help. Technology itself must counteract and reverse its own unanticipated consequences.
60 This predicament points at once to a subsequent paradox: captivity means survival. The question is not one of whether we should let the beasts roam free in the wild. We have already seen to it that they cannot. The elephant has no room. The tiger is
65 vanishing. The panda relies on bamboo shoots for food, but bamboo groves themselves will soon be extinct. Rainforests are turning into subsistence farms.

The one thing we must hold in mind is the
70 awesome truth that we have, in effect, already captured all the animals. We have already captured the entire ecosphere in a network of unstoppable human development and expansion. The question, then, is whether we have the will to make of captivity
75 an ark that will protect the remaining creatures from the floodtide of humanity.

It is with the honest recognition of this heavy responsibility for preservation that we must now turn to the creation of animal habitats. Habitats are not
80 cosmetic playgrounds meant to rationalize human domination; they are intentional survival zones created in rational response to that domination. They are sanctuaries of hope, not fuzzy optimism. These habitats provide a reasonable chance for modern
85 nature—actual nature, not a "lost" nature sentimentalized by the stuffed animals in the make-believe worlds of small children and big-game hunters.

1

Lines 13-23 are primarily concerned with showing us that the "natural" habitats

A) provide more livable, miniature environments for animals in captivity.
B) are inhumane enclosures that taunt animals with reminders of lost freedom.
C) enable us to appreciate animal life without interposing our own misconceptions.
D) lull us into disregarding our own involvement in the containment of animals.

2

As used in line 23, "containing" most nearly means

A) having.
B) including.
C) enclosing.
D) encompassing.

3

In lines 27-29, the author asserts that one of the reasons that people go to zoos is to

A) learn about the variety of species in danger of becoming extinct.
B) reflect on the transformations of evolution and our own place in its course.
C) observe animal behavior in a controlled, artificial environment.
D) relieve the monotony of everyday urban life.

4

In lines 29-33, the author implies that in our ordinary lives we

A) are so preoccupied that we hardly notice the nature of life itself.
B) are absorbed in the detailed observation of gradual changes in the natural world.
C) flee from any contemplation of ultimate reality.
D) find meaning and purpose in the larger framework of evolutionary development.

5

The word "pitting" in line 34 most nearly means

A) juxtaposing.
B) facing.
C) mimicking.
D) challenging.

6

Lines 73-76 emphasize the point that

A) we can make a conscious choice to safeguard animals.
B) we must decide whether it is we or the animals who will survive.
C) we are the only ones who can rescue ourselves from the fate of the animals.
D) we are capable of saving the animals because now so few of them are left.

7

The author of Passage 2 would most likely agree with which one of the following assertions?

A) Animals in captivity give up the aggressive behaviors characteristic of their natural way of life.
B) Unlike zoos, habitats let us imagine the remote strangeness of nature without having to expose ourselves to danger.
C) Ideally, habitats ought to help us face up to our responsibility for the planetary destruction of wildlife.
D) City zoos let us relate to caged animals more as unruly house pets than as creatures from the natural world.

8

Which choice provides the best evidence for the answer to the previous question?

A) lines 43-45 ("We… condition")
B) lines 46-49 ("As… precious")
C) lines 51-52 ("There… technology")
D) lines 57-59 ("Technology… consequences")

9

In contrast to Passage 2, the author of Passage 1 discusses the significance of animal habitats from the standpoint of

A) the cultural value of zoos in modern urban centers.
B) the captive animals themselves.
C) the need for a global understanding of the reality of species extinction.
D) the responsibility of technology to remedy the predicament of the natural world.

10

Which choice provides the best evidence for the answer to the previous question?

A) lines 13-14 ("Animals… habitats")
B) lines 14-16 ("These… them")
C) lines 16-17 ("We… them")
D) lines 18-23 ("With… them")

11

Whereas the author of Passage 1 views habitats as an attempt by humans to ignore the reality of imprisoned animals, the author of Passage 2 sees them primarily as

A) a logical necessity of conservation.
B) a needed escape from the pressures of life in a big city.
C) a way to change people's attitudes about nature.
D) attractive exhibits intended to educate the public about environmental concerns.

Reading Summary

Reading the Passages

- As you are reading and analyzing a passage, acknowledge the role of the writer. Try to determine the writer's opinion on the passage's topic. Ask yourself: Why did the writer choose to write the passage as he or she did?

- **Stay engaged**. Do not read passively, waiting for the passage to reveal information to you. Instead, interact directly with the passage and think about what the author is saying or trying to convey.

- **Map the Passage**. Develop an organized understanding of a Reading passage by finding the main idea of each paragraph.

- Treat paired passages as two separate passages.

  1. Read the first passage and answer the questions for it.

  2. Read the second passage and answer the questions for it.

  3. Answer the questions that concern both passages.

Answering the Questions

- Ask questions while you read.

- Understand the question before you look at the answer choices.

- Make sure that you've found the **best** answer, not just a good one. Reading questions, especially difficult ones, will usually contain at least one or two choices that are "almost right."

Reading Practice

Questions 1-11 are based on the following passage.

This passage is adapted from a novel about a young woman's evolving relationship with her mother.

My mother rested one hip against the rumbling clothes-dryer in her basement, her face impassive. Only her quick fingers moved, pressing sharp folds into my sister's maroon-and-gold cheerleading
5 uniform. Upstairs, my sister and stepfather were enjoying a warm May afternoon, but the basement was already dark. Racks of winter clothes lurked in the shadows.

A bulb hanging over the washer lent Mom's wavy
10 hair and fine skin a yellow cast. Before we'd come to this house, and its basement laundry room, she had lived many years in the desert. There, in the constant sun, her hair had permanently faded to a honey brown, while her cheeks were always warmer than
15 mine, even in the summer when I worked outdoors and she sat in her office all day. Her fingers were long like mine, with the same improbably beautiful knobs at the knuckles. We'd both inherited them from her grandmother, who in her eighties was still
20 crocheting jewelry boxes and afghans for my ever-growing army of cousins. Unbreakable, precise hands. Hers had laid aside the uniform, turned their attention to a pair of gray slacks. Mine folded beneath my chest.

25 I set one bare, trembling foot against a box of books I'd brought home from school and waited for her face to move. The gray slacks lay flat beside the shiny gold pleated skirt. A faded pair of jeans, mine, danced crisply in the air between us.

30 "Rook is picking me up at midnight," I said. The jeans collapsed atop the slacks, the hands stilled momentarily.

"What about your job at the paper?" She sounded as tired as she looked. "Karl was counting on you to
35 pick up your old beat."

I tried to hide my reaction. Before leaving for Berkeley the year before, I had worked a freelance beat at the local paper. Karl, my editor, was counting on me not only to pick up the beat for the summer,
40 but also to turn in a long profile for the front page in about 24 hours. Karl had given me my first job, and I hated letting him down. But not enough to spend my nineteenth summer living at home, covering town meetings and scouring police logs for "Man Bites
45 Dog" tidbits.

"He can live without me," I shrugged. "He's been doing just fine all year. This is the chance I've been dreaming of forever."

She turned away at that, her hands waking as her
50 face remained unreadable. A brightly patterned bedsheet took up the space between us. The

conversation was over. Automatically I reached out for the sheet's edge, joining her in the simple Dance of Bedsheet Folding we'd been practicing since I was
55 a tiny child.

The chance I was taking was an unplanned trip to New Orleans with some friends. It had the makings of a Great American Road Trip: thirteen people, one brightly muralled van and an amorphous destination
60 somewhere in New Orleans. The call had come late Friday, from Rook, a man I'd known only a few weeks but already adored. School had been out all of three days, and I was restless at home, anxious for Rook's promised visit. Instead, he called and asked
65 me to travel to New Orleans. They were leaving Monday morning. It was Sunday afternoon now, and I'd just told my mother I'd be going with them.

I watched her face, imagining envy in the exhaustion lining her beloved features. This
70 movement – running, traveling, tripping, movement – was becoming a family tradition. At my age, the woman now refusing to look at me had dropped out of college to move to San Diego in an old VW with her boyfriend, two friends, two dogs, and an injured
75 owl. It was 1970. She'd spent the summer touring as a roadie with a music festival, and California was calling her. She made it as far as Arizona.

After eleven years in the lush desert outside of Tucson, Mom took us back to the boring safety of her
80 mother's home, where my great-grandmother tried to educate her great-granddaughters in what she called "the art of being a lady," while instead we learned about junk food and cable television.

From there we moved where her job pushed us,
85 coming to rest in a quiet town north of Boston. Now, my mother had a nice house by the water, an office job she claimed to love, a husband who rubbed her feet when they sat on the couch in the evenings, health insurance for her kids. Now, I was taking a
90 definitive step away from that creeping normalcy. The sheet was folded – she took it from me without looking up, and I turned away.

1

When the narrator calls her mother's face "impassive" (line 2) she most likely means that

_____

_____

_____

_____

2

The description of the hands (lines 16-22) primarily serves to

_____

_____

_____

_____

3

The statement that the mother's "hands stilled momentarily" (lines 31-32) implies that

_____

_____

_____

_____

4

Which lines provide the best evidence for the answer to the previous question?

_____

_____

_____

_____

5

When her mother mentions Karl, the narrator tries to hide her reaction because she

A) regrets disappointing him.
B) doesn't particularly like him.
C) wants to continue the conversation.
D) knows that he is her mother's friend.

6

Which choice provides the best evidence for the answer to the previous question?

A) Lines 38-41 ("Karl…hours")
B) Lines 41-42 ("Karl…down")
C) Lines 46-47 ("He…year")
D) Lines 60-62 ("The…adored")

7

The narrator's statement in line 47-48, "this is the chance I've been dreaming of forever" refers to her

A) college education at Berkeley.
B) move to Arizona.
C) impending travel plans.
D) summer job at the newspaper.

8

The word "amorphous," as it is used in line 59, most likely means

A) shapeless.
B) metaphysical.
C) undetermined.
D) ephemeral.

9

The narrator describes her mother's youth (lines 71-77) in order to

A) discredit her mother's opinion.
B) relate an interesting story.
C) define her mother's character.
D) demonstrate their common ground.

10

All of the following might be seen as examples of what the narrator calls "creeping normalcy," (line 90) EXCEPT

A) a family health insurance plan.
B) a nine-to-five job.
C) a stable relationship.
D) a 1970's VW mini-van.

11

It can be inferred from the last paragraph (lines 84-92) that the narrator

A) is not going to New Orleans after all.
B) dislikes folding sheets.
C) feels more connected to her mother.
D) will follow in her mother's footsteps.

Questions 12-22 are based on the following passage.

This passage is adapted from an article about an area containing a number of rare marine fossils.

The ecosystems of shallow marine waters—coral reefs would be a good example—are the most diverse in the modern oceans, and they have probably been so throughout the history of life. And yet, they are
5   not well represented in the fossil record. Environments that are rich in life are also rich in the means of destroying it. When a shrimp or fish dies, it is rapidly devoured by scavenging crustaceans and decomposed by bacteria, and every trace of the
10   organism is destroyed in the process. In order for a fossil to be left, the dead organism must somehow be sheltered from the grave-robbing crabs, starfish, and bacteria that thrive in shallow-water environments. An animal stands a much better chance of being
15   preserved as a fossil in deep water, where there are fewer bacteria and no scavengers.

The discovery known as the Burgess Shale is an exception. A lucky series of accidents, about 530 million years ago, transported shallow-water animals
20   by the hundreds of thousands from their normal environment into much deeper water. They were killed in the process but came to lie in a place where their trace could be preserved. The means was probably a mudslide: the animals, it is thought, were
25   living at the edge of a cliff made of mud, and when the cliff collapsed it carried down with it an avalanche of shallow-water animals into the depths. The Burgess Shale fossil locality is now eight thousand feet up a mountain quarry in British
30   Columbia, Canada. It was first discovered in 1909 by Charles Walcott.

Walcott never had the time to work on the fossils he discovered as thoroughly as he wished, but he did make some preliminary observations. These
35   observations were highly influential. Walcott placed all the Burgess Shale fossils into already known groups of animals, noticing resemblances to shrimp, crabs, and so on. This seemed to make sense to many people. After all, you might expect that if you traced
40   life back over 500 million years, you would come to some ancestors of species that exist in the present day.

But this did not turn out to be true. Walcott did not place the fossils so much as shoe-horn them into
45   these groups. In 1966, a Cambridge geologist named Harry Whittington reexamined the fossils. He discovered they had a three-dimensional structure, preserved within the rocks. Walcott had thought the fossils were squashed flat on the rock surface, but
50   Whittington drilled down with a dentist's drill and

found there was more structure below. He was thus able to reconstruct the animals in much more detail.

In a series of painstaking drawings, Whittington reconstructed the animals preserved as fossils in the
55   Burgess Shale. He drew one of them, the Opabinia, to look something like a cross between a worm and a shrimp; it had no legs, and its gills were attached laterally on each body segment. It also had five eyes, four of them on stalks, and a flexible nozzle with
60   claws on the end—rather like an elephant's trunk with pincers. But among all of Whittington's reconstructions, the strangest animal is the Wiwaxia. It is probably best to look at the drawings he made, because the Wiwaxia is so surreal that everyone will
65   come up with a different way of describing it. The animal was shaped like a disc, or the shell of a turtle, and the disc was covered with hundreds of shapes like nut shells and two rows of what look like bent knife blades along the back.

70   The animals turned out to be very different from what Walcott had believed. Scientists who studied Whittington's drawings have come to the conclusions that these were not primitive versions of modern animals. These animals, they believe, were related to
75   modern forms, but as separate early radiations within a broad category and not as ancestors.

Some of the more astonishing Burgess animals do not even fit into modern categories at all. The Opabinia and Wiwaxia are recognizable as animals,
80   but they belong to groups that are no longer represented in our oceans. What were the factors that drove them into extinction? Why did other groups survive when they did not? Scientists may never know, but these questions raise an important point
85   about the nature of evolution. It may have been mainly a matter of luck which groups survived and which did not.

The animals which happen to be alive today are probably the fortunate survivors of a series of
90   contingent accidents. And this, no doubt, is true of every species. There is nothing inevitable about the evolution of complex living things, and whole groups of animals have been lost in its twists and turns. This seems also to be true of humans. From the evidence
95   of the Burgess Shale, it is clear that even we are not the climax of a predictable, progressive, evolutionary drama.

12

According to the author of this passage, animals from the most heavily populated ocean environments tend not to be preserved as fossils because

A) the sedimentary deposits necessary for fossilization are not present in coral reefs.
B) these populations do not occupy deep water.
C) their remains are eaten.
D) shallow-water environments do not contain enough bacteria.

13

Which choice provides the best evidence for the answer to the previous question?

A) Lines 1-4 ("The…life")
B) Lines 7-9 ("When…bacteria")
C) Lines 18-21 ("A…water")
D) Lines 22-24 ("The…mud")

14

The author describes the accidents in the second paragraph as "lucky" (line 18) because they

_____

_____

_____

_____

15

By using the word "shoe-horn" in line 44 the author implies that

_____

_____

_____

_____

16

According to the author, the interpretation of the Burgess Shale fossils changed most dramatically after the discovery that

A) the fossils were not two-dimensional.
B) the fossils had been preserved in a deep-water environment.
C) certain species were extinct 500 million years ago.
D) regions thousands of feet above sea level could contain marine fossils.

17

According to the passage, what was the most important contribution Whittington made to the scientific understanding of the Burgess Shale fossils?

A) He classified the fossils within existing groups of modern animals.
B) He developed a new theory of evolutionary accident to account for both their existence and their eventual destruction.
C) He was able to dissect the Opabinia and the Wiwaxia.
D) He studied the fossils and made detailed drawings of what the animals might have looked like.

18

Which choice provides the best evidence for the answer to the previous question?

A) Lines 35-38 ("Walcott…on")
B) Lines 39-42 ("After…day")
C) Lines 50-52 ("Whittington…detail")
D) Lines 77-78 ("Some…at all")

19

The word "radiations" in line 75 most nearly means

A) variations.
B) contaminations.
C) generations.
D) accidents.

20

The author claims that "we are not the climax of a predictable, progressive, evolutionary drama" in lines 95-97 in order to

A) demonstrate the precise order of evolution.
B) highlight the importance of his findings.
C) present his findings from a theatrical perspective.
D) dispute the common human-centric view of the world.

21

Based on the passage, which of the following statements best describes how the Burgess Shale fossils have influenced scientific theories about evolution?

A) They have encouraged scientists to postulate a greater role for random chance in evolution.
B) The strange groups of animals represented there have changed our modern system of classification and thus our understanding of life in general.
C) They have expanded scientific understanding of the specific causes that drove some animal groups to extinction.
D) Scientists have been able to identify in the fossils a previously unprecedented variety in anatomical design.

22

The author of this passage would most likely agree with which of the following hypotheses about evolution?

A) Early groups of terrestrial vertebrates were never meant to survive.
B) Modern animals did not evolve in distinct groups.
C) Humanity is the goal or conclusion of millions of years of evolution.
D) The accidental extinctions of species give other species the chance to survive and evolve.

Questions 23-32 are based on the following passage.

This passage is from a short story by Willa Cather.

I first met Myra Henshawe when I was fifteen, but I had known about her ever since I could remember anything at all. She and her runaway marriage were the theme of the most interesting stories that were
5 told in our family. My mother and aunts still heard from Myra Driscoll, as they called her, and Aunt Lydia occasionally went to New York to visit her. Myra had been the brilliant and attractive figure among the friends of their girlhood, and her life had
10 been as exciting and varied as ours was monotonous.

Though she had grown up in our town, Myra Henshawe never, after her elopement, came back but once. It was in the year when I was finishing High School, and she must then have been a woman of
15 forty-five. She came in the early autumn, with brief notice by telegraph. Her husband, who held an executive position in the corporate offices of a large Eastern railroad, was coming west on business, and they were going to stop over for two days. He was to
20 stay at the Parthian, as our new hotel was called, and Mrs. Henshawe would stay with Aunt Lydia.

I was a favorite with my Aunt Lydia. She had three big sons, but no daughters, and she thought my mother scarcely appreciated me. She was always
25 giving me what she called "advantages," on the side. My mother and sister were asked to dinner at Aunt Lydia's on the night of the Henshawes' arrival, but she had whispered to me: "I want you to come in early, an hour or so before the others, and get
30 acquainted with Myra."

That evening I slipped quietly in at my aunt's front door and while I was taking off my wraps in the hall I could see, at the far end, a short, plump woman in a black velvet dress, seated upon the sofa and
35 softly playing on Cousin Bert's guitar. She must have heard me, and, glancing up, she saw my reflection in a mirror; she put down the guitar, rose, and stood to await my approach.

I hastened across the room with so much
40 bewilderment and concern in my face that she gave a short laugh as she held her hand out to me.

I could not meet the playful curiosity of her eyes at all, so I fixed my stare on a necklace of carved amethysts she wore inside the square cut neck of her
45 dress. I suppose I stared, for she said suddenly, "Does this necklace annoy you? I'll take it off if it does."

I was utterly speechless. I could feel my cheeks burning. Seeing that she had hurt me, she was sorry,
50 threw her arm impulsively around me, drew me into the corner of the sofa and sat down beside me.

By the time her husband came in I had begun to think she was going to like me. I wanted her to, but I felt I didn't have half a chance with her; her
55 charming, fluent voice, her clear enunciation bewildered me. And I was never sure whether she was making fun of me or of the thing we were talking about. Her sarcasm was so quick, so fine at the point – it was like being touched by a metal so cold that
60 one doesn't know whether one is burned or chilled. I was fascinated, but very ill at ease, and I was glad when Oswald Henshawe arrived from the hotel.

He came directly into the room without taking off his overcoat and went directly up to his wife, who
65 rose and kissed him. Again I was some time in catching up with the situation; I wondered whether they might have come down from Chicago on different trains; for she was clearly glad to see him – glad not merely that he was safe and had got round
70 on time, but because his presence gave her lively personal pleasure. I was not accustomed to that kind of feeling in people long married.

23

The narrator uses the phrase "runaway marriage" (line 3) in order to

A) demonstrate how strange the narrator thinks Myra is.
B) foreshadow the narrator's own marriage.
C) contrast Myra's exciting life with the narrator's own.
D) express disapproval over the idea of moving to New York City.

24

Which choice provides the best evidence for the answer to the previous question?

A) Lines 5-7 ("My…her")
B) Lines 8-10 ("Myra…monotonous")
C) Lines 11-13 ("Though…once")
D) Lines 24-25 ("She…side")

25

The author mentions in lines 16-18 that Myra's husband works in the corporate offices in order to

_____

_____

_____

_____

26

The word "advantages" (line 25) most nearly means

_____

_____

_____

_____

27

The first three paragraphs of the passage serve primarily to

A) set up the narrator's first meeting with Myra Henshawe.
B) describe the lavish lifestyle the Henshawes led.
C) demonstrate the narrator's fondness for Aunt Lydia.
D) show the reader how happy the narrator is.

28

The phrase "it was like being touched. . . burned or chilled" in lines 59-60 refers to

A) Myra Henshawe's curious eyes.
B) Myra's sarcastic sense of humor.
C) Aunt Lydia's disapproval of the narrator's actions.
D) the mysterious stones of the necklace.

29

Which choice provides the best evidence for the answer to the previous question?

A) Lines 48-49 ("I…burning")
B) Lines 52-54 ("I…her")
C) Lines 56-58 ("And…point")
D) Lines 60-62 ("I…hotel")

30

It can be inferred from the passage that the narrator was "glad when Oswald Henshawe arrived" (lines 61-62) because

_____

_____

_____

_____

31

The last sentence of the passage (lines 71-72) implies that people in the narrator's own family

A) are not likely to get married.
B) do not like Myra Henshawe.
C) stop talking to one another when they marry.
D) lose romantic interest in their spouses over time.

32

Based on the information in the passage, all of the following statements are true EXCEPT:

A) The narrator is Lydia's niece.
B) Myra, Lydia and the narrator's mother are all related.
C) Myra Henshawe is a considerate person.
D) The narrator is intrigued by Myra's life.

Questions 33-43 are based on the following passage.

This passage is adapted from an article about archaeological research on the development of permanent settlements and agriculture.

The rise of cities during the Neolithic Period was a significant event in human prehistory. However, just why people started living in cities rather than in isolated family groups is a topic of intense research.
5　Archeological finds at the Neolithic town of Çatalhöyük in modern-day Turkey suggest that agricultural practices may not have been the driving force in this transition, as they were once thought to be.

10　Until recently, many archaeologists thought that the transition from nomadic life to settlements and the transition from hunting and gathering to farming and animal domestication were part of one process: the Neolithic Revolution. Since crops and animals
15　would have required that early farmers stay nearby, it would have made sense for these farmers to create permanent settlements. Settled farming would have created agricultural surpluses that permitted some people to quit farming and become full-time artisans
20　or members of other professions, and new social and economic relationships resulting from this division of labor would have encouraged people to group together in larger towns.

4500 years older than the Egyptian pyramids,
25　Çatalhöyük harbored as many as 10,000 people across nearly 30 acres of land. At the time of its discovery, Çatalhöyük surpassed all other known settlement sites in terms of age and size, prompting its discoverers to hail it as the world's oldest known
30　city. However, more careful excavations in the 1990s have suggested that, despite its population, Çatalhöyük shows little evidence of the social and agricultural advances that archaeologists' theories regarding the Neolithic Revolution predict would be
35　found in an early city.

Although the homes in Çatalhöyük have similar structures and floorplans, there is evidence that families constructed their own homes rather than relying on specialized builders. Microscopic studies
40　of the plaster and mud bricks from different houses reveal significant variation in the components used, indicating that there was no standardized way of producing these materials. Although it was originally believed that the highly crafted obsidian objects
45　found in the homes – such as carefully worked blades and mirrors – must have been the work of specialized artisans, the discovery of obsidian flakes on the floors of homes suggests that this work was in fact carried out in individual dwellings. Furthermore, the recent
50　excavations have unearthed no public buildings that would suggest a shared civic life.

Agriculture seems to have been at a relatively early stage in Çatalhöyük. Plant remains in and near the dwellings indicate that inhabitants relied largely
55　on wild plants and seeds that grew in the nearby wetlands. Some grains may have been cultivated, but there is no evidence that they were ground for bread, and it is unlikely that crops were irrigated. While earlier studies suggested that cattle were
60　domesticated early in the life of Çatalhöyük and were numerous in the city, recent analysis of bones indicates that sheep, which are known to have been domesticated much earlier, were actually far more numerous than cattle.

65　These findings, along with similar evidence from some other Near East sites, call into question the link between settled life and agriculture proposed by the Neolithic Revolution. Ian Hodder, who leads the Çatalhöyük Research Project, has puzzled over the
70　relationship between sedentism and the development of agriculture. According to Hodder, a major site with such a large population but such little domestic agriculture contradicts common sense, since the natural resources around Çatalhöyük could have been
75　more easily exploited by a dispersed population. "Since Çatalhöyük, there's been a change in my mind," says Hodder. "If agriculture didn't cause the settled life, then what did? One possibility is that sites like this were built around ritual." The people of
80　Çatalhöyük and other Neolithic settlements must have had reasons for coming together, and further research at these sites may produce the foundations for a new theory of city origins.

33

According to archaeologists' theories of the Neolithic Revolution, as described in the second paragraph, how did farming result in new divisions of labor?

A) Larger farms produced a need for specialized assistants who could run them effectively.
B) Because farming requires tools, its rise produced a need for blacksmiths, woodworkers, and other artisans.
C) Farmers clustered together to make large settlements that were economically reliant on the crops produced.
D) Because a small number of farmers can feed a large number of people, some people were able take up jobs other than farming.

34

The passage most strongly suggests that the archaeologists who discovered Çatalhöyük initially believed that

A) their early excavations were not careful enough.

B) Çatalhöyük's size and age would prove that Neolithic people went through a revolution of agricultural development.

C) agriculture in Çatalhöyük was at a primitive stage of development and depended primarily on foraging for wild plants.

D) larger and older cities were likely to be found in the surrounding areas.

35

Which choice provides the best evidence for the answer to the previous question?

A) lines 30-35 ("However,…city.")

B) lines 43-49 ("Although… dwellings.")

C) lines 58-64 ("While… cattle.")

D) lines 71-75 ("According…population.")

36

Within the context of the passage, the main purpose of the second paragraph (lines 10-23) is to

A) offer historical background for contextualizing recent archaeological findings.

B) introduce a rejected theory of city development as a basis for explaining a more recently accepted theory of city development.

C) explain a process in order to showcase an example of that process.

D) present a theory in order to show how recent discoveries have invalidated it.

37

The author develops the third paragraph (lines 24-35) by presenting

A) scientific evidence followed by a hypothesis.

B) controversial findings that are then dismissed.

C) general claims followed by specific assessments.

D) an accepted view that is called into question.

38

As used in line 45, "worked" most nearly means

A) fashioned.

B) labored.

C) operated.

D) performed.

39

As it is used in line 56, "cultivated" most nearly means

A) reined.

B) trained.

C) farmed.

D) promoted.

40

The discovery that sheep were more common than cattle at Çatalhöyük (lines 58-64) is mentioned in order to

A) counter the claim that agriculture was at a more advanced stage in the settlement.

B) distinguish advances in crop farming from advances in animal domestication.

C) characterize a long-standing debate about whether sheep or cattle were domesticated earlier.

D) introduce evidence in favor of the Neolithic Revolution.

41

According to lines 65-83, why is it surprising that Çatalhöyük had both a large population and limited agriculture?

A) Usually cities were centered around the rituals of farm life.

B) We do not understand the reasons that Neolithic people had for coming together in cities.

C) Relying on the wild plants or animals would have been easier if people spread out.

D) The development of agriculture didn't cause the settled life.

42

The author includes the quote from Ian Hodder (lines 76-79) primarily to

A) provide a view about the origins of Çatalhöyük that is incompatible with the views discussed elsewhere in the passage.
B) emphasize that researchers have not yet fully developed explanations that are alternatives to the Neolithic Revolution.
C) suggest that archaeologists may never find answers to some of their questions.
D) contrast his uncertainty with the certainty of the scientific research being conducted at Çatalhöyük.

43

Which choice provides the best evidence for the answer to the previous question?

A) lines 2-4 ("However… research.")
B) lines 14-17 ("Since… settlements.")
C) lines 17-23 ("Settled… towns.")
D) lines 26-30 ("At the time…city.")

Questions 44-54 are based on the following passage.

This passage is adapted from an article about the discovery of penicillin.

Despite the common adulation of individual genius, the advancement of scientific knowledge is nearly always an incremental, collaborative process. Progress tends to be slow and spotty at first. Early
5 research reveals clues which lead to theories; theories drive further research; promising ideas are tested and rejected. Finally, usually after the community has had time to ponder and build understanding, practical applications arise that solve real-world problems.
10 The process may take years or decades, but mainstream society cannot be bothered to follow every turn. We tend to wait for the big breakthroughs, streamline the details, and heap our admiration on lone figures, often leaving the most important work
15 as footnotes.

Sir Alexander Fleming, his Nobel complimented by knighthood, became an object of scientific lore following the successful mass production of penicillin, perhaps the most important turning point
20 in the history of modern medicine. It is the sort of tale that makes otherwise esoteric science not merely digestible, but popular. When Fleming, a bacteriologist on staff at a Scottish hospital, left for his August vacation in 1928, he hastily stacked his
25 cultures of staphylococci bacteria on a bench in the corner of his untidy laboratory. Upon returning one month later, he was surprised to find that a mold had developed on some of the cultures, and that the bacteria nearest to this mold had died while his other
30 samples remained healthy. Fleming came to recognize the miraculous mold as a member of the Penicillium genus; dubbing the material it released penicillin, he set about experimenting with its ability to treat bacterial infections in humans. His early
35 results were promising; penicillin not only reversed the spread of staphylococci, it was also shown to kill the bacteria that caused many other destructive diseases of the age, including scarlet fever, pneumonia, meningitis, diphtheria, and gonorrhea.
40 Fleming published his results in the *Journal of Experimental Pathology* in 1929, but they received little attention from the broader community. Because he lacked the proper facilities and scientific expertise necessary to work with penicillin, Fleming found the
45 mold difficult to produce in quantity, and he struggled to isolate its antibiotic agent. Furthermore, Fleming was working with a type of penicillin that acted rather slowly on infectious bacterias, and he worried that the finicky substance would not survive
50 once inside the human body. Discouraged, Fleming eventually abandoned his research into penicillin.

Fortunately, Oxford University Professor Howard Florey stumbled upon Fleming's paper in 1938, as he searched for a cure to bacterial infections
55 on behalf of the British and American militaries. Florey assembled a team of expert researchers in one of Britain's most well-equipped laboratories; among the most capable of his employees was a young biochemist named Ernst Chain. During the summer
60 of 1940, the scientists tested a new penicillin mold extract on a collection of 50 mice infected with streptococcus; the mice injected with penicillin recovered and survived. Florey believed the results promising enough to move to human trials, but there
65 was still the problem of producing enough penicillin to treat larger organisms.

The first person treated by Florey and Chain was Albert Alexander, a local police constable who had developed an infection after suffering a small cut to
70 his face while working in his rose garden. Alexander's condition had worsened quickly; streptococci and staphylococci had spread first to his eyes and scalp, and then to his shoulder and lungs. Having heard of Alexander's condition from
75 colleagues at the Radcliffe Institute, Florey and Chain suggested trying penicillin. Five days after his initial treatment, Alexander's infections had begun to retreat; but further doses of penicillin were required, and because Florey and Chain could not possibly
80 produce their antibiotic solution fast enough, Alexander ultimately died. It was another member of the Oxford team, Norman Heatley, who was most instrumental in developing the x-ray technologies and filtration techniques necessary to mass produce
85 penicillin.

When news reports touting the new wonder-drug swept the world in 1941, it was the story of Fleming's chance discovery that captivated the public. Years of challenging technical work by the
90 Oxford team, whose efforts that had made the breakthrough possible, were largely ignored. The modest Fleming did his best to share the spotlight, but it is his name alone that graces the lips of millions of school-age children, often mentioned alongside the
95 likes of Louis Pasteur, Percy Julian, and Jonas Salk. Fleming was a dedicated biologist who made a fortunate discovery, but it took a team of top scientists to advance antibiotics from an interesting observation to a revolutionary treatment.

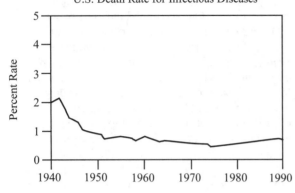

U.S. Death Rate for Infectious Diseases

44

Based on the passage, which choice best describes the relationship between Fleming's work and that of the Oxford researchers?

A) Fleming made an initial discovery that was the basis for work by the Oxford researchers.
B) Fleming and the Oxford researchers arrived independently at similar discoveries.
C) Fleming proposed a scientific theory that was challenged by the Oxford researchers.
D) Fleming refined a scientific technique pioneered by the Oxford researchers.

45

Which choice provides the best evidence for the answer to the previous question?

A) Lines 7-9 ("Finally... problems")
B) Lines 16-20 ("Sir Alexander... medicine")
C) Lines 40-42 ("Fleming... community")
D) Lines 96-99 ("Fleming... treatment")

46

Which description of penicillin is supported by the passage?

A) Penicillin is a virus that spreads quickly among humans.
B) Penicillin is extracted from mold and used to combat bacterial infections.
C) Penicillin is a bacteria grown from staphylococci.
D) Penicillin does not occur naturally and must be synthesized inside of a laboratory.

47

Which choice provides the best evidence for the answer to the previous question?

A) Lines 81-85 ("It was... penicillin")
B) Lines 4-7 ("Progress... rejected")
C) Lines 71-73 ("Alexander's... lungs")
D) Lines 30-34 ("Fleming... humans")

48

As used in line 4, "spotty" most nearly means

A) stained.
B) microscopic.
C) inconsistent.
D) abbreviated.

49

Lines 10-15 ("The process... footnotes.") draw a distinction between

A) the work of amateur scientists and that of trained professionals.
B) the advancement of scientific knowledge and public perception of such progress.
C) conducting scientific research and writing for scientific journals.
D) previously held beliefs and modern scientific knowledge.

50

The passage most strongly suggests that the "community" mentioned in lines 7 and 42 is composed of

A) research scientists.
B) medical patients.
C) people living in close proximity to the Radcliffe Institute.
D) citizens of Britain and the United States of America.

51

In relation to the rest of the passage, the primary function of first paragraph is to

A) explain a scientific principle that is subsequently refuted by the author.
B) consider an event that contradicts a theory presented in the following paragraph.
C) introduce a problem for which a solution is described later in the passage.
D) present a claim that is illustrated in the remainder of the passage.

52

The author probably considers Fleming to have been

A) a brilliant researcher at the top of his field.
B) a fraud who manipulated the public to achieve fame.
C) an unremarkable scientist who made an auspicious discovery.
D) an under-appreciated genius whose achievements have only recently begun to gain recognition.

53

Data in the graph following the passage most strongly support which of the following statements?

A) Penicillin usage has declined since the mid-1970s.
B) Penicillin usage has declined since the early 1940s.
C) The widespread usage of penicillin brought a decline in the mortality of infectious diseases.
D) The widespread usage of penicillin brought an increase in the mortality of infectious diseases.

54

Which of the following best describes the role of Norman Heatley in the development of penicillin?

A) Heatley was the first person to be treated with penicillin.
B) Heatley developed new techniques for producing penicillin.
C) Heatley was the first researcher to publish a scientific paper on penicillin.
D) Heatley lobbied the British military to adopt penicillin.

Questions 55-65 are based on the following passage.

This passage is adapted from an article on the potential dangers and prevention of tin whisker growth in electronic devices.

For decades, electronic components—in everything from radios to the International Space Station—have been soldered together using a tin-lead alloy. However, in 2006 the European Union
5   directive for the Reduction of Hazardous Substances (RoHS) was put in place. This law banned the use of lead in all electronic assemblies, and will inevitably catalyze broader changes in the global electronics industry. It is a shift that, according to George
10   Galyon of IBM, "may expose the next generation of electronic equipment to massive field service failure rates." In addition to the increased costs and concerns over the changes in electronic assembly methods that the new alternative solder formulations might entail,
15   many in the industry are now concerned about other disasters that the use of lead-free solders might usher in: failing cell phones, unreliable missile launch systems, and GPS satellites falling from orbit. And what is the cause of such doomsday scenarios?
20   Whiskers. Tin whiskers.

Tin whiskers are filamentary growths that sprout spontaneously from electroplated tin surfaces, producing fine nanowire "whiskers" with diameters ranging from one to five microns. These whiskers can
25   grow to upwards of 5,000 microns (5mm) in length, bridging gaps between closely spaced electrical conductors on circuit boards. If this occurs, the highly conductive tin whiskers can readily short out electrical components. While pure tin solders are
30   observed to produce whiskers, the tin-lead alloy solders that have been used for decades (typically an amalgam of 63% tin and 37% lead) show a reduced propensity for sprouting whiskers.

There has been a long history of whisker-related
35   electronic failures due to pure solders with no lead content. During World War II, radios and other communication devices used cadmium-plated electrical contacts that were subject to similar shorting. A 1951 report compiled after the war by
40   K.G. Compton at Bell Laboratories triggered a series of long-term research projects into how, and under what conditions, these whiskers form. Tin, it was soon discovered, produces whiskers similar to cadmium's. Foremost in the minds of the researchers
45   during the 1950s was the development of whisker mitigation practices, one effect of which was the widespread adoption of tin-lead solders by the electronics industry. As the decade progressed, new experimental tools such as the SEM (scanning
50   electron microscope) and the TEM (transmission

electron microscope) were used to gain new insights into the physics of whisker formation. With the advent of electron microscopy, scientists were able to observe tin whiskers growing: they appeared as
55   extrusions from the substrate, pushed up from material at the base rather than accreted at the tip of the whisker. Various mechanisms were proposed to explain the formation of such whiskers, including the effects of recrystallization of the metal, dislocations,
60   and the formation of thin areas or cracks in the oxide layer on the surface of the metal through which the tin whiskers might emerge preferentially.

The increased reliance on electronics in the 21st-century world and the enactment of the RoHS
65   legislation in Europe have both served to spur an upsurge in whisker-related research. Focused ion beam (FIB) microscopy and micro-focus X-ray diffraction (XRD) have the potential to allow direct measurement of the stresses that cause the formation
70   of metallic whiskers and to provide detailed depictions of the various habits of whisker growth. The well-intentioned ban on lead-based solders is certainly laudable—lead exposure, even at low levels, is known to produce harmful effects on
75   children, including lowered IQs and reduced attention spans. However, concerned scientists such as Galyon are no less justified in worrying that the ban might result in unmitigated whisker growth that could cause higher rates of failure for all manner of mission-
80   critical devices, not just electric razors.

The table shows statistics of the growth of tin whiskers on 200 samples of tin monitored over one year. 100 samples were kept at room temperature, and 100 samples were kept in an oven at a constant temperature.

Growth of Tin Whiskers		
Environmental Conditions	Oven (52° C)	Room Temperature (23° C)
Mean	0.81 mm	1.31 mm
Standard Deviation	0.30 mm	0.42 mm
Maximum	1.62 mm	1.96 mm
Minimum	0.43 mm	0.54 mm

55

Which of the following is mentioned in the passage as an example of a device or system that is susceptible to failure due to the formation of metallic whiskers?

A) Radio
B) Satellite phone
C) Microscope
D) Computer network

56

The author of this passage would most likely agree that

A) lead poisoning is a more serious threat than any danger posed by tin whisker formation.
B) excessive regulation in the European Union has reduced the potential for economic growth.
C) additional whisker-mitigation research, similar to studies carried out in the 1950s, should be encouraged.
D) adoption of cadmium-based solders might alleviate the tin whisker problem.

57

Which choice provides the best evidence for the answer to the previous question?

A) Lines 4-12 ("However, . . . rates.")
B) Lines 39-42 ("A 1951 report... whiskers form.")
C) Lines 42-44 ("Tin, it was soon... cadmium.")
D) Lines 72-80 ("The well-intentioned... razors.")

58

As used in line 8, "catalyze" most nearly means

A) rush.
B) crystalize.
C) cause.
D) steepen.

59

Which of these statements is refuted by information in the passage?

A) X-ray diffraction was developed in the 20th century.
B) Electron microscopes were in use before World War II.
C) The TEM was developed before the SEM.
D) The scanning electron microscope was invented in the 21st century.

60

Based on the information in the passage and in the table, which of the following would be most likely to grow harmful tin whiskers?

A) Pure tin at 20° Celsius
B) Pure tin at 50° Celsius
C) Tin-lead alloy at 20° Celsius
D) Tin-lead alloy at 50° Celsius

61

What main effect does the rhetorical question in lines 19-20 have on the tone of the passage?

A) The question introduces an element of doubt by making the reader second-guess his or her beliefs.
B) The choice of words paints a gloomy picture of the future.
C) The question casts doubt on the reliability of both research and regulation.
D) The answers offered add a light-hearted note to an otherwise serious subject.

62

As used in line 73, "laudable" most nearly means

A) amplified.
B) praiseworthy.
C) extolled.
D) ridiculous.

63

The passage is written from the perspective of someone who is

A) proposing further regulation to protect the environment.
B) worried by the complacency of the European Union.
C) urging that a solution be found to a widespread problem.
D) warning of possible unintended consequences of legislation.

64

Which choice provides the best evidence for the answer to the previous question?

A) Lines 4-9 ("However,… industry")
B) Lines 12-17 ("In addition… usher in:")
C) Lines 73-76 ("lead exposure… spans")
D) Lines 76-80 ("However, concerned… razors.")

65

The passage's mention of Compton's report serves to

A) indicate a contrast to present-day slipshod research into whisker growth.
B) provide an example of research that spurred further research.
C) encourage the development of research facilities on the model of Bell Laboratories.
D) hint at the inadequacy of early research in the field.

Questions 66-76 are based on the following passage.

Passage 1 is adapted from Elizabeth Cady Stanton, "The Solitude of Self." Passage 2 is from Sojourner Truth, "Ain't I a Woman?"

Passage 1

The point I wish plainly to bring before you on this occasion is the individuality of each human soul. In discussing the rights of woman, we are to consider, first, what belongs to her as an individual, in a world

5 of her own, the arbiter of her own destiny, an imaginary Robinson Crusoe with her woman Friday on a solitary island. Her rights under such circumstances are to use all her faculties for her own safety and happiness.

10 The isolation of every human soul and the necessity of self-dependence must give each individual the right to choose his own surroundings. The strongest reason for giving woman all the opportunities for higher education, for the full

15 development of her faculties, her forces of mind and body; for giving her the most enlarged freedom of thought and action; a complete emancipation from all forms of bondage, of custom, dependence, superstition; from all the crippling influences of fear

20 is the solitude and personal responsibility of her own individual life. The strongest reason why we ask for woman a voice in the government under which she lives; in the religion she is asked to believe; equality in social life, where she is the chief factor; a place in

25 the trades and professions, where she may earn her bread, is because of her birthright to self-sovereignty; because, as an individual, she must rely on herself…

Nothing strengthens the judgment and quickens the conscience like individual responsibility. Nothing

30 adds such dignity to character as the recognition of one's self-sovereignty; the right to an equal place, everywhere conceded—a place earned by personal merit, not an artificial attainment by inheritance, wealth, family and position. Conceding then that the

35 responsibilities of life rest equally on man and woman, that their destiny is the same, they need the same preparation for time and eternity. The talk of sheltering woman from the fierce storms of life is the sheerest mockery, for they beat on her from every

40 point of the compass, just as they do on man, and with more fatal results, for he has been trained to protect himself, to resist, to conquer…

Is it, then, consistent to hold the developed woman of this day within the same narrow political

45 limits as the dame with the spinning wheel and knitting needle occupied in the past? No, no! Machinery has taken the labors of woman as well as man on its tireless shoulders; the loom and the spinning wheel are but dreams of the past; the pen,

50 the brush, the easel, the chisel, have taken their places, while the hopes and ambitions of women are essentially changed.

Passage 2

Well, children, where there is so much racket there must be something out of kilter. I think that

55 'twixt the negroes of the South and the women at the North, all talking about rights, the white men will be in a fix pretty soon. But what's all this here talking about?

That man over there says that women need to be

60 helped into carriages, and lifted over ditches, and to have the best place everywhere. Nobody ever helps me into carriages, or over mud-puddles, or gives me any best place! And ain't I a woman? Look at me! Look at my arm! I have ploughed and planted, and

65 gathered into barns, and no man could head me! And ain't I a woman? I could work as much and eat as much as a man—when I could get it—and bear the lash as well! And ain't I a woman? I have borne thirteen children, and seen most all sold off to

70 slavery, and when I cried out with my mother's grief, none but Jesus heard me! And ain't I a woman?

Then they talk about this thing in the head; what's this they call it? [member of audience whispers, "intellect"] That's it, honey. What's that

75 got to do with women's rights or negroes' rights? If my cup won't hold but a pint, and yours holds a quart, wouldn't you be mean not to let me have my little half measure full?

Then that little man in black there, he says

80 women can't have as much rights as men, 'cause Christ wasn't a woman! Where did your Christ come from? Where did your Christ come from? From God and a woman! Man had nothing to do with Him.

If the first woman God ever made was strong

85 enough to turn the world upside down all alone, these women together ought to be able to turn it back, and get it right side up again! And now they is asking to do it, the men better let them.

Obliged to you for hearing me, and now old

90 Sojourner ain't got nothing more to say.

66

Which of the following arguments is advanced by both Stanton and Truth?

A) Women who work alongside men should be treated as their male colleagues are treated.
B) Women should be granted additional rights because men and women have similar responsibilities in society.
C) Women should not be forced to work in physically demanding occupations that are better suited to men.
D) The duties of men and women are distinct but should be recognized as equally challenging.

67

Within Passage 1, the primary purpose of the second paragraph (lines 10-27) is to

A) discuss the impact of employment on women's self-esteem.
B) illustrate the ways in which government policies discourage women from becoming educated.
C) specify the areas in which women's rights and opportunities should be expanded.
D) relate the experiences of women to the experiences of enslaved African-Americans.

68

An important difference between the demands made by Stanton and Truth is that

A) Stanton argues that men and women should be treated equally, while Truth believes that women should be treated with more care than should men.
B) Stanton encourages women to utilize their power in government to create change, while Truth advocates the use of social disobedience.
C) Stanton is concerned with the rights of all women, while Truth argues only for the rights of enslaved women.
D) Stanton focuses on the rights of women, while Truth advocates for the rights of both women and African-Americans.

69

In lines 37-42 ("The talk… conquer…"), Stanton draws a distinction between

A) the extents to which men and women are affected by the hardships they face.
B) the abilities of men and women to survive in the wilderness on their own.
C) the ways in which men and women deserve to be treated.
D) the appropriate roles of men and women in armed conflicts.

70

According to Passage 1, the evolving role of women in society has been hastened by

A) technological advances that have allowed women to take on new roles in the economy.
B) new laws granting women the right to an education.
C) acclaimed literary works portraying women as strong individuals.
D) a weakened economy that required women to enter the workforce.

71

Which choice provides the best evidence for the answer to the previous question?

A) Lines 28-29 ("Nothing… responsibility")
B) Lines 34-37 ("Conceding… eternity")
C) Lines 37-42 ("The talk… conquer")
D) Lines 47-52 ("Machinery… changed")

72

Within Passage 2, what is the main rhetorical effect of repeating the question "And ain't I a woman?"

A) Emphasize that all women should be treated equally, regardless of the prestige of their work.

B) Assert that women and men can only achieve equality when they do the same work.

C) Note the hypocrisy of those who claim that women deserve special care but do not extend such courtesies to all women.

D) Draw attention to the mistreatment of enslaved African-Americans.

73

Based on the passages, how would Stanton probably view the question posed by Truth in lines 75-78 ("If my... full?")?

A) Stanton would agree with the notion that men and women have different intellectual capacities.

B) Stanton would agree that the differences between men and women can be quantified.

C) Stanton would agree that women should be given every chance to meet their fullest intellectual potentials.

D) Stanton would disagree that women and African-Americans face similar levels of discrimination.

74

Which choice provides the best evidence for the answer to the previous question?

A) Lines 1-2 ("The point... soul")

B) Lines 3-7 ("In discussing... island")

C) Lines 7-9 (Her rights... happiness")

D) Lines 10-12 ("The isolation... surroundings")

75

As used in lines 8 and 15, "faculties" most nearly means

A) teachers.

B) evidence.

C) abilities.

D) members.

76

As used in line 65, the phrase "and no man could head me" indicates that

A) Truth was able to outsmart her male colleagues.

B) Truth performed the same amount of work as did the men with whom she was enslaved.

C) Truth refused to walk behind the men in her family.

D) Truth's height made her more productive than most female slaves.

Questions 77-87 are based on the following passage.

This passage is adapted from a book about a famous amusement park outside of New York City.

Coney Island: the name can still echo with a sense of excitement, the reverberations from an earlier age. Once commanding two miles of beach on the southwestern end of Long Island, the
5 amusement center has shrunk to a comparatively small area sixteen blocks long and two wide. Coney Island now lives largely on the borrowed capital of its past. It wears an air of faded glory, making it a favorite subject of magazine articles and anecdotal
10 tributes. But despite the nostalgia Coney Island arouses, scholars have neglected the historical context in which it established its enduring national reputation. Its true significance has scarcely been grasped.
15 The era of Coney Island began in 1895, and its heyday in the early twentieth century coincided with a critical period of American history, when the nation came of age as an urban-industrial society and its citizens eagerly but painfully adjusted to the new
20 structure of American life. Indeed, so major was the cultural upheaval Coney Island dramatized that it is difficult to recapture the age that went before it.

Nineteenth-century America was governed by a set of values which were in many respects more
25 thoroughly "Victorian" than the England over which Queen Victoria reigned. American culture before the age of Coney Island was dominated by an elite of genteel reformers who had taken it as their mission to refine and instruct the American working class.
30 These reformers labored to inculcate the Victorian virtues of "character" — morality, self-control, seriousness, and hard work. Perhaps most importantly, they believed that all leisure activities should be ultimately constructive, legitimized not for
35 their own sake but for their moral and social utility. Relatively few entertainers dared to violate Victorian respectability. Even P.T. Barnum presented his attractions in a way that always seemed consistent with the values of the period; he designed his circus
40 so the events appeared morally elevated and culturally refined, as well as scientifically instructive.

By the end of the nineteenth century, however, this cultural order had begun to crumble, and the nation's entertainers, who had previously helped to
45 support the authority of Victorian values, discovered new opportunities outside those confines. By the turn of the century, the managers of mass culture sensed new markets in the urban middle class and the growing working class, all eager to respond to
50 amusement in a less earnest cultural mood — a more exuberant, uninhibited, and irreverent mood.

Examples of this transformation abound. But the most striking expression of this change in American culture emerged in the new amusement parks that
55 were developed at the turn of the century. Made possible by swelling urban populations, as well as an increase in leisure time and spending power, and spurred by the development of electric trolley systems that allowed inexpensive excursions from the
60 city, amusement parks grew rapidly throughout the country. Dominating them all in size, scope, and fame was New York's Coney Island.

Amusement parks at Coney Island and elsewhere gathered together a variety of popular attractions and
65 pastimes, all of which reflected the changing cultural mood. These might include bathing facilities, band pavilions, dance halls, and circus attractions. The special distinction of these parks, however, lay in the new mechanical amusements they offered — the
70 Ferris wheels, the early roller coasters, and so on — and the response these received from the huge crowds that would line up to ride them. In most entertainment of the period, from baseball contests to vaudeville theaters, the public remained in the role of
75 the spectator. At Coney Island and other amusement parks, by contrast, audience and activity could merge. Customers were intimately involved in the spectacle of their own entertainment.

Coney Island quickly became a symbol not only
80 of fun and frolic but also of major changes in American manners and morals. It thus offers a case study of the growing cultural revolt against Victorian tastes and standards that would swell to a climax in the 1920s. The new amusement park and its patrons
85 attracted the attention of a variety of critics, artists, and reformers. In studying Coney Island, these observers believed they were confronting the face of a new mass culture. They pondered the nature of this culture and wondered what rules and restraints would
90 replace those which had been swept away. Coney Island precipitated a debate that has continued up to our own time over the role and significance of popular amusement in a democracy. Far from being an object of nostalgia, the resort stands as a symbol
95 of modernity, and its story illuminates the character of the mass culture that would soon dominate American life.

77

The author of this passage is interested in Coney Island chiefly because it was

A) developed by members of the new urban class.
B) the most famous amusement park in the nation.
C) the product of the Victorian era in America.
D) symptomatic of a social transition.

78

Which choice provides the best evidence for the answer to the previous question?

A) Lines 3-6 ("Once... wide")
B) Lines 8-10 ("It... tributes")
C) Lines 15-20 ("The... life")
D) Lines 26-29 ("American... class")

79

In lines 7-8 the author uses the phrase "borrowed capital of its past" to indicate that Coney Island

A) costs too much to maintain in its original size and scope.
B) had first become famous in its original location in the state capital.
C) has not yet made enough money to pay back the loans needed for its restoration.
D) survives mainly because of nostalgia and historical interest in its heyday.

80

The word "air" in line 8 most nearly means

A) wind.
B) façade.
C) aura.
D) reputation.

81

According to lines 42-51, at the turn of the century, people in the entertainment business

A) responded to the popular trend away from tasteless recreation.
B) effectively created a new mood in the general public.
C) discovered that mechanical amusements were marketable to all classes of society.
D) tried to match the services they provided to the changes in the moods of the populace.

82

According to lines 72-78, amusement parks such as Coney Island differed from other entertainments of the period in being

A) non-transportable.
B) instructive.
C) participatory.
D) exhilarating.

83

The author would consider all of the following statements true of the era represented by Coney Island EXCEPT

A) The public was less interested in entertainment that had moral and social utility.
B) Working people with less time on their hands were increasingly employed in factories.
C) Members of the middle class and the working class in America had more money to spend.
D) The number of people living in cities was rapidly increasing, thus expanding the market for entertainment near urban areas.

84

The word "precipitated" in line 91 most nearly means

A) clouded.
B) epitomized.
C) started.
D) decided.

85

Why does the author of this passage consider Coney Island "a symbol of modernity" (lines 94-95)?

A) It introduced spectacular amusements that captured the imagination of the general public.

B) It was the first form of mass entertainment to capitalize on the public's nostalgia for the past.

C) It attracted a mass audience with diversions reflecting controversial new values.

D) It was the first amusement park made accessible by a modern mass transit system.

86

Which choice provides the best evidence for the answer to the previous question?

A) Lines 58-60 ("Spurred…city")

B) Lines 67-69 ("The…offered")

C) Lines 79-81 ("Coney…morals")

D) Lines 84-86 ("The…reformers")

87

Which one of the following statements most contradicts the author's conclusion that Coney Island is not an object of nostalgia?

A) The culture of the past has been replaced by new types of entertainment.

B) Coney Island heralded a period of sweeping social changes.

C) Victorian values lost their relevance in the age of the mechanical amusement park.

D) Coney Island reminds us of a feeling, now lost, of thrilling liberation from outdated conventions.

Questions 88-98 are based on the following passage.

Passage 1 is adapted from an article describing a journey into the jungles of the Democratic Republic of the Congo. Passage 2 is adapted from an article about Jane Goodall's research on chimpanzees.

Passage 1

I followed Trinidad Garcia, a researcher from the University of Madrid, into the verdant jungle. She moved deftly through the thick leaves and vines, and at times I lost sight of the outline of her shoulders,
5 bouncing ahead of me in the dense morning fog. Suddenly she froze, and I nearly collided with her leather pack as I rounded a mossy trunk. In a single smooth gesture, she motioned for me to lower myself from sight and quickly yanked the sweaty red
10 Cardinals cap from my head. "Shhh . . ." she cautioned. "I told you, you didn't need this;" she scolded, "they will see us."

Clustered in the tree branches thirty feet above us were the objects of our endeavor: bonobos, *Pan*
15 *paniscus,* the reclusive and endangered relatives of the chimpanzee, only found in this small area on the north bank of the Luo River, here in the Democratic Republic of the Congo.

Everyone has heard of chimpanzees, but few
20 know about the bonobos, who carry a reputation as the "make love, not war" member of the ape family. They are more diminutive and considered less bellicose than their cousins south of the river, but I was surprised by what I saw next. The group of seven
25 or eight bonobos appeared transfixed on a smaller monkey – a black mangabey, my escort told me later – clinging to the side of a tree. Moving across trunks and through the branches in what seemed like a coordinated dance, they encircled the poor animal
30 from above and below, stalking ever closer. I watched in amazement as they worked together like a veteran team. Monitoring the jerking movements of the frightened little monkey, only those bonobos at the monkey's back moved while the others remained
35 still in an apparent attempt to appear nonthreatening. Then, just as they appeared to be within reach of their prey, the mangabey launched itself straight back from the trunk; eluding his captors by mere inches, the monkey vaulted and grabbed a hanging vine in
40 midair before dropping safely onto the fog-encased forest floor. The bonobos let out fearsome shrieks as they watched their chosen breakfast disappear; these were not the passive primates I had imagined.

"Hunting behavior, really unusual," Trinidad
45 whispered as the apes scrambled away. "You are very lucky." I had been in Africa for only three days, and already my expectations of the peaceful bonobo were bending to reality in the wild.

Passage 2

Jane Goodall was just twenty-six years old in the
50 summer of 1960, when she first entered the Gombe Stream National Park, deep in the jungles of Tanzania. Goodall was not a trained scientist, but her research was supported by renowned Kenyan archeologist and paleontologist Louis Leakey, who
55 suspected that chimpanzee behavior might shed light on the lives of early hominids. Goodall's unorthodox approach was apparent from the beginning. Instead of numbering her subjects, she gave them names like Greybeard, Goliath, Mike and Gigi, and in each she
60 recognized distinct personality traits.

"It isn't only human beings who have personality, who are capable of rational thought and emotions like joy and sorrow," Goodall would later recount. Her insights into the chimpanzee's social
65 structure, a balance of hierarchical and cooperative relationships, revolutionized how scientists view animal societies. The chimps hugged, kissed, and even tickled, actions that indicated true affection; but Goodall also witnessed the darker side of chimpanzee
70 nature. When the group she was observing split into two rival clans, a murderous conflict ensued that came to be known as the Gombe Chimpanzee War. The tension began when Goliath was deposed as the group's leader by Mike, a younger male. Goliath led
75 a small group of males and females to settle in the north section of the Gombe, but Goliath and his male co-conspirators returned repeatedly to attack and kill males who had remained with the original clan.

Goodall's reports of organized conflict between
80 chimpanzees in their natural habitat were not universally accepted in the scientific community. Her practices came under fire from traditionally-trained scientists like Margaret Power, who argued in her book *The Egalitarians – Human and Chimpanzee: An*
85 *Anthropological View of Social Organization* that Goodall had created the conflict she saw by setting up feeding stations. Designed to attract the animals for easier observation, this unnatural food source may have also disrupted the chimpanzees' complex social
90 order. Goodall herself acknowledged that the feeding stations may have contributed to aggression within and between chimpanzee groups, but insisted that the stations only served to intensify a natural tendency. Even years after Goodall ended her thirty year study
95 of the Gombe chimpanzees, scientists are still reexamining her records and challenging her interpretations; debate continues over the true nature of our closest animal relatives.

88

Passage 1 was likely written by

A) a researcher returning to a preferred location for wildlife observation.
B) a young primatology student embarking on his first field study.
C) a park ranger patrolling an assigned route.
D) an anthropologist observing animals in a controlled setting.

89

The primary purpose of the description given in lines 22-23 ("They are more diminutive and considered less bellicose than their cousins south of the river") is to

A) describe the animals that bonobos hunt for food.
B) remind readers of the differences between bonobos and modern humans.
C) compare bonobos to a similar species.
D) compare two populations of bonobos that live on opposite sides of the Luo River.

90

As used in line 39, "vaulted" most nearly means

A) locked.
B) struggled.
C) leapt.
D) ran.

91

In Passage 1, the effect of the final paragraph (lines 44-48) is to

A) contrast the tendencies of two closely related species.
B) establish that a particular observation was rare and unanticipated.
C) present an alternative explanation for a phenomenon.
D) describe the setting in which an animal was seen.

92

In Passage 2, the main purpose of the third paragraph (lines 79-98) is to

A) discuss the concerns of Goodall's critics in the scientific community.
B) introduce a new scientific principle that supports Goodall's conclusions.
C) contrast Goodall's published work with her initial findings.
D) detail a more recent observation that confirms one of Goodall's original hypotheses.

93

As described in Passage 2, the Gombe Chimpanzee War was

A) a series of violent encounters between two groups of chimpanzees.
B) a military conflict between Tanzania and Kenya.
C) an effort to prevent chimpanzee poaching in the Gombe Stream National Park.
D) a scientific debate over the natural behavior of chimpanzees.

94

The concerns presented by Margaret Power are primarily a critique of Goodall's

A) research methods.
B) choice of research subjects.
C) interpretation of a scientific principle.
D) use of names to identify research subjects.

95

One difference between the approaches of the researchers in the two passages is that, unlike the researcher in Passage 1, the researcher in Passage 2

A) presented her subjects with a puzzle to solve.
B) significantly altered her subjects' natural environment.
C) intervened to protect her subjects from danger.
D) observed her subjects exclusively in their natural habitat.

96

Which choice provides the best evidence for the answer to the previous question?

A) Lines 67-68 ("The chimps… affection")
B) Lines 70-72 ("When… War.")
C) Lines 87-90 ("Designed… order.")
D) Lines 57-60 ("Instead… traits.")

97

Both passages consider the behavior of primates in terms of their

A) curiosity and intellect.
B) emotions and gender roles.
C) habitat and communication.
D) endangered status.

98

As used in line 56, "unorthodox" most nearly means

A) novel.
B) nonreligious.
C) inappropriate.
D) personal.

Questions 99-108 are based on the following passage.

This passage is from U.S. president John F. Kennedy's inaugural address, January 20, 1961.

We observe today not a victory of party but a celebration of freedom, symbolizing an end as well as a beginning, signifying renewal as well as change. For I have sworn before you and Almighty God the
5   same solemn oath our forebears prescribed nearly a century and three-quarters ago.

The world is very different now. For man holds in his mortal hands the power to abolish all forms of human poverty and all forms of human life. And yet
10   the same revolutionary beliefs for which our forebears fought are still at issue around the globe – the belief that the rights of man come not from the generosity of the state but from the hand of God.

We dare not forget today that we are the heirs of
15   that first revolution. Let the word go forth from this time and place, to friend and foe alike, that the torch has been passed to a new generation of Americans, born in this century, tempered by war, disciplined by a hard and bitter peace, proud of our ancient heritage,
20   and unwilling to witness or permit the slow undoing of those human rights to which this nation has always been committed, and to which we are committed today at home and around the world.

Let every nation know, whether it wishes us well
25   or ill, that we shall pay any price, bear any burden, meet any hardship, support any friend, oppose any foe to assure the survival and the success of liberty.

This much we pledge – and more.

To those old allies whose cultural and spiritual
30   origins we share, we pledge the loyalty of faithful friends. United, there is little we cannot do in a host of cooperative ventures. Divided, there is little we can do; for we dare not meet a powerful challenge at odds and split asunder.
35   To those new states whom we welcome to the ranks of the free, we pledge our word that one form of colonial control shall not have passed away merely to be replaced by a far more iron tyranny. We shall not always expect to find them supporting our view.
40   But we shall always hope to find them strongly supporting their own freedom; and to remember that, in the past, those who foolishly sought power by riding the back of the tiger ended up inside.

To those people in the huts and villages of half
45   the globe struggling to break the bonds of mass misery, we pledge our best efforts to help them help themselves, for whatever period is required – not because the communists may be doing it, not because we seek their votes, but because it is right. If a free
50   society cannot help the many who are poor, it cannot save the few who are rich…

Finally, to those nations who would make themselves our adversary, we offer not a pledge but a request: that both sides begin anew the quest for
55   peace, before the dark powers of destruction unleashed by science engulf all humanity in planned or accidental self-destruction…

All this will not be finished in the first one hundred days. Nor will it be finished in the first one
60   thousand days, nor in the life of this Administration, nor even perhaps in our lifetime on this planet. But let us begin.

In your hands, my fellow citizens, more than mine, will rest the final success or failure of our
65   course. Since this country was founded, each generation of Americans has been summoned to give testimony to its national loyalty. The graves of young Americans who answered the call to service surround the globe…
70   Can we forge against these enemies a grand and global alliance, North and South, East and West, that can assure a more fruitful life for all mankind? Will you join in that historic effort?

In the long history of the world, only a few
75   generations have been granted the role of defending freedom in its hour of maximum danger. I do not shrink from this responsibility; I welcome it. I do not believe that any of us would exchange places with any other people or any other generation. The energy,
80   the faith, the devotion which we bring to this endeavor will light our country and all who serve it – and the glow from that fire can truly light the world.

And so, my fellow Americans: ask not what your country can do for you – ask what you can do for
85   your country.

My fellow citizens of the world: ask not what America will do for you, but what together we can do for the freedom of man.

99

Based on the passage, Kennedy's attitude toward foreign conflict can best be described as

A) an aggressor eager to expand the American empire.
B) an idealist seeking to spread American influence while avoiding military conflict.
C) an altruist seeking out and combating injustice across the globe.
D) a disaffected observer analyzing and comparing the outcomes of recent foreign wars.

100

Which choice provides the best evidence for the answer to the previous question?

A) Lines 52-57 ("Finally… self-destruction")
B) Lines 63-65 ("In your… course")
C) Lines 74-76 ("In the long… danger")
D) Lines 79-82 ("The energy… world")

101

As used in line 45, "bonds" most nearly means

A) connections.
B) promises.
C) shackles.
D) investments.

102

Kennedy's assertion that "the rights of man come not from the generosity of the state but from the hand of God" (lines 12-13) is primarily intended to convey that

A) all people deserve to live under governments that respect human rights.
B) Americans must acknowledge the important influence that Christian principles have had on our legal system.
C) the United States was founded in order to protect religious minorities from oppression.
D) religious values demand that all nations work to combat poverty wherever it occurs.

103

In the eighth paragraph (lines 44-51), Kennedy draws a distinction between

A) people who live in small villages and those who live in large cities.
B) the respect for human rights and the oppression of religious minorities.
C) populations that revolt against injustice and those that accept it.
D) the fight against communism and a moral necessity.

104

Which of the following is the most likely reason that Kennedy reminds his audience that "In your hands, my fellow citizens, more than mine, will rest the final success or failure of our course" (lines 63-65)?

A) To encourage Americans to become active in the country's struggles.
B) To deflect blame for the numerous crises facing the country.
C) To remind Americans that he is unlikely to fulfill all of his promises.
D) To promote friendly relations with foreign nations vital to the fight against communism.

105

Which of the following best describes the intended audience for Kennedy's address?

A) Members of Congress and other attendees to the inauguration ceremony.
B) The American people and people of foreign nations.
C) Foreign leaders and dignitaries.
D) Impoverished people in the United States and across the world.

106

Which choice provides the best evidence for the answer to the previous question?

A) Lines 1-4 (We observe… change")
B) Lines 24-27 ("Let… liberty")
C) Lines 44-51 ("To those… rich")
D) Lines 83-88 ("And so…man")

107

What message does Kennedy direct to nations hostile to the United States?

A) He suggests a plan to prevent the further development of nuclear weapons.
B) He encourages them to restart attempts at peace.
C) He threatens to respond to any aggression with overwhelming force.
D) He proposes an agreement to share technological secrets.

108

Which of the following is a rhetorical strategy repeatedly employed by Kennedy?

A) He makes commitments to particular groups.
B) He critiques unpopular philosophies.
C) He cites legal precedents.
D) He uses intricate, extended metaphors.

Questions 109-118 are based on the following passage.

This passage is from Mahatma Gandhi, on his conviction for sedition, March 23, 1922.

I owe it perhaps to the Indian public and to the public in England, to placate which this prosecution is mainly taken up, that I should explain why from a staunch loyalist and cooperator, I have become an
5 uncompromising disaffectionist and non-cooperator. To the court too I should say why I plead guilty to the charge of promoting disaffection toward the government established by law in India.

My public life began in 1893 in South Africa in
10 troubled weather. My first contact with British authority in that country was not of a happy character. I discovered that as a man and as an Indian, I had no rights. More correctly, I discovered that I had no rights as a man because I was an Indian.

15 But I was not baffled. I thought that this treatment of Indians was an excrescence upon a system that was intrinsically and mainly good. I gave the government my voluntary and hearty cooperation, criticizing it freely where I felt it was faulty but never
20 wishing its destruction.

I came reluctantly to the conclusion that the British connection had made India more helpless than she ever was before, politically and economically. A disarmed India has no power of resistance against
25 any aggressor if she wanted to engage in an armed conflict with him. So much is this the case that some of our best men consider that India must take generations before she can achieve Dominion status. She has become so poor that she has little power of
30 resisting famines. Before the British advent, India spun and wove in her millions of cottages, just the supplement she needed for adding to her meager agricultural resources. This cottage industry, so vital for India's existence, has been ruined by incredibly
35 heartless and inhuman processes as described by English witnesses. Little do town dwellers know how the semi-starved masses of India are slowly sinking to lifelessness. Little do they know that their miserable comfort represents the brokerage they get
40 for the work they do for the foreign exploiter, that the profits and the brokerage get sucked from the masses. Little do they realize that the government established by law in British India is carried on for the exploitation of the masses. No sophistry, no jugglery
45 in figures can explain away the evidence that the skeletons in many villages present to the naked eye. I have no doubt whatsoever that both England and the town dwellers of India will have to answer, if there is a God above, for this crime against humanity, which
50 is perhaps unequaled in history. The law itself in this country has been used to serve the foreign exploiter.

My unbiased examination of the Punjab Martial Law cases has led me to believe that ninety-five per cent of the convictions were wholly bad. My experience
55 of political cases in India leads me to the conclusion that in nine out of every ten the condemned men were totally innocent. Their crime consisted in the love of their country. In ninety-nine cases out of a hundred, justice has been denied to Indians as against
60 Europeans in the courts of India. This is not an exaggerated picture. It is the experience of almost every Indian who has had anything to do with such cases. In my opinion the administration of the law is thus prostituted, consciously or unconsciously, for
65 the benefit of the exploiter.

In fact, I believe that I have tendered a service to India and England by showing in non-cooperation the way out of the unnatural state in which both are living. In my opinion, non-cooperation with evil is as
70 much a duty as is cooperation with good. But in the past, non-cooperation has been deliberately expressed in violence to the evildoer. I am endeavoring to show to my countrymen that violent non-cooperation only multiplies evil, and that as evil can only be sustained
75 by violence, withdrawal of support for evil requires complete abstention from violence. Non-violence implies voluntary submission to the penalty of non-cooperation with evil. I am here, therefore, to invite and submit cheerfully to the highest penalty that can
80 be inflicted upon me for what in law is a deliberate crime, and what appears to me to be the highest duty of a citizen. The only course open to you, the judge, is either to resign your post, and thus dissociate yourself from evil, if you feel that the law you are
85 called upon to administer is an evil, and that in reality I am innocent, or to inflict upon me the severest penalty, if you believe that the system and the law you are assisting to administer are good for the people of this country, and that my activity is,
90 therefore, injurious to the public weal.

109

Which of the following best describes Gandhi's attitude toward his conviction?

A) He admits his wrongdoing and regrets his actions.
B) He believes that there is insufficient evidence to prove his guilt.
C) He accepts his guilt but rejects the legitimacy of the legal system.
D) He claims that he was falsely accused and has never broken the law.

110

The phrase "troubled weather" in line 10 is a reference to

A) a deadly storm that struck on the day that Gandhi was born.
B) an ongoing military struggle between South Africa and England.
C) oppression Gandhi faced as an Indian living in British-controlled South Africa.
D) racism inherent to the British practice of colonization.

111

As used in line 19, "freely" most nearly means

A) without effort.
B) without payment.
C) without thought.
D) without apprehension.

112

According to Gandhi, which of the following best describes the "town dwellers" mentioned in lines 36 and 48?

A) Indians who are ignorant of the cruelty of the British system they support.
B) Wealthy foreigners who exploit rural Indians for economic gain.
C) Socially conscious British citizens who oppose the occupation of India on moral grounds.
D) Victims of a famine that struck the Indian countryside.

113

The main rhetorical effect of the two phrases that begin the sentence in lines 44-46 ("No sophistry, no jugglery in figures") is to

A) characterize attempts to defend the current legal system as dishonest.
B) place blame for an inequity on Indian citizens as opposed to the British.
C) distinguish the pastimes of rural Indians from those enjoyed by the British.
D) highlight that the actions of the British are both unjust and sinful.

114

Which of the following is most analogous to the situation described in lines 52-60 ("My unbiased examination… courts of India.")?

A) A university admissions board consistently denies admission to a particular demographic of students, regardless of the students' qualifications.
B) An auto mechanic repeatedly fails to properly repair a particular brand of vehicle.
C) A teacher is more likely to assign perfect scores to student work that she grades in the evenings.
D) A police officer frequently ridicules the female drivers he stops for traffic violations.

115

What is the main purpose of the final paragraph (lines 66-90)?

A) Provide a detailed example of a common problem.
B) Examine and refute a popular misconception.
C) Promote a course of action for resolving a crisis.
D) Enumerate the causes of a particular injustice.

116

According to the passage, Gandhi's initial response to his mistreatment by British authorities was to

A) work to establish solidarity between the lower classes in India and South Africa.
B) call for all Indians to peacefully resist the British occupation.
C) organize a violent rebellion against the British military.
D) support the British system and hope for natural reform.

117

Which choice provides the best evidence for the answer to the previous question?

A) Lines 9-10 (My public… weather")
B) Lines 10-12 ("My first… character")
C) Lines 15-17 ("I thought… good")
D) Lines 17-20 ("I gave… destruction")

118

Which of the following quotes from the passage best describes Gandhi's ultimate approach to the British?

A) Lines 72-77 ("I am endeavoring… violence.")
B) Lines 17-20 ("I gave... destruction.")
C) Lines 46-50 ("I have… history.")
D) Lines 30-33 ("Before… resources.")

SUMMIT
EDUCATIONAL
GROUP

Writing and Language Overview

- ❑ The SAT Writing and Language Test

- ❑ The PSAT Writing and Language Test

- ❑ Test Structure

- ❑ Scoring and Scaling

- ❑ Setting Your Goal

- ❑ The Instructions

- ❑ Working Through the Writing and Language Test

- ❑ General Tips

The SAT Writing and Language Test

❑ The SAT Writing and Language Test tests your skill at evaluating and improving 400-450-word essays. You've likely been practicing most of these skills on school assignments for years.

Format	44 questions 4 passages multiple-choice
Content	Standard English Conventions - Conventions of Usage - Sentence Structure - Conventions of Punctuation Expression of Ideas - Development - Organization - Effective Language Use
Scoring	Evidence-Based Reading and Writing score: 200-800 Writing and Language Test score: 10-40
Time	35 minutes

❑ Writing and Language Test questions divide into two content areas:

Content Area	Questions	Sample Topics
Standard English Conventions	20	
Conventions of Usage		pronoun clarity, possessive determiners, agreement, frequently confused words, logical comparison
Sentence Structure		sentence boundaries, subordination and coordination, parallel structure, modifier placement, shifts in verb tense, mood, voice, and pronoun person and number
Conventions of Punctuation		end-of-sentence, within-sentence, possessive, items in series, nonrestrictive and parenthetical, unnecessary
Expression of Ideas	24	
Development		proposition, support, focus, quantitative information
Organization		logical sequence, introduction, conclusions, transitions
Effective Language Use		precision, concision, style and tone, syntax

The PSAT Writing and Language Test

❑ The PSAT Writing and Language Test has the same timing and number of questions as the SAT Writing and Language Test.

Format	44 questions 4 passages multiple-choice
Content	Standard English Conventions - Conventions of Usage - Sentence Structure - Conventions of Punctuation Expression of Ideas - Development - Organization - Effective Language Use
Scoring	Evidence-Based Reading and Writing score: 160-760 Writing and Language Test score: 8-38
Time	35 minutes

❑ The PSAT and SAT are scored on vertically aligned scales. This means, for instance, that a student scoring 550 on the PSAT is demonstrating the same level of achievement as a student scoring 550 on the SAT. It does <u>not</u> mean that the same student is predicted to score a 550 on the SAT. The PSAT is reported on a slightly lower scale (160-760), reflecting the fact that the exams test the same body of skills, but at age-appropriate levels.

Test Structure

❑ Questions generally follow the order of the passage, but do not progress from easy to difficult.

35 Minutes

MULTIPLE-CHOICE																					
Passage 1											Passage 2										
1	2	3	4	5	6	7	8	9	10	11	12	13	14	15	16	17	18	19	20	21	22
NOT IN ORDER OF DIFFICULTY																					

MULTIPLE-CHOICE																					
Passage 3											Passage 4										
23	24	25	26	27	28	29	30	31	32	33	34	35	36	37	38	39	40	41	42	43	44
NOT IN ORDER OF DIFFICULTY																					

❑ You are asked to read 4 essays of roughly the same length and answer questions about grammar, style, and strategy. There are 11 questions related to each essay.

The essays range in complexity from grades 9-10 to college-level.

❑ Each test includes one passage in each of the following content areas: careers, history/ social studies, humanities, and science. The passages appear in the following types: 1-2 argument, 1-2 informative/explanatory, 1 nonfiction narrative.

Scoring and Scaling

You'll receive an Evidence-Based Reading & Writing section score from 200-800, a Writing & Language Test score from 10-40, and subscores in Words in Context, Command of Evidence, Expression of Ideas, and Standard English Conventions. The subscores will be reported on a 1-15 scale. Some of the questions will also count toward one of the two cross-test subscores called Analysis in Science and Analysis in History/Social Studies. College admissions offices will care most about the 200-800 Evidence-Based Reading & Writing section score.

1 Total Score (400-1600 scale)	SAT			
2 Section Scores (200-800 scale)	Evidence-Based Reading & Writing		Math	
3 Test Scores (10-40 scale)	Reading	Writing & Language	Math	
2 Cross-Test Scores (10-40 scale)	Analysis in Science			
	Analysis in History / Social Studies			
7 Subscores (1-15 Scale)	Words in Context		Heart of Algebra	
	Command of Evidence		Passport to Advanced Mathematics	
		Expression of Ideas	Problem Solving & Data Analysis	
		Standard English Conventions		

- ❑ **How Your Score is Calculated** – You receive 1 raw point for a correct answer. You lose nothing for incorrect answers. Your **raw score** is calculated by adding up raw points. Your raw score is then converted to a scaled Writing and Language **test** score from 10-40 (8-38 for PSAT). This test score is combined with your Reading Test score to generate an overall Evidence-Based Reading and Writing **section** score from 200-800 (160-760 for PSAT).

- ❑ **Never leave a question blank**. Since there is no penalty for wrong answers, you should answer every single question on the SAT.

Setting Your Goal

Set a goal. Envision where you want to be when you've finished your SAT preparation. Using your diagnostic results and previous test scores, work with your instructor to set a realistic score goal.

❑ Set your targets in the table below.

My Targets

My overall SAT Goal: _____

My Evidence-Based Reading and Writing Goal: _____

My Writing and Language Test Goal: _____

How many questions do I need to answer correctly (raw score)? _____

The Instructions

❑ The instructions are the same on every SAT. Familiarize yourself with the instructions before you take the test. At test time, you can skip the instructions and focus on the problems.

DIRECTIONS

Each passage below is accompanied by a number of questions. For some questions, you will consider how the passage might be revised to improve the expression of ideas. For other questions, you will consider how the passage might be edited to correct errors in sentence structure, usage, or punctuation. A passage or a question may be accompanied by one or more graphics (such as a table or graph) that you will consider as you make revising and editing decisions.

Some questions will direct you to an underlined portion of a passage. Other questions will direct you to a location in a passage or ask you to think about the passage as a whole.

After reading each passage, choose the answer to each question that most effectively improves the quality of writing in the passage or that makes the passage conform to the conventions of standard written English. Many questions include a "NO CHANGE" option. Choose that option if you think the best choice is to leave the relevant portion of the passage as it is.

> Answer the questions as you read through the passage. Although the SAT suggests you read the entire passage before you answer the questions, this approach is unnecessary and time-consuming.

SUMMIT
EDUCATIONAL
GROUP

Working Through the Writing and Language Test

❑ **Focus on one passage at a time**.

Answer all of the questions to a passage before you move onto the next.

❑ On average, each passage of 11 questions should be completed within 8 minutes.

❑ Within each passage, maximize your score by focusing on the easier questions first. Each question is worth 1 raw point. Regardless of its difficulty, every question counts the same.

Would you rather earn $20 working for 1 hour or earn $20 working for 10 minutes? The answer is easy, right? Similarly, on the Writing and Language Test, you should spend your time earning points as efficiently as you can. Put your time and energy into the questions within your capabilities, starting with the easiest and finishing with the hardest.

❑ **Focus on one question at a time**.

The SAT is timed, so it's normal to feel pressure to rush. Resist the temptation to think about the 10 questions ahead of you or the question you did a minute ago. Relax and focus on one question at a time. **Patience** on the SAT is what allows you to work more quickly and accurately.

❑ **Use the Two-Pass Approach for <u>each passage</u>.**

Step 1: Answer the questions as you read the passage. We do NOT recommend reading the passage before answering the questions.

On your first pass through a passage, answer all of the questions you can, but don't get bogged down on an individual question. If you're stuck or unsure, mark it in your test booklet and move on. Remember: Each question is worth the same amount – 1 raw point. Don't get caught battling a difficult question at the expense of answering easier questions.

Step 2: Make a second pass.

If you skipped and/or marked any, go back and work on these questions – it shouldn't be more than 1-3 per passage. Focus first on the ones you think you have the best chance of answering correctly. For some, you'll find the right answer fairly easily. For the others, aggressively eliminate answer choices and make educated guesses.

Note: Having read the complete passage, you are now in a much better position to answer some of the questions that require an understanding of main idea and author's purpose.

Step 3: Don't leave any answers blank.

At this point, you shouldn't have any questions unanswered, but if you do, make guesses before you move on to the next passage. Even if you feel like you really don't know the answer, it will be easier to guess while you're still thinking about the passage.

❑ There is no penalty for guessing, so make sure you answer every question. With about 30 seconds remaining for the test, make guesses any remaining questions.

General Tips

Learn to use the following array of strategies. You'll become a proactive test-taker, and you'll improve your ability to solve the more difficult questions.

☐ **Use Process of Elimination (POE).** Even if you can't find the correct answer, you'll almost always be able to eliminate one or two incorrect answers. Sometimes you'll "hear" the error, and other times certain answer choices will be written in an obviously incorrect way. The more answer choices you can eliminate, the greater the likelihood you'll get the right answer.

IMPORTANT: Once you have eliminated an answer, cross if out in the test booklet. Crossing out answers prevents you from wasting time looking at eliminated answers over and over again.

☐ **Shorter is often better.** The SAT prefers writing that is precise and concise. Answer choices with convoluted or redundant writing will be incorrect. On the Writing and Language Test, the shortest answer choice is often the correct answer.

> For much of human history, <u>it was believed by people</u> that coral are plants.
>
> A) NO CHANGE
> B) people believed it that
> C) people believing
> D) people believed

☐ If there are two errors in a question, deal with one at a time. Eliminate all of the choices that contain one error, and then repeat the process with the second error.

A question on the Writing and Language Test will never test more than two errors.

> Also mentioned in the referendum <u>was:</u> the requirement that townspeople pay extra taxes and the demand that the speed limit in school zones be reduced.
>
> A) NO CHANGE
> B) was
> C) were:
> D) were

❑ **Don't always trust your ear.** Standard written English may be more formal than what you are used to hearing.

Even if something sounds right the first time you read through it, double check for frequently tested grammatical errors. There are certain things that you might say, hear, or write in everyday life that contain grammatical errors.

> The bread from the bakery around the corner from my grandmother's house is always better <u>then our bakery</u>.
>
> A) NO CHANGE
> B) than our bakery.
> C) then the bread from our bakery.
> D) than the bread from our bakery.

❑ **Don't find errors where none exist.** Just because something is underlined doesn't mean that it contains an error. "NO CHANGE" is correct approximately ¼ of the time it appears as an answer choice – just as frequently as any other answer choice.

❑ **When there is an actual question, read it carefully**. The keys to the correct answer often lie within the question.

> Underline the part of the following question that gives a clue about what you should focus on as you solve the question.
>
> "The writer wants to convey an attitude of genuine interest. Which answer choice best accomplishes this goal?"

❑ Questions about the main idea or author's intent or purpose will often require reading the entire paragraph or beyond.

❑ Try to spot and fix the error before looking at the answer choices.

SUMMIT
EDUCATIONAL
GROUP

Writing and Language

❏ Standard English Conventions

Conventions of Usage

- ❏ Pronouns
- ❏ Subject-Verb Agreement
- ❏ Comparisons
- ❏ Idioms
- ❏ Diction

Sentence Structure

- ❏ Fragments
- ❏ Run-Ons
- ❏ Conjunctions
- ❏ Parallelism
- ❏ Modifiers
- ❏ Verb Tense

Conventions of Punctuation

- ❏ Semicolons & Colons
- ❏ Commas
- ❏ Apostrophes

❏ Expression of Ideas

Development

- ❏ Main Idea
- ❏ Addition
- ❏ Deletion

Organization

- ❏ Organization
- ❏ Transitions

Effective Language Use

- ❏ Wordiness
- ❏ Style

Data Graphics

Pronouns

Pronoun questions often require you to determine if a particular pronoun should be singular or plural. They may also test your knowledge of proper apostrophe usage. Challenging pronoun questions involve more than one noun to which the pronoun could refer.

❏ Pronouns can be used as subjects, objects, or possessives.

Subject	Object	Possessive
I	me	my, mine
you	you	your, yours
he, she	him, her	his, her, hers
we	us	our, ours
they	them	their, theirs
who	whom	whose
it	it	its
one	one	one's

Pronoun used as a subject: *He is going to the store.*

Pronoun used as an object: *They took him to the store.*

Pronoun used as a possessive: *That is his store.*

❏ **Pronoun Agreement** – A pronoun must agree with the noun it refers to in number, gender, and person.

> The energy company is cutting payroll in order to increase (*its* / *their*) profits.

Similarly, nouns that relate to the same thing must agree in number.

> Incorrect: After a vote by the entire team, both Tania and Jeanette were selected as the captain.
>
> Correct: _____
>
> _____

❑ **Ambiguous Pronouns** – A pronoun must clearly refer back to the noun or nouns it represents. If there is no antecedent or more than one possible antecedent, the pronoun is ambiguous.

> Incorrect: According to the governor's son, he had not yet decided to run for re-election.
>
> Correct: According to the governor's son, _____
>
> _____

❑ **Compound Phrase** – To check for the proper form in a compound phrase, remove the rest of the group.

> After school, Sam asked Louis and (*I/me*) if we wanted to go climbing with him.

❑ **Pronoun Case** – In order to determine whether a pronoun is a subject or object, try plugging in an easier pronoun (such as "he/him") and see which works better. If the objective-case pronoun ("him") works better, use the objective case for the pronoun in question ("whom"). This is called the "M test," because many object pronouns have the letter *m*.

A pronoun that follows a preposition requires the objective case and not the subjective case.

> Before buying birthday gifts for my twin sister and (*I/me*), my father e-mailed us to get our shoe sizes.

The pronoun "who" always refers to the subject. The pronoun "whom" always refers to an object.

> The characters in Charles Dickens's stories were people (*who/whom*) lived poor, ordinary lives.

❑ **Relative Pronouns** – Don't use *that* or *which* when referring to people. People are always *who* or *whom*.

> The scientist (*that/who*) discovered the cause is famous around the world.

❑ **Its vs It's** – "It's" is always a contraction of "it is." Also, "its" is always a possessive pronoun.

Similarly, "they're" is a contraction of "they are," and "their" is a possessive pronoun.

"You're" is a contraction of "you are," and "your" is a possessive pronoun.

> Heisenberg's experiment is reliable in (*it's / its*) setup and execution.

❑ **One and You** – Pronouns *one* and *you* are not interchangeable. Whichever of these pronouns is being used must be carried throughout the sentence.

> If you decide that you're not going to apply to graduate school, then (*one / you*) need not take an entrance exam.

PUT IT TOGETHER

In 1973, sci-fi author Arthur C. Clarke declared his oft-cited law: "Any sufficiently advanced technology is indistinguishable from magic." The implication of Clarke's law is that people **1** who do not understand a new technology's scientific basis will see the innovation as a marvelous wonder. Since **2** it's declaration, Clarke's law has been regarded as a cultural truism, but do modern scientific advancements still bring such awe and wonder?

In the past, science has often been mistaken for magic. With **3** their many discoveries and inventions, Thomas Edison was popularly known as a "wizard," as though his electrical wonders were the product of sorcery rather than of natural physics. Today, the advances of technology evoke less wonder. This situation exists not because modern innovations are any less revolutionary, but because **4** its not treated as spectacles.

Modern consumers obsess over new technologies but also expect this technology to integrate seamlessly into **5** one's daily lives. Therefore, the goal of many modern inventors is to streamline technology so that it goes mostly unnoticed. In this sense, Clarke's law is still accurate, though we have to change our interpretation of "magic." Rather than being like a magician's spectacular stunt, our modern technology is used to create something more like a fantasy world where everything seems a bit simpler, a bit better, and a bit more magical.

1
A) NO CHANGE
B) whom
C) that
D) which

2
A) NO CHANGE
B) its
C) their
D) they're

3
A) NO CHANGE
B) they're
C) his
D) its

4
A) NO CHANGE
B) it's
C) their
D) they're

5
A) NO CHANGE
B) our
C) his or her
D) their

Subject-Verb Agreement

❑ Singular subjects require singular verbs, and plural subjects require plural verbs. Singular verbs usually end in *s*.

The <u>teacher</u> of the school's chemistry and physics classes <u>assigns</u> too much homework.

The other <u>teachers</u>, whom I prefer, usually <u>assign</u> little or no homework.

❑ **Ignore the Extras** – To simplify sentences, remove all extra information between the subject and the verb. Then, make sure the subject and verb agree.

The mastodon, ~~an early elephant-like animal with shaggy fur and huge, circular tusks,~~ was once common to parts of northern Europe and Asia.

> The list of books, authors, and publishers (*was / were*) sitting on the table.

❑ **Compound Subjects** – Subjects grouped by "and" are plural, even if the "and" joins two singular words.

> Sometimes, strong wind and freezing rain (*cause / causes*) power failures.

You may simplify compound subjects by replacing them with a plural pronoun.

Incorrect: He and my brother <u>goes</u> to school.

Simplified: <u>They</u> ...   ... (*go/goes*) to school.

Correct: He and my brother <u>go</u> to school.

❑ **Delayed Subject** – When the subject follows the verb, flip the sentence to put the subject first.

> Opposite the train station (*is / are*) a large shopping mall and a playground for children.

> Over there (*is / are*) the hiking equipment and the mountain bikes.

❑ **Indefinite Pronouns** – Pronouns containing "one," "body," or "thing" are singular.

> Anyone who (*want / wants*) to become a police officer should get a degree in criminal justice.

PUT IT TOGETHER

In few industries **1** are the pressure of logistics as demanding as in the dairy industry. Milk, cheese, yogurt, and other dairy products are particularly vulnerable to spoilage due to time and environmental factors. The journey from the farms to the refrigerators **2** include shipment of raw materials to processing plants, warehousing, and delivery to retailers. At each step, special hygienic conditions are necessary. Transporters and handlers must prevent microbial growth, altered acidity, and spoilage. When any one of these conditions **3** arise, they are detrimental to quality and may render the product unsellable. Cool temperatures and timely delivery are vital to providing fresh, top-quality dairy foods to customers.

Dairy producers and retailers must rely on logistics firms that specialize in developing efficient, coordinated systems. Decades ago, business savvy and ingenuity **4** was the basis for this type of work. Nowadays, logistics firms utilize cutting-edge computer software to find optimal solutions to extremely complex systems. Something as simple as a supermarket shelf full of milk cartons **5** relies on a wide range of professional expertise, from agriculture and shipping to economic analysis and computer programming.

1

A) NO CHANGE
B) is the pressure
C) have the pressure
D) has the pressures

2

A) NO CHANGE
B) includes
C) including
D) included

3

A) NO CHANGE
B) arises, they are
C) arises, it is
D) arise, it is

4

A) NO CHANGE
B) were
C) is
D) are

5

A) NO CHANGE
B) are relied
C) relying
D) rely

Comparisons

❑ Make sure that comparisons are logical and parallel. The same types of ideas should be compared to each other.

> Incorrect:　Warren's stories are more exaggerated and rambling than most children.
>
> Correct:　Warren's stories are more exaggerated and rambling than _____
>
> _____

❑ When comparing someone (or something) to a group that she is a part of, you can't just compare her to the whole group. Remember to use "other," comparing her to the rest of the group, not to herself.

> Incorrect:　Although he is pleasant sometimes, he is still more obnoxious than any boy in his class.
>
> Correct:　Although he is pleasant sometimes, he is still more obnoxious than _____
>
> _____

❑ Use the comparative form of an adjective to compare two things. Comparative forms add either "-er" or are preceded by "more." (e.g., quicker, more courageous)

Use the superlative form of an adjective to compare three or more things. Superlative forms add either "-est" or are preceded by "most." (e.g., quickest, most courageous)

> Of the three possible routes to Rangeley, the interstate is the (_less / least_) scenic, and
>
> between the other two, the county road is the (_quicker / quickest_).

PUT IT TOGETHER

Buying tomatoes from the market has become a dilemma. Do I pay more for a tastier, uglier organic, or do I save money on a tasteless, bio-engineered beauty? With the modern advent of genetically modified organisms (GMOs), scientists have been able to create crops that are insect-resistant, virus-resistant, vitamin-enriched, and drought-tolerant. Yet, despite the current and potential benefits of genetic modification, many consumers prefer organic, heirloom produce simply because it tastes better. Surely, GMO companies can find some way to create crops that are, compared to heirloom organic foods, **1** more nutritious and better tasting. Unfortunately, in the current state of GMO advancements, maximizing profits has been a bigger focus than **2** any concern.

The issue of flavor results from changes to natural processes caused by genetic modification. When crops have small yields, each plant or fruit receives a large portion of the available nutrients. Furthermore, when plants are exposed to insect and microbial pests, they respond by producing chemicals that repel these threats; these chemicals are the sources of flavor and aroma in natural foods. Genetic modification is often aimed at increasing yields and reducing pests. Consequently, genetic modification leads to less flavorful produce than **3** methods of organic farming do.

It is time for a shift in agricultural practices. My hope is for a future in which all produce reaches the pinnacle of culinary senses. We have the capability of engineering the most flavorful crops ever known, so why not use those abilities to their fullest extent?

1
A) NO CHANGE
B) mostly
C) most
D) more of

2
A) NO CHANGE
B) anything
C) any
D) any other concern

3
A) NO CHANGE
B) organic farming methods
C) methods of organic farming
D) of farming methods that are organic

> Carefully consider the logic of what is being compared.

Idioms

Idioms are combinations of words that, taken together, have agreed upon meanings.

❑ The idiom questions on the SAT will often involve prepositions. Make sure the correct preposition is being used.

> Dawn desperately wanted to participate _____ the post-game festivities.

> Each molecule of water consists _____ two hydrogen atoms and one oxygen atom.

❑ On the SAT, if you see an underlined verb and preposition or just an underlined preposition, look for an idiom error.

❑ Make sure you are familiar with commonly used idioms:

accuse of	agree to	agree with	agree on
apologize for	apply to	apply for	approve of
arrive at	blame for	care about	care for
compare to	compare with	consist of	contribute to
count on	cover with	decide on	depend on
differ from	different from	distinguish from	excuse for
forgive for	give to	insist on	participate in
prevent from	prohibit from	provide with	rely on
respond to	substitute for	wait for	wait on

❑ Native English speakers will usually "hear" idiom errors. Non-native speakers will have to work harder to notice these. Reviewing a list of common verb-preposition pairs can help you spot such problems.

PUT IT TOGETHER

Even if you never venture to outer space, your life will be affected **1** by the work done during the "Space Race" between NASA and its Soviet counterpart, the RFSA. In addition **2** with the work these organizations have done exploring the cosmos, or rather because of that work, their many inventions and new technologies have trickled down to much of the world in common industrial and commercial use. Furthermore, the exploration of space has served **3** for a common goal for many world powers, leading to improved national relations.

1
A) NO CHANGE
B) from
C) on
D) for

2
A) NO CHANGE
B) to
C) for
D) as

3
A) NO CHANGE
B) to be
C) like
D) as

Diction

❏ Diction is the choice of words used. Many English words are commonly misused in casual conversation, so make sure you understand the proper ways to use them.

❏ Know the proper usage of the following words.

Accept: to approve or receive (verb)

Except: excluding, besides (preposition)

> I like every flavor (*accept/except*) coconut.
>
> I (*accept/except*) your proposal.

Affect: to influence (verb)

Effect: result or consequence (noun)

> The lyrics of his songs still (*affect/effect*) me.
>
> That story had a strong (*affect/effect*) on people.

Than: in comparison with

Then: at that time

> A kilogram is heavier (*than/then*) a pound.
>
> I exercised, and (*than/then*) I rested.

Lose: to fail or cease to have

Loose: not firm

> The bolt had a (*lose/loose*) fit.
>
> We might (*lose/loose*) this game.

Lie: to pause for rest

Lay: to set down

> Please (*lie/lay*) the package on the table.
>
> After a marathon, I (*lie/lay*) in bed all day.

Lead: present tense of "to lead"

Led: past tense of "to lead"

> Now, the tour guides (*lead/led*) us down the path.
>
> Yesterday, our GPS (*lead/led*) us in circles.

Principle: an accepted rule

Principal: leader

> Sincerity is a (*principle/principal*) of good conduct.
>
> The (*principle/principal*) was late to the meeting.

Number: countable quantity

Amount: measurable quantity

> A large (*number/amount*) of people had a party.
>
> A large (*number/amount*) of flour is used in cake.

Fewer: a countable difference

Less: an uncountable difference

> The express aisle allows 15 items or (*fewer/less*).
>
> After going to the circus, I have (*fewer/less*) fear of clowns and elephants.

Between: in a comparison or in the space separating two objects

Among: in the midst of more than two objects

> The only difference (*between/among*) the two refrigerators is how much they cost.
>
> He wants to build a cabin in the wilderness (*between/among*) all those elm trees.

PUT IT TOGETHER

The goal of freeze drying is to eliminate water from a product, such as food or medicine. Freeze drying creates a product much lighter and **1** heartier then the original, rendering it easier to store and transport, as well as more resistant to spoilage. Water is eliminated through sublimation: the direct transition of a substance from solid to gas. Thus, the first step is to make all water in a product become solid, which is, of course, done by freezing. Although it is easier to sublimate large crystals of ice, food producers use flash-freezing methods to prevent the creation of ice crystals, which cause damage to food cells and **2** effect the flavor and nutrition.

The "drying" portion of the freeze-drying process is performed in large vacuum chambers. At a pressure below 0.006 atm, solid ice is converted directly into its gas phase when heated. A **3** large amount of water vapor is drawn off, rendering the original products almost completely dry.

Freeze drying dates as far back as 1250 BC, when the Peruvian Incas froze crops in the mountains. Due to the high elevation, air pressure was low and the crops would **4** loose much of their moisture as they thawed, preserving the stored food for months, or even years. In the late 1930s, Brazil harvested an **5** excess of coffee beans, which led to Nestle producing freeze-dried brewed coffee. Nowadays, freeze-dried foods are commonly used when it is critical to reduce the weight of transported foods, such as for expeditions by hikers and astronauts.

1
A) NO CHANGE
B) heartier than
C) hardier than
D) hardier then

2
A) NO CHANGE
B) effecting
C) affect
D) affecting

3
A) NO CHANGE
B) large number
C) largeness
D) number

4
A) NO CHANGE
B) lose
C) lost
D) losing

5
A) NO CHANGE
B) excess to
C) access of
D) access to

Fragments

A complete sentence must have a subject (who or what does the action) and a predicate (the action) and must form a complete idea. Any sentence missing one of these elements is a fragment.

❑ **Where's the Verb?** – A verb ending in *ing* is not a complete verb. An *ing* verb creates a fragment if the sentence does not include another, complete verb.

> Incorrect: The CEO of the corporation, after great deliberation, deciding to acquire the software company.
>
> Correct: _____
>
> _____

❑ **Relative Pronouns** – Be careful with relative pronouns, such as *who*, *which*, and *that*. They may create incomplete ideas by changing how the action of the sentence relates to the subject.

> Incorrect: Severe drought conditions, which caused a significant drop in the orange grove's production.
>
> Correct: _____
>
> _____

PUT IT TOGETHER

In the wake of the Scientific Revolution of the 17th century, the first modern **1** chemists setting out to establish new ways of thinking about changes between states of matter. *Phlogiston* was a term created in one of the first attempts to better understand the phenomenon of combustion, or burning. Phlogiston was considered to be the element of combustion, present in any physical object capable of catching fire. As the fire burned, so the theory went, the burning object released phlogiston. Chemists believed that highly combustible materials, such as wood or oil, **2** comprising more phlogiston than were less combustible materials, such as stone or iron. This theory, generally accepted for most of the 1700s, unraveled in the face of repeated scientific testing.

One of the primary challenges to phlogiston theory was its measurable inconsistency. Some objects like charcoal would burn away almost completely and leave very little solid mass behind. This phenomenon would seem to indicate that all the phlogiston had been released. But other objects, like the metal magnesium, were actually heavier after burning than before! At first, supporters of phlogiston theory attempted to explain away these inconsistencies. Eventually, however, phlogiston theory gave way to a new, and provable, understanding of combustion as an oxygen-dependent process.

Those early chemists who gave birth to and supported phlogiston **3** theory, who may have been incorrect, but we are still indebted to them. Though their hypotheses were proven false, they led us to better understandings of the world around us.

1
A) NO CHANGE
B) chemists who set
C) chemists set
D) chemists, they set

2
A) NO CHANGE
B) was comprised of
C) were comprised of
D) which comprised

3
A) NO CHANGE
B) theory. Who may
C) theory, and which
D) theory may

Run-ons

Because run-on errors are fixed with the proper use of punctuation or transition words, it is important to understand the proper usage of periods, semicolons, commas, and transitions.

❑ Run-on sentences result when multiple independent clauses are improperly joined.

You can correct run-ons in a variety of ways, including the three below:

1. Add a period and create two sentences.

2. Add a comma and a conjunction.

3. Use a semicolon.

Incorrect:	They were best friends they haven't spoken to each other in years.
Correct:	They were best friends. They haven't spoken to each other in years.
Correct:	They were best friends, but they haven't spoken to each other in years.
Correct:	They were best friends; they haven't spoken to each other in years.

❑ **Comma Splice** – When two independent clauses are joined with a comma but without a conjunction, this mistake is called a comma splice. Fix a comma splice by replacing the comma with a semicolon, a period, or a comma and a conjunction.

Incorrect:	My history professor is brilliant, I've learned a lot from her.
Correct:	_____

❑ **Relative Pronouns** – Some run-on sentences are best fixed with the addition of relative pronouns, such as *who*, *which*, and *that*.

Incorrect:	Several banks provided long-term funding to Eurotunnel, the company was close to bankruptcy while building a tunnel connecting England to France.
Correct:	Several banks provided long-term funding to Eurotunnel, _____

_____

PUT IT TOGETHER

At some point between the years 1400 and 1600, a significant change occurred in the way that speakers of English pronounced **1** vowels, named the Great Vowel Shift, the accumulated modifications resulted in some identifiable patterns. Some vowels began to be pronounced as *dipthongs,* single syllables which include two distinct vowel sounds. The other significant change was the tendency to raise the tongue higher when pronouncing certain vowels.

These changes in English pronunciation were identified based on the consistent use of rhyme in Middle English **2** writing, scholars noticed that, through the 15th and 16th centuries, different pairings of words were used in rhymes. The rhyming patterns pointed to an evolution in the way these words had been pronounced. An example of these clues is seen in the 14th century poem *Canterbury Tales*, which constructs rhymes between *melody* and *eye*, **3** words that were once pronounced with similar vowel sounds.

1
A) NO CHANGE
B) vowels, but named
C) vowels named
D) vowels. Named

2
A) NO CHANGE
B) writing scholars noticed that. Through
C) writing, scholars noticed that through
D) writing. Scholars noticed that, through

3
A) NO CHANGE
B) these words
C) words
D) DELETE the underlined portion

Conjunctions

Conjunctions are used to connect ideas within and between sentences. Pay attention to the relationship between clauses that are joined by conjunctions. Do the clauses describe things that are basically the same, or that are opposites? Does one clause cause the other? Make sure you use the most appropriate conjunction.

❑ **Coordinating Conjunctions** – The most common conjunctions can be remembered with the acronym FANBOYS: *for, and, nor, but, or, yet,* and *so.*

> Steffi Graf was one of the most successful tennis players of this century, (*or / but*) toward the end of her career she experienced a dramatic decline in her game.

❑ **Subordinating Conjunctions** – Certain conjunctions can be used at the beginning of dependent clauses. These include *although, because, before, since, unless, until, whereas, whether, which,* and *while.*

> (*Unless / Although / Because*) they are detailed and sincere, the stories about alien abduction are frequently believed.

❑ **Paired Conjunctions** – Certain conjunctions are used to connect two paired ideas. Use proper phrasing with paired conjunctions.

both . . . and	not only . . . but also	not . . . but
either . . . or	neither . . . nor	whether . . . or
as . . . as		

> The guide not only provides readers with a brief overview of common accounting mistakes (*but / and also / but also*) suggests ways to correct them.

PUT IT TOGETHER

1 <u>Because</u> people can be impatient in their need for information, a successful news outlet relies on a reputation of being the first to publish a story. In the time before the Internet, when publication required timely printing, the quickest way to get a newspaper on the shelves was to write about an event before it happened. For big, popular stories, such as sports championships and political elections, some news outlets would write multiple articles, one for each potential outcome. These editions would be readied and printed in **2** <u>advance. They would contain</u> just enough information to disguise the fact they were based purely on speculation. Once the game ended or the vote was counted, the proper edition would be immediately shipped. For every accurate story sold to readers, there was another discarded story documenting an event that never occurred.

Print journalists must be careful to publish only information that they can verify. An error or mistake that is physically printed cannot be unwritten, **3** <u>because,</u> in the world of online news, stories can grow organically, with edits and corrections made at any time. There has been a growing trend of real-time stories, which start as a loose collection of details and rumors and then evolve with regular updates as any new information becomes available. With these real-time reports, the news outlet becomes both a collection of researchers **4** <u>but also</u> a source of public chatter. Such journalism isn't necessarily a problem. Perhaps it is time to stop expecting journalism in the form of finished stories and embrace the idea of news reporting as a process, one that is adaptable and prone to assumptions.

1
A) NO CHANGE
B) Although
C) Unless
D) DELETE the underlined portion and begin the sentence with the proper capitalization.

2
Which choice most effectively combines the sentences at the underlined portion?
A) advance and this contains
B) advance, containing
C) advance; those which contain
D) advance, which contain

3
A) NO CHANGE
B) whereas
C) unless
D) until

4
A) NO CHANGE
B) but
C) or
D) and

Parallelism

Parallelism questions are easiest to identify when they appear as a list. Trickier questions will involve comparisons that must be made parallel so the same types of things are being compared.

❑ Sentence elements and ideas that are alike in function should also be the same in grammatical form so that they are "parallel."

❑ **Lists** – Use parallel structure with elements in a list or in a series.

> Incorrect: The social customs emphasized mutual aid, cooperative labor, and sharing of responsibilities.
>
> Correct: The social customs emphasized mutual aid, cooperative labor, and _____
>
> _____

❑ **Paired Conjunctions** – Conjunctions used in pairs (e.g., not only… but also, both… and, either… or, neither… nor) require that the words following each conjunction be parallel.

> Incorrect: His duties as shift manager included not only the supervision of two employees but also required him to assist in food preparation.
>
> Correct: His duties included not only _____
>
> but also _____

❑ **Comparisons** – Use parallel structure with elements being compared.

> Incorrect: Every year, more tourists travel to Disney World than the Louvre.
>
> Correct: Every year, more tourists travel <u>to</u> Disney World than <u>to</u> the Louvre.

> Incorrect: To leave now is worse than betraying your country.
>
> Correct: To leave now is worse than _____.

PUT IT TOGETHER

Modern fishermen are currently weathering an unusual period; in an industry that expects the unexpected, the future is dangerously uncertain. A career in fishing is marked by stress, not only from physical strain **1** as also the strict regulations that are a part of modern fishing. Many traditional fishing families have begun to question whether they should allow their children to work in the fishing industry. The job is typified by working long hours at sea, taking frequent trips away from family, and **2** they risk physical injury without a guarantee of profit. Many fishermen, however, still believe that the gains outweigh the sacrifices. They love the job despite the time commitment, difficulties, and risks that come along with it, and believe the hardships are balanced by the satisfaction of doing something they truly love.

Perhaps because commercial fishing is a difficult and dangerous occupation, many fishermen hold fast to superstitions. Some fishermen will turn with or against the sun in order to create good luck. Some will depart for fishing trips only on Fridays. **3** Turkeys and bananas are prohibited from some of their boats. The most common custom is to ban whistling on a fishing boat. While some fishermen believe the whistling ban is steeped in the practical, such as the necessity of listening to one's engine, others fear that "whistling up a wind" might stir up a storm. The diversity of superstitions among fishermen – some serious, some silly – reflects the challenging but high-spirited nature of the fishing industry.

1

A) NO CHANGE
B) and also with
C) but also has
D) but also from

2

A) NO CHANGE
B) risking
C) to risk
D) risk

3

Which choice best maintains the pattern established by previous sentences in the paragraph?

A) NO CHANGE
B) Prohibited from some of their boats are turkeys and bananas.
C) Some of their boats will prohibit turkeys and bananas.
D) Some will prohibit turkeys and bananas from their boats.

Modifiers

A modifier is a descriptive word or phrase. Modifier questions require careful consideration of sentence logic. Make sure that modifiers are properly placed so they describe the right things.

❑ **Faulty Modification** – Modifiers should be placed next to what they modify. Misplaced modifiers create ambiguity or cause a change in meaning.

Incorrect:	<u>Biking to school</u>, the wind nearly blew me over.
Correct:	Biking to school, I was nearly blown over by the wind.
Correct:	As I biked to school, the wind nearly blew me over.
Correct:	The wind nearly blew me over as I biked to school.

Incorrect:	Because it is similar to other ailments, doctors often have difficulty diagnosing Lyme Disease.
Correct:	Because it is similar to other ailments, _____
	_____

❑ **Dangling Modifier** – Check for modifying phrases that appear at the beginning of a sentence and ask who or what is being modified. The subject that directly follows the modifier should be what the modifier describes.

Smashed flat by a passing truck, Big Dog sniffed at what was left of the half-eaten hamburger.

What is the modifying phrase? _____

Who or what is being modified? _____

Write the sentence correctly: _____

_____

PUT IT TOGETHER

A hunter, outdoorsman, and boxer, **1** Ernest Hemingway's reputation is partly due to his larger-than-life persona. His writing showed an obsession with a wide range of dangerous activities, including war, safaris, and bullfighting. In the public's eye, he became a symbol of such activities. He became known as something of a caricature, the personification of "manliness." This image earned him, in addition to much fame and praise, some harsh criticism.

Hemingway was eager to defend his masculine identity against detractors. When well-known writer and critic Max Eastman claimed that Hemingway's persona was an act to cover insecurity, Hemingway personally responded. **2** Hemingway was enraged and, upon meeting the critic, the critic's own book was used to strike Eastman across the face. Such actions added to Hemingway's fame and further strengthened the popular image of the brawny writer.

1

A) NO CHANGE
B) Ernest Hemingway developed a reputation that was partly due to his larger-than-life persona.
C) Ernest Hemingway's larger-than-life persona was partly responsible for developing his reputation.
D) the development of Ernest Hemingway's reputation is partly due to his larger-than-life persona.

2

A) NO CHANGE
B) Upon meeting the critic, Hemingway was enraged and struck Eastman across the face with the critic's own book.
C) Upon meeting the critic, the critic's own book was used by an enraged Hemingway to strike Eastman across the face.
D) Hemingway was enraged and Eastman was struck across the face with the critic's own book upon meeting the critic.

Verb Tense

Most verb tense questions test for consistency of tense within and among sentences.

❑ Verb tenses should remain consistent unless the sentence indicates a change in time.

❑ When trying to determine whether there might be a verb tense error, pay attention to clues about time. Is the action happening in the past, present, or future? Is the action ongoing or is it finished?

❑ **Has or Had** – The most challenging verb tense questions typically require an understanding of the difference between past, past perfect, and present perfect tenses.

Past tense is used to describe completed actions.

> John *cooked* breakfast yesterday morning.

Present perfect tense is used to describe past actions that are still continuing. Present perfect verbs use the auxiliary verbs "has" or "have."

> John *has cooked* breakfast every Sunday since he was 12 years old.

Past perfect tense is used to describe completed actions that occurred before other actions. Past perfect verbs use the auxiliary verb "had."

> Until last year, when he decided to stop eating breakfast, John *had cooked* breakfast every Sunday.

> For the past 100 years or more, the town of Concord, Massachusetts, (*had stood / has stood*) for the American patriotism which New Englanders embrace so strongly.

PUT IT TOGETHER

In early 1692, the Salem Witch Trials **1** begun in the Massachusetts Bay colony. Two teenage girls had accused a handful of adults of practicing witchcraft. Within a short time, an increasing number of people were accused, and by the time the frenzy ended in mid-1693, twenty-four people **2** have lost their lives. All but six of the accused were pardoned in 1711, and in 1992 the state legislature passed a bill acquitting the rest. However, these pardons do not undo the harm brought against the accused "witches."

In recent years, this rich history **3** has begun attracting hordes of tourists. The Halloween revelry alone includes parades and festivals, making October the town's most lucrative month of the year.

1
A) NO CHANGE
B) began
C) begins
D) have begun

2
A) NO CHANGE
B) had lost
C) were lost
D) lose

3
A) NO CHANGE
B) had begun
C) begins
D) beginning

Semicolons

Semicolon questions test your skills with fragments and run-ons. These questions often ask you to choose whether a semicolon, comma, or no punctuation should sit between certain clauses.

❑ Semicolons, like periods, are used between two independent clauses. A semicolon indicates that two ideas are related. Semicolons and periods are usually interchangeable.

❑ **Run-Ons** – Use semicolons to fix comma splices and other run-on errors.

> Incorrect: The railroad played a major role in expanding the country's borders, it made the western frontier accessible to everyone.
>
> Correct: The railroad played a major role in expanding the country's borders _____
>
> _____

❑ **Misused Semicolons** – Be on the lookout for semicolons that are used with conjunctions or where commas or colons should be used.

> Incorrect: Smokejumpers are not often deployed; but their work is very dangerous.
>
> Correct: _____

Colons

The key to correcting most colon errors is determining whether the clauses before and after the punctuation are independent or dependent.

❑ **Before the Colon** – Colons should be used only at the end of a complete sentence.

> Incorrect: The classic polymath, Galileo made innovations in: many fields, including physics, mathematics, and, most famously, astronomy.
>
> Correct: _____
>
> _____

❑ **After the Colon** – Colons are most commonly used to introduce lists, but they may also be used to present information that clarifies or elaborates on the independent clause.

> Correct: Of all the countries represented at the summit, only one spokesman offered an alternative to the proposal: the ambassador from Japan.

PUT IT TOGETHER

Art experts use their knowledge of artists to help determine if paintings are authentic or forgeries. They look at many **1** details: such as clothing and furnishings in the painting and pigments or canvas used, to conclude if they match those used during the time period of the artist. They also look at the painting's provenance, or documentation of ownership, and if available, the **2** *catalogue raisonné*; a comprehensive, annotated listing of an artist's works. Talented art forgers take advantage of the lack of a methodological approach to analysis. With their own study of the artist and techniques to make a painting look real, they can fool the experts of the subject.

If authentication from art experts does not suffice, a technical analysis of the painting can take place. Various techniques are used to determine **3** authenticity; they use high-resolution cameras, digital scans, microscopic analysis, and carbon dating are all commonly employed by art authenticators. Ultraviolet and infrared analysis will show a painting beneath a painting, and x-ray analysis will show fingerprints or newer material. In one case, an infamous art forger was finally caught when he used paint mixed with unlabeled titanium white, a pigment used after the time of the artist he was copying.

1
A) NO CHANGE
B) details;
C) details,
D) details

2
A) NO CHANGE
B) *catalogue raisonné*; and it was
C) *catalogue raisonné*: being
D) *catalogue raisonné*:

3
A) NO CHANGE
B) authenticity. They use:
C) authenticity, using:
D) authenticity;

Commas

Many questions on the SAT Writing test involve commas. Even questions that deal with other grammatical rules will sometimes ask you to make a decision about proper comma placement.

❑ **Scene Setters** – If a sentence begins with a phrase that sets time, place, or purpose, then the phrase should be followed by a comma.

> Incorrect: After the heavy rain frogs emerged from the ground.
>
> Correct: _____

❑ **Independent Clauses and Conjunctions** – When two independent clauses are joined by a conjunction, there should be a comma placed before the conjunction.

> Incorrect: Many people assume that eating tomatoes originated in Italy but the fruit originated in South America.
>
> Correct: _____
>
> _____

❑ **Nonrestrictive Clauses** – Clauses that provide nonessential information about a subject are offset by commas. Nonessential clauses can also be offset by parentheses or dashes.

> Correct: The new findings, which seem to disprove the modern understanding of the universe, confused the astronomers.
>
> Correct: Hawaii was governed by monarchies until 1893, when it was annexed by the United States.

When a name is paired with an identifier, carefully consider whether the name or the identifier provides information essential to understanding the reference.

> Correct: My best friend, Irene, is taking the bus.
>
> Correct: Successful industrialist Andrew Carnegie is known for his philanthropy.

❑ **Series** – Commas separate items in a list.

> Incorrect: During dinner, we discussed cake recipes my parents and Ben Franklin.
>
> Correct: During dinner, we discussed _____.

PUT IT TOGETHER

In 1966, half a century after his last **1** <u>race, former Olympic runner, Shizo Kanakuri,</u> received an odd invitation. The Olympic committee asked that he complete a 54-year-old race. Kanakuri was 75 years old at the time and far from the athletic form of his youth, but he decided to accept the invitation and return to Stockholm, Sweden.

For the Swedish National Olympic Committee, the return of Shizo Kanakuri was also the resolution to a 54-year mystery. Back in 1912, Kanakuri had **2** <u>competed,</u> in the Olympic games in Stockholm. He had a world-record qualifying time of 2 hours, 32 minutes, and 45 seconds, nearly half an hour faster than the previous **3** <u>record –</u> and many spectators expected him to take the gold medal. For Kanakuri, the 1912 race was far below expectations. During the Olympic games, a heat wave brought temperatures of 40 degrees C (104 degrees F); more than half of the runners were afflicted with heat stroke. Suffering from **4** <u>travel fatigue, stomach, illness</u> and heat exhaustion, Kanakuri lost consciousness partway through the race. Unable to continue, he stumbled into the garden of a local farming family. The family cared for him, giving him orange juice and allowing him to rest. **5** <u>Kanakuri, too ashamed to continue the race</u> left for Japan the next day without notifying the race officials. For decades, Swedish authorities were puzzled by his disappearance. He became a local legend – "the missing marathoner."

More than half a century later, Kanakuri was happy to return and finally complete what he had started. Television crews crowded the sides of the streets to capture the aging athlete's smile as he happily ran the rest of his marathon. His time was announced as 54 years, 8 months, 6 days, 5 hours, 32 minutes, and 20.3 seconds, the longest time on record. Kanakuri remarked, "It was a long trip. Along the way, I got married, had six children and ten grandchildren."

1
A) NO CHANGE
B) race, former Olympic runner, Shizo Kanakuri
C) race, former Olympic runner Shizo Kanakuri
D) race former Olympic runner Shizo Kanakuri

2
A) NO CHANGE
B) competed;
C) competed,
D) competed

3
A) NO CHANGE
B) record:
C) record,
D) record;

4
A) NO CHANGE
B) travel, fatigue stomach, illness
C) travel fatigue, stomach illness,
D) travel, fatigue, stomach, illness,

5
A) NO CHANGE
B) Kanakuri, too ashamed to continue the race,
C) Kanakuri too ashamed to continue the race,
D) Kanakuri, too ashamed, to continue the race

Apostrophes

Apostrophes are used to indicate possession or to take the place of missing letters in contractions.

- ❑ **Singular Possessive** – When the possessor is a singular noun, possession can be indicated by adding *'s.*

    Correct: Is that <u>Bob's</u> dog or is it <u>James's</u>?

- ❑ **Plural Possessive** – When the possessor is a plural noun ending in *s*, possession can be indicated by adding an apostrophe. Plural nouns that do not end in *s* can be made possessive by adding *'s.*

    (*Children's / Childrens'*) joy often comes from not having to handle many responsibilities.

- ❑ **Pronouns** – Pronouns do not require apostrophes to indicate possession. Rather, pronouns have their own possessive forms.

    Incorrect: The apple tree may be her's, but the fruit is now their's.

    Correct: The apple tree may be _____, but the fruit is now _____.

    There is one exception to this rule: the possessive form of the indefinite pronoun *one* requires an apostrophe

    Incorrect: It is not in <u>ones</u> best interest to throw rocks at a beehive.

    Correct: It is not in <u>one's</u> best interest to throw rocks at a beehive.

- ❑ **Contractions** – There are many contractions in English, all of which require apostrophes.

    The following is a short list of common contractions.

    It's = It is   You're = You are   They've = They have

    They're = They are   She'll = She will   He'd = He had; He would

    Who's = Who is   Won't = Will not

PUT IT TOGETHER

1 Its' difficult to overestimate the impact of clean water on our health. World population growth has strained fresh water availability, forcing governments and scientists to seek new solutions. Desalination, the process of removing salt from seawater, has become one major focus of global efforts to provide usable water. Nearly 98% of **2** Earth's water contains salt, but municipal governments and private industry have struggled to develop cost-effective methods for desalinating seawater.

Various factors contribute to the extraordinary expense of desalination; specialized facilities must be constructed, and these plants use large quantities of energy to create the pressure necessary to force water through salt-filtering membranes. Much of the cost associated with desalination depends on a number of regional considerations. The price of labor is yet another consideration: a plant in the United States must devote over 60% of **3** their budget to worker's wages.

1
A) NO CHANGE
B) It's
C) Its
D) It

2
A) NO CHANGE
B) Earths water contain's
C) Earths' water contains
D) Earths' water contain's

3
A) NO CHANGE
B) they're budget to workers'
C) its budget to workers'
D) it's budget to workers

> Apostrophe questions often involve pronoun agreement.

Main Idea

The main idea is the central point, opinion, or purpose of a passage or a portion of a passage. Main idea questions may require you to choose a sentence that best states the main idea or to choose information that is most relevant to the focus of the passage.

Many Expression of Ideas questions will require an understanding of the passage's main idea.

❑ **Stay on Point** - Every portion of a passage should contribute to the main idea. Do not choose to include a detail just because it is related to the general topic of the passage.

> Whenever you cannot think of the right word to express yourself, rest assured that it might not be your fault; you can blame the limits of your language. Even with an estimated one million unique words, the English language does not have a word for everything. Online databases are used to record and organize the vast English vocabulary, along with each word's origins. More than five thousand languages have been developed to describe the many experiences and ideas of human life, but no single language does it all. Among different languages, there are "lexical gaps," or words that do not have equivalents in other languages. For example, English has no word for the anxious anticipation of waiting for someone to visit you. In Inuit, this word is *iktsuarpok*. In Yaghan, the word *mamihlapinatapai* refers to a look shared between two people when they share a silent understanding. We can translate these words, but only with complicated explanations.
>
> Certainly, each language is largely a product of the culture from which it originates, and thus a language's range of expressible ideas is representative of that culture. Further, speakers' minds may be limited by what words are available to them. Anthropologists Edward Sapir and Benjamin Lee Whorf hold that the structure and limits of a language affect how its speakers can formulate ideas and world views. Their hypothesis of linguistic relativity poses that our language affects our perceptions and interpretations. In short, your language and vocabulary may determine how you think.

What is the main idea of the first paragraph?

What is the main idea of the second paragraph?

What information in the first paragraph should be removed?

❑ Before you can answer a main idea question, you may need to reread part of the passage.

SUMMIT
EDUCATIONAL
GROUP

PUT IT TOGETHER

[1] At best, critics judge a remake as being inferior or lacking the same impact as the original. At worst, they condemn a remake as disrespectful or insulting to the classic it's based on. In response to a recent blockbuster film based on a children's cartoon show from decades ago, some fans were outraged, even going so far as to claim that the new film "ruined" their childhood. The problem here is that critics have lost their objectivity. Upon reviewing a new work, we must not make the mistake of prejudice. All too often, it seems that critics are expecting a remake to fail to capture the magic of the original before it has even been seen.

This issue is one of nostalgia. Many of us have convinced ourselves that the classics are flawless works that modern recreations can only spoil. I don't see any problem with remaking, updating, or reimagining classics. Artists have always borrowed from previous [2] artists, a practice which helps preserve certain artistic styles and movements. We shouldn't assume that the classics are perfect, nor should we discourage new art that is inspired by the classics. Instead, we should encourage the artists who are bold and brave enough to take a classic work and try to improve upon it by envisioning it in a new way.

1

Which choice most effectively establishes the main focus of the paragraph?

A) Instead of criticizing remakes, our criticism should focus on the flaws of classic art.

B) Critics should be more accepting of remakes of classic works of art.

C) Remakes make improvements on the classics on which they are based.

D) Artists should be more respectful of classics and should not try to remake them.

2

Which choice provides the most relevant detail?

A) NO CHANGE

B) artists, as much as copyright laws allow.

C) artists, except for those who are in emerging fields and must be entirely innovative.

D) artists to build on previous strengths and expand into new artistic possibilities.

Addition

Most addition questions will ask you to find the best place to include a sentence. Difficult questions ask you to judge the role and importance of a sentence and the potential effects of adding, or choosing not to add, the sentence.

❑ **The Right Place** – Added sentences must logically connect to the sentences around them.

> The writer wants to add the following sentence to the paragraph.
>
> > "But inflation's opposite, deflation, can be just as detrimental."
>
> Indicate where the sentence should be placed.
>
>   The key to economic stability is maintaining the status quo. ____ In times of inflation, the value of money falls and prices seem higher. ____ Deflation causes prices to effectively decrease, which means that businesses' profits drop. ____ While cheaper merchandise might seem desirable to consumers, paying ten thousand dollars for a car that will be worth half that amount in a short time isn't. ____ Deflation causes businesses to decrease paychecks and employ fewer people. ____ In the end, a stable economy is better than one in which either inflation or deflation are unchecked.

❑ **Relevance** – Added sentences must be relevant to the focus of passage and should support and strengthen the passage's ideas. It does not matter if the addition is interesting or well-stated; it must make sense where it would be added in the passage.

❑ Some addition questions ask whether a sentence or phrase should be added to the passage and also ask for a reason why the addition should or should not be made. For these questions, first eliminate half of the answer choices by determining whether the addition works well in the passage. Then consider the reasoning of the two remaining answer choices.

PUT IT TOGETHER

[1] Even though he is often given credit for it, Thomas Edison did not invent the light bulb. [2] More than a dozen other inventors had created electric incandescent bulbs before him. [3] The idea of creating light by passing electricity through thin filaments of metal had been known nearly 80 years before Edison's attempt at the light bulb. [4] Inventors such as Humphry Davy, James Lindsay, and Warren de la Rue all made advancements in electric lighting decades before Edison, but their experiments were limited by their interest in other inventions or by the expense of making the filaments, which were made of platinum in early versions of the light bulb. [5] Edison's improvements allowed electric light bulbs to be used throughout the world. **1**

Our control of light is closely tied to great periods of human advancement. Lighting technologies freed us from our dependence on solar cycles for productivity. Before the electric light bulb became the standard source of lighting, gas lighting was the norm. Being cheaper and more effective than candles, gas lighting changed 19th-century society. **2** In the 20th century, electric lighting made it even more convenient for us to be able to work as capably during the night as we do during the day.

1

The writer wants to add the following sentence to the first paragraph.

What Edison managed to do was improve on these other inventors' designs and create a light bulb that was more practical and effective.

The best placement for the sentence is before

A) sentence 2.
B) sentence 3.
C) sentence 4.
D) sentence 5.

2

At this point, the writer is considering adding the following sentence.

By allowing people to stay up later at night to read or work, gas lighting brought about an increase in literacy and industrialization of the time.

Should the writer make this addition here?

A) Yes, because it provides a clear transition between the topic of inventors and the topic of gas lighting.
B) Yes, because it provides more information to support the main point of the paragraph.
C) No, because the details are redundant and unnecessary.
D) No, because the details are not relevant to the focus of the paragraph.

Deletion

Deletion questions ask you to judge the role and importance of a sentence and the potential effects of deleting, or choosing not to delete, the sentence.

❑ **Cut the Excess** – Sentences should be deleted if they are not relevant to the focus of the passage or do not support and strengthen the passage's ideas.

> Which of the sentences should be deleted from the paragraph? _____
>
> [1] Although viruses share some of the distinctive properties of living organisms, they are not technically alive. [2] They are unable to grow or reproduce in the same way that living creatures do. [3] Instead, they act like parasites in order to reproduce. [4] After locating and making contact with the right kind of cell, a virus injects its genetic material. [5] It then uses the host cell, which is unable to distinguish the virus' genes from its own, to replicate. [6] DNA and RNA viruses differ in which part of the cell they replicate. [7] This process kills the cell, creating a new virus organism.

❑ Some deletion questions ask whether a sentence or phrase should be deleted from the passage and also ask for a reason why the deletion should or should not be made. For these questions, first eliminate half of the answer choices by determining whether the deletion would improve the passage. Then consider the reasoning of the two remaining answer choices.

PUT IT TOGETHER

[1] During the Victorian Era, British upper society faced an unusual new problem. [2] This period is named for Queen Victoria of England, who became a figure of social restraint and morality. [3] With the developments of the 19th century came an increase in luxury and leisure for the privileged upper class, and these wealthy men and women had too much free time. [4] In order to fight off the boredom, these ladies and gentlemen invented new parlor games. [5] In one of these new games, a row of books was lined up across the middle of a table and two more books were used to hit a ball shaped from a champagne cork. [6] The ball was hit back and forth across the table, over the row of books in the center. [7] The game was named "wiff-waff," for the sound made by the books smacking the cork ball. [8] Today, the game is more commonly known as "table tennis" or "ping-pong." **1**

The game of table tennis has changed greatly since its creation. **2** It is an Olympic Sport, and many spectators complain that the game is too fast to follow. Celluloid plastic balls replaced the corks and golf balls that had originally been used. A racket, made of a flat wooden paddle covered with a sheet of rubber, replaced books and cigar box lids. Special tables and nets were made to replicate tennis courts, though the game is still very different from traditional tennis. Within a couple decades, the game went from a simple, amusing diversion to an aggressively competitive sport.

1

Which sentence should be deleted from the essay because it contains information that is not related to the essay's central focus?

A) Sentence 2
B) Sentence 3
C) Sentence 4
D) Sentence 5

2

The writer is considering deleting the underlined sentence. Should the sentence be deleted from this paragraph?

A) Yes, because it contradicts the central argument of the paragraph.
B) Yes, because it contains information that is not relevant to the main focus of the paragraph.
C) No, because the sentence provides a necessary example of how table tennis differs from traditional tennis.
D) No, because the sentence helps explain why the sport of table tennis has changed over time.

Organization

Organization questions ask you to make a clear progression of ideas. You may be asked to reorganize sentences in a paragraph or parts of a sentence to create the most logical order.

❑ **Get in Order** – When organized properly, an essay's ideas should build upon each other and transition naturally.

> Read the passage and then note where each of the sentences following the passage belongs in the paragraph.
>
> Long ago, the world's tallest mountain range, the Himalayas, was actually a pair of beaches. _____ Between the two continents lay the Tethys Ocean, which was narrowing by approximately 10 cm per year. _____ Normally, when two tectonic plates collide, one is subducted under the other and sinks into the Earth's mantle. However, sedimentary materials of the Asian and Indian continents were both low in density. Neither could be forced downward into the mantle. _____ The pressure of this collision causes frequent earthquakes and has, over time, created the Himalaya mountain range, which boasts the famous Mount Everest. Evidence of the region's past can be found in fossilized ocean life in the stones of the Himalayan mountains.
>
> 1) Instead, the land was folded, faulted, and lifted.
>
> 2) 50 million years ago, India was an island continent drifting north toward Asia.
>
> 3) The two continents eventually collided, thus eliminating the Tethys Ocean and creating incredible tectonic pressure.

❑ When you see numbered sentences, be prepared for an organization question. As you read, look for sentences that seem out of order.

❑ When considering an organization question, reread the passage with the changes based on each answer choice.

PUT IT TOGETHER

[1] In 1978, construction workers in Mexico City stumbled upon a surprising discovery. [2] Buried below the city's main square was a large carving of Coyolxauhqui, the Aztec moon goddess. [3] As archaeologists began excavating the site, they realized the ancient carving was part of a much larger discovery. [4] By chance, they had discovered the ruins of Templo Mayor, a massive temple of the ancient Aztec Empire. **1**

Templo Mayor had been the most important religious site in Tenochtitlán, the capital of the Aztec Empire. The temple was made larger and larger over time as a symbol of the city's growing prosperity. It had been a monument to the success of a great civilization. However, the prosperity of Tenochtitlán was not to last.

2 [1] The Templo Mayor was seized and destroyed in 1521 by the Spaniard Hernán Cortés. [2] Cortés, a Spanish explorer, was at first impressed and amazed by the beauty and grandeur of the Aztec city. [3] Cortés destroyed Tenochtitlán to erase all traces of the Aztec religion. **3** [4] <u>However, he was also horrified by the Aztec's religious practices, so he laid siege to the city.</u> [5] In short time, a Spanish city was built over the remains of the Aztec city.

Now, Templo Mayor is more than an archaeological interest; it is a recovery of Aztec heritage.

1

The writer wants to add the following sentence to the paragraph:

> The construction workers did not recognize the figure, but the image would have been familiar to the people who lived there 500 years earlier.

The best placement for the sentence is immediately

A) before sentence 1.
B) after sentence 1.
C) after sentence 2.
D) after sentence 3.

2

In order to emphasize the extent of the destruction by Cortés, the writer intends to add to the following sentence this phrase:

> along with much of the rest of Tenochtitlán

The phrase, with proper punctuation added, would most effectively serve the writer's purpose if added

A) after *Templo Mayor*.
B) after *seized and*.
C) after *1521*.
D) after *Hernán Cortés*.

3

To make this paragraph most logical, sentence 4 should be placed

A) where it is now.
B) before sentence 1.
C) before sentence 2.
D) before sentence 3.

Transitions

Transition questions will ask you to choose the most appropriate and logical way to shift from one idea to another. These questions may ask you to choose the most appropriate transition between two clauses, sentences, or paragraphs.

❑ Transitions show whether one idea contrasts, supports, or causes another.

Contrasting	Supporting	Cause/Effect
but	and	because
however	thus	consequently
instead	similarly	if
despite	furthermore	therefore
although	indeed	since
nevertheless	; (semicolon)	subsequently

❑ **Connect Ideas** – Pay attention to the ideas that come before and after a transition.

> Write transitions in the following passage.
>
> Our sun is approximately halfway through its 10 billion year lifespan. Over the next half of its life, our sun will get hotter and larger, growing several billion times larger in volume. Eventually, its outer layers will swell into a colossal nebula of ionized gases that will spread outward through our solar system. Our planet might survive all of this, but no life on Earth will. _____, scientists are looking for other planets that might support life when our planet will no longer be able to. With the latest imaging technologies, scientists have been scanning our galaxy in hope of finding planets that may harbor life. The results have been very encouraging. Based on current data, planets are plentiful throughout the universe, _____ many of them (as many as two billion!) are similar to Earth. _____, these planets are very far away. At present, we don't have the technology needed to travel to another solar system, _____ we must find a way. As the NASA administrator has said, "The goal is... extending the range of human habitat... In the long run, a single-planet species will not survive."

PUT IT TOGETHER

Today's image of the American Old West is wild and adventurous, a chaotic blend of pioneers, cowboys, Native Americans, outlaws, and wild animals. **1** However, like many images of history, this idea of the Wild West is not entirely accurate. The mundane facts of life have been overlooked in favor of dramatizing the more exciting and entertaining aspects of 19th-century western America.

The Wild West is mostly a myth, which has been shaped over the years by movies, television, and fictional stories, which exaggerate the real western frontier. Above all, the legend of the Wild West was created and spread by William F. Cody, also known as Buffalo Bill. Buffalo Bill's own life certainly matched the wild image of the **2** West: he was a gold-seeker, a hunter, an Army scout, and a cowboy. In 1883, he founded "Buffalo Bill's Wild West," a spectacular, circus-like show in which performers would reenact historical battles, display tricks, tell stories, and showcase wild animals in front of huge audiences.

3 The intention of the Wild West show was to present the American west in an educational way. Buffalo Bill hoped to preserve the western culture he fondly grew up in. He saw the show as a public lesson in history and culture. Arguably, with its many stunts, races, and attractions, the show placed more emphasis on entertainment than education. **4** As such, an embellished view of the American West was popularized, commercialized, and cemented into the cultural history of America.

1
A) NO CHANGE
B) Similarly
C) Further
D) Additionally

2
A) NO CHANGE
B) West: in contrast, he
C) West: therefore, he
D) West: nevertheless, he

3
Which choice provides the smoothest transition between the second and third paragraphs?
A) NO CHANGE
B) Such a performance required incredible coordination.
C) As many as 500 performers and staff traveled together.
D) The production moved from city to city by train.

4
A) NO CHANGE
B) Likewise,
C) In other words,
D) For instance,

Wordiness

On the SAT Writing Test, concise and economic language is usually better. Wordiness questions require you to eliminate redundancies and irrelevant information.

Simpler questions will have synonyms placed next to each other. More complicated questions will have ideas that are described multiple times or that are unrelated to the main focus of the passage.

❑ **Avoid redundancy** – Eliminate details that are unnecessarily repeated. Look out for synonyms that do not add new information.

Wordy:	Of all the teachers in the school, he is the most popular teacher.
Concise:	_____

Wordy:	Each year, the financier makes an annual analysis of prospects.
Concise:	_____

❑ **Get to the Point** – Eliminate stalling or unnecessary phrases.

Wordy:	When the media portray an athlete as greedy, this is when people rush to judge his or her character.
Concise:	_____

PUT IT TOGETHER

Given the importance of electricity in modern society, we must anticipate potential risks to our power grids. We are accustomed to worrying about the impact of drastic weather. Insurance plans can cover losses due to damages from tornadoes, flooding, and other **1** common disasters that occur regularly. There is, however, no insurance against the extreme weather of outer space.

Our sun is not as stable and kindly as it seems. The sun's surface occasionally erupts, shooting gas and radiation. Known as a coronal mass ejection (CME), these powerful outbursts can involve billions of tons of charged particles traveling at seven million miles per hour. When a CME strikes Earth, it causes a geomagnetic storm in our atmosphere. A weak CME may cause an aurora, such as the famous Northern Lights. In 1859, an enormous CME caused aurora lights across the world. Because of the strength of this **2** powerful storm of solar energy, telegraph systems were overloaded and damaged. With the extensive electrical systems of the modern world, the potential damage is much greater. A geomagnetic storm caused by a powerful CME could bring year-long electric blackouts to entire nations.

Measures must be taken to prepare for the potential damage of CMEs. Investments need to be made to modernize and strengthen power grids, especially in high population areas. Satellites can be employed to monitor solar activity and warn electric grid operators before a CME strikes. While these precautions can mitigate the damage, **3** we currently do not, at present, have any guaranteed protection against these solar storms. We may have to simply accept the consequences and—when the inevitable occurs—rebuild, just as we do with the hurricanes and tornados that we regularly endure.

1
A) NO CHANGE
B) recurrent disasters, which commonly occur.
C) common disasters that can be damaging.
D) common disasters.

2
A) NO CHANGE
B) solar storm caused by the sun's energy,
C) storm that created widespread aurorae,
D) storm,

3
A) NO CHANGE
B) we do not currently have any guaranteed protection at this time
C) right now we do not currently have any guaranteed protection
D) we currently have no guaranteed protection

SUMMIT
EDUCATIONAL
GROUP

Style

Style questions ask you to make sure that portions of the passage are precise, effective, and appropriate. Most of these questions require you to choose the most suitable of several related words. Others will ask you to choose between several phrases that range in tone, formality, or complexity.

❑ **Word Choice** – When choosing between synonyms, carefully consider the exact meaning of each word in the context of the passage. You will often need to know the main idea of the passage in order to understand the writer's intended meaning of a word.

> When Picasso painted *Guernica*, it firmly (*implanted / authorized / established*) him as one of the premier artists of the twentieth century.

❑ **Tone** – Make sure the language of passages is consistent in tone. Avoid language that is too complex or too informal.

> For everyday problems, humans have the ability to (*extrapolate / develop / get*) a solution.

> The complicated problem of long-term homelessness in advanced nations has proven too (*bad / formidable*) for any one solution.

PUT IT TOGETHER

Modern clinical and public health faces an ironic dilemma: through the treating of illness, there is the potential to make illnesses untreatable. The past half-century has seen the rise of antibiotic use, as well as newly resistant diseases. A prime example is *Staphylococcus aureus*, a pathogenic bacteria that has evolved to be resistant to many types of antibiotics, which makes it very difficult to treat. The development of bacteria like *Staphylococcus aureus* has brought new recognition of the consequences of antibiotic use. We are facing a **1** vital medical concern if we continue our current methods of treatment.

Bacteria are pervasive and essential throughout the biological world. In our zeal to heal and disinfect, we have lost sight of the **2** natural microbial ecosystem. Antibiotic medication does not **3** erase all bacteria from a patient (nor should it, as so many of our biological processes rely on bacteria). The remaining microbial life is left to thrive. Similarly, the use of antibacterial agents, such as hand sanitizer, in the home sets the stage for an altered microbial environment in which certain bacteria are allowed to flourish because their competition has been eliminated. To curb this problem, we must **4** promote the growth of diverse flora that can compete with the resistant organisms.

We are entering the post-antibiotic era. Recognizing that we cannot win a battle against bacteria, we are **5** admitting new tactics. Recent years have seen the rapid rise of the use of probiotics. By encouraging the growth of benign bacteria, we are creating healthier environments without the risk of spawning drug-resistant epidemics.

1

Which of the following is most consistent with the rest of the first paragraph?

A) NO CHANGE
B) dire
C) hurtful
D) standard

2

A) NO CHANGE
B) likely
C) commonplace
D) customary

3

A) NO CHANGE
B) eradicate
C) waste
D) massacre

4

A) NO CHANGE
B) aggrandize
C) help out
D) venerate

5

A) NO CHANGE
B) adopting
C) raising
D) permitting

Data Graphics

Each SAT Writing Test contains at least one chart or table. Data graphic questions will ask you to connect the information shown in the graphic to the information in the passage. In order to understand this connection, you will have to know the main idea of the passage.

❑ **Accuracy** – Information in the passage must accurately reflect the data in the graphic.

Use the Process of Elimination and remove any answer choices that do not match the data.

❑ **Relevance** – Information in the passage must be relevant to the main idea.

Use the Process of Elimination and remove any answer choices that do not apply to the central focus of the passage.

❑ Let the answer choices guide you.

Do not analyze all of the information in a data graphic, because this is usually too time-consuming. Instead, note the labels so you understand what the graphic is showing, and then use the answer choices to determine what data to focus on.

PUT IT TOGETHER

In spite of the numerous benefits of laboratory-grown meat (derisively called "shmeat"), there seems to be little hope for its commercial future. Why would we want to have scientists, rather than ranchers, make burgers? Because raising animals for slaughter is highly inefficient. Producing one kilogram of conventional beef requires as much as twenty kilograms of feed, which is a significant loss of resources. Raising livestock also leads to significant emissions of greenhouse gases. With a quickly rising global population and an average consumption of over 200 pounds of meat per adult in industrialized nations, our current meat-eating trend is, at best, impractical and, at worst, unsustainable. By comparison, laboratories can grow meat using **1** twice the energy and a tenth of the water needed for an equivalent amount of conventional beef.

Lab-grown meat is more practical, but it will not likely be widely accepted. **2** Furthermore, consumers are picky about their meat. We have certain expectations for flavor and texture. Current laboratory methods are not yet capable of replicating the blood vessels, fat, gristle, and other tissues that are key to certain cuts of meat. Traditional recipes often utilize specific meats or organs, and many people will be unwilling to compromise.

1

Which choice most accurately represents the information in the graph?

A) NO CHANGE
B) half the energy and a tenth of the water
C) half the energy and ten times the water
D) an equivalent amount of energy and water

2

At this point, the writer wants to include relevant and accurate information from the graph to support the main claim made in this paragraph. Which choice best accomplishes this goal?

A) Consumers will be reluctant to pay for lab-grown meat, which is twice the price of conventional beef.
B) Conventionally-raised chicken is more affordable than beef or pork.
C) Growing meat in a laboratory results in less greenhouse gas emissions than does conventional meat production.
D) Lab-grown meat requires less energy use than does any conventional meat production.

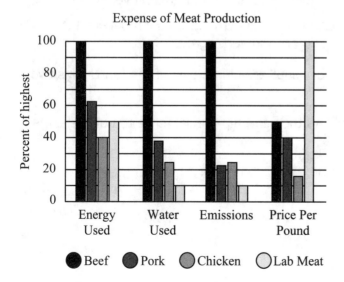

Expense of Meat Production

(Bar graph — y-axis: Percent of highest, from 0 to 100; x-axis categories: Energy Used, Water Used, Emissions, Price Per Pound; legend: Beef, Pork, Chicken, Lab Meat)

Writing and Language Summary

Pronouns

- ❑ **Pronoun Agreement** – A pronoun must agree with the noun it refers to in number, gender, and person. Similarly, nouns that relate to the same thing must agree in number.

- ❑ **Ambiguous Pronouns** – A pronoun must clearly refer back to the noun or nouns it represents. If there is no antecedent or more than one possible antecedent, the pronoun is ambiguous.

- ❑ **Compound Phrase** – To check for the proper form in a compound phrase, remove the rest of the group.

- ❑ **Pronoun Case** – In order to determine whether a pronoun is a subject or object, try plugging in an easier pronoun (such as "he/him") and see which works best.

  A pronoun that follows a preposition requires the objective case and not the subjective case. The pronoun "who" always refers to the subject. The pronoun "whom" always refers to an object.

- ❑ **Relative Pronouns** - Don't use *that* or *which* when referring to people. People are always *who* or *whom*.

- ❑ **Its vs It's** – "It's" is always a contraction of "it is." Likewise, "its" is always a possessive pronoun. Similarly, "they're" is a contraction of "they are," and "their" is a possessive pronoun. "You're" is a contraction of "you are," and "your" is a possessive pronoun.

- ❑ **One and You** – Pronouns *one* and *you* are not interchangeable. Whichever of these pronouns is being used must be carried throughout the sentence.

Subject-Verb Agreement

- ❑ Singular subjects require singular verbs, and plural subjects require plural verbs.
- ❑ **Ignore the Extras** – To simplify sentences, remove all extra information between the subject and the verb. Then, make sure the subject and verb agree.
- ❑ **Compound Subjects** – Subjects grouped by "and" are plural, even if the "and" joins two singular words.
- ❑ **Delayed Subject** – When the subject follows the verb, flip the sentence to put the subject first.
- ❑ **Indefinite Pronouns** – Pronouns containing "one," "body," or "thing" are singular.

Comparisons

❏ Make sure that comparisons are logical and parallel. The same types of ideas should be compared to each other.

❏ When comparing someone (or something) to a group that she is a part of, you can't just compare her to the whole group. Remember to use "other," comparing her to the rest of the group, not to herself.

❏ Use the comparative form of an adjective to compare two things. Comparative forms add either "-er" or are preceded by "more." (e.g., quicker, more courageous)
Use the superlative form of an adjective to compare three or more things. Superlative forms add either "-est" or are preceded by "most." (e.g., quickest, most courageous)

Idioms

❏ The idiom questions on the SAT will often involve prepositions. Make sure the correct preposition is being used.

Diction

❏ Diction is the choice of words used. Many English words are commonly misused in casual conversation, so make sure you understand the proper ways to use them.

Fragments

❏ **Where's the Verb?** – A verb ending in *ing* is not a complete verb. An *ing* verb creates a fragment if the sentence does not include another, complete verb.

❏ **Relative Pronouns** – Be careful with relative pronouns, such as *who, which*, and *that*. They may create incomplete ideas by changing how the action of the sentence relates to the subject.

Run-ons

❏ Run-on sentences result when multiple independent clauses are improperly joined.
You can correct run-ons in a variety of ways, including the three below:
1. Add a period and create two sentences.
2. Add a comma and a conjunction.
3. Use a semicolon.

❏ **Comma Splice** – When two independent clauses are joined with a comma but without a conjunction, this mistake is called a comma splice. Fix a comma splice by adding a semicolon, a period, or a comma and a conjunction.

❏ **Relative Pronouns** – Some run-on sentences are best fixed with the addition of relative pronouns, such as *who, which*, and *that*.

Conjunctions

- ❑ **Coordinating Conjunctions** – The most common conjunctions can be remembered with the acronym FANBOYS: *for, and, nor, but, or, yet,* and *so.*

- ❑ **Subordinating Conjunctions** – Certain conjunctions can be used at the beginning of dependent clauses. These include *although, because, before, since, unless, until, whereas, whether, which,* and *while.*

- ❑ **Paired Conjunctions** – Certain conjunctions are used to connect two paired ideas. Use proper phrasing with paired conjunctions.

Parallelism

- ❑ Sentence elements and ideas that are alike in function should also be the same in grammatical form so that they are "parallel."

- ❑ **Lists** – Use parallel structure with elements in a list or in a series.

- ❑ **Paired Conjunctions** – Conjunctions used in pairs (e.g., not only... but also, both... and, either... or, neither... nor) require that the words following each conjunction be parallel.

- ❑ **Comparisons** – Use parallel structure with elements being compared.

Modifiers

- ❑ **Faulty Modification** – Modifiers should be placed next to what they modify. Misplaced modifiers create ambiguity or cause a change in meaning.

- ❑ **Dangling Modifier** – Check for modifying phrases that appear at the beginning of a sentence and ask who or what is being modified. The subject that directly follows the modifier should be what the modifier describes.

Verb Tense

- ❑ Verb tenses should remain consistent unless the sentence indicates a change in time.

- ❑ **Has or Had** – The most challenging verb tense questions typically require an understanding of the difference between past, past perfect, and present perfect tenses.

Semicolons

❑ Semicolons, like periods, are used to link two independent clauses. A semicolon indicates that two ideas are related. Semicolons and periods are usually interchangeable.

❑ **Run-Ons** – Use semicolons to fix comma splices and other run-on errors.

❑ **Misused Semicolons** – Be on the lookout for semicolons that are used with conjunctions or where commas or colons should be used.

Colons

❑ **Before the Colon** – Colons should be used only at the end of a complete sentence.

❑ **After the Colon** – Colons are most commonly used to introduce lists, but they may also be used to present information that clarifies or elaborates on the independent clause.

Commas

❑ **Scene Setters** – If a sentence begins with a phrase that sets time, place, or purpose, then the phrase should be followed by a comma.

❑ **Independent Clauses and Conjunctions** – When two independent clauses are joined by a conjunction, there should be a comma placed before the conjunction.

❑ **Nonrestrictive Clauses** – Clauses that provide nonessential information about a subject are offset by commas. Nonessential clauses can also be offset by parentheses or dashes.

When a name is paired with an identifier, carefully consider whether the name or the identifier provides information essential to understanding the reference.

Apostrophes

❑ When the possessor is a singular noun, possession can be indicated by adding *'s*.

❑ When the possessor is a plural noun ending in *s*, possession can be indicated by adding an apostrophe. Plural nouns that do not end in *s* can be made possessive by adding *'s*.

❑ Pronouns do not require apostrophes to indicate possession. Rather, pronouns have their own possessive forms.

There is one exception to this rule: the possessive form of the indefinite pronoun *one* requires an apostrophe

Main Idea

- ❑ **Stay on Point** - Every portion of a passage should contribute to the main idea. Do not choose to include a detail just because it is related to the genearl topic of the passage.

Organization

- ❑ **Get in Order** – When organized properly, an essay's ideas should build upon each other and transition naturally.

Transitions

- ❑ Transitions show whether one idea contrasts, supports, or causes another.

- ❑ **Connect Ideas** – Pay attention to the ideas that come before and after a transition.

Addition

- ❑ **The Right Place** – Added sentences must logically connect to the sentences around them.

- ❑ **Relevance** – Added sentences must be relevant to the focus of passage and should support and strengthen the passage's ideas.

Deletion

- ❑ **Cut the Excess** – Sentences should be deleted if they are not relevant to the focus of the passage or do not support and strengthen the passage's ideas.

Wordiness

- ❑ **Avoid redundancy** – Eliminate details that are unnecessarily repeated. Look out for synonyms that do not add new information.

- ❑ **Get to the Point** – Eliminate stalling or unnecessary phrases.

Style

- ❑ **Word Choice** – When choosing between synonyms, carefully consider the exact meaning of each word in the context of the passage. You will often need to know the main idea of the passage in order to understand the writer's intended meaning of a word.

- ❑ **Tone** – Make sure the language of passages is consistent in tone. Avoid language that is too complex or too informal.

Data Graphics

- ❑ **Accuracy** – Information in the passage must accurately reflect the data in the graphic.

- ❑ **Relevance** – Information in the passage must be relevant to the main idea.

Writing and Language Practice

Questions 1-11 are based on the following passage.

Detectives of the 21st Century

Cyber-intruders hack into a national retailer's online records and steal millions of customers' credit card information. Hackers circumvent a defense contractor's database security to pilfer data. Cyber-criminals coordinate "Distributed Denial of Service" attacks on a technology company's website. **1** In fact, the companies affected will turn to their information security analysts.

[1] Much like their cybersecurity counterparts in the government, **2** protection of the integrity of online information is maintained by information security analysts, particularly by focusing on a company's infrastructure. [2] To address this security concern, the company would hire an information security analyst to conduct penetration testing: simulated attacks meant to detect vulnerabilities. [3] Analysts research available tools, seek out vulnerabilities in software, hardware, and network personnel, **3** and strengthen weak points. [4] For example, a news organization may have a list of experts and anonymous informants that it keeps behind a firewall so that only its journalists can see the list; however, the organization might notice some unfamiliar requests coming through its servers. [5] Having found a point of weakness, the analyst would then write a report to senior staff detailing the nature of the potential breach and recommending methods for shoring up security protocols **4** based on the use of information technology and its recent trends. **5**

1

A) NO CHANGE
B) In each case,
C) Despite these facts,
D) In addition,

2

A) NO CHANGE
B) the integrity of online information is protected by information security analysts,
C) the work information security analysts do protects the integrity of online information,
D) information security analysts work to protect the integrity of online information,

3

A) NO CHANGE
B) strengthening
C) to strengthen
D) for the strengthening of

4

A) NO CHANGE
B) based on recent trends in information technology.
C) based on trends from the most recent times in information technology.
D) based on recent modern trends occurring in information technology.

5

To make this paragraph most logical, sentence 2 should be placed

A) where it is now.
B) before sentence 1.
C) after sentence 3.
D) after sentence 4.

Information security analysts may work exclusively for individual companies, or they may be brought in as [6] helpers on a case-by-case basis. While a [7] person, who lives in a small town could become an analyst, many of the jobs are located in Washington, D.C., New York, and Silicon Valley. More often than not, analysts do a great deal of diagnostic investigation and then work closely with security engineers, architects, and administrators, [8] all of whom implement the analyst's suggestions and recommendations.

Universities are responding to the need for security analysts by tailoring computer science programs to this career path. However, for most analysts, a bachelor's degree in computer science, programming, or a comparable major [9] are sufficient, especially when they're combined with work experience in a related field; many analysts begin their careers as network or systems administrators. An MBA can also be useful, and generally will require an additional two years of study.

[6]

A) NO CHANGE
B) go-getters
C) consultants
D) subordinates

[7]

A) NO CHANGE
B) person, who lives in a small town could,
C) person who lives in a small town could,
D) person who lives in a small town could

[8]

A) NO CHANGE
B) all of who
C) each of which
D) whom

[9]

A) NO CHANGE
B) is sufficient, especially when they're combined
C) is sufficient, especially when it's combined
D) are sufficient, especially when it's combined

10 Demand for information security analysts is particularly high in the financial sector. According to a recent survey of 170 U.S. banks conducted by the American Banking Association, **11** over 60% of data breach attacks on midsize banks were successful. Given the increasing volume of cyberattacks, this figure is not surprising. This sort of crisis makes information security a growth industry.

Bank Institution Data Breaches in 2009

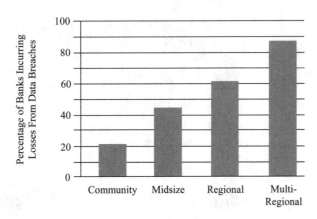

Size of Banking Institution

10

Which choice most effectively establishes the main topic of the paragraph?

A) Unlike information security analysts, software developers are the creative minds behind computer programs.

B) In May of 2012, the median annual wage for information security analysts was $86,170.

C) There are many challenges that a skilled analyst must overcome in order to advance on the career path.

D) Many industries are expected to increase their use of security analysts in the coming years.

11

Which choice is an accurate interpretation of the data presented in the chart?

A) NO CHANGE

B) in 2009, over 90% of the largest banks incurred losses in data breaches.

C) data breaches at community banks have increased over 20% since 2009.

D) less than 15% of multi-regional banks were safe from data breach attacks.

Questions 12-22 are based on the following passage.

A Focus on the Everyday

A 1982 documentary about distinguished photographer André Kertész shows the artist wandering around a Parisian **12** courtyard, and an Olympus camera slung around his neck. He pauses, leans over, and looks left and right; he seems to be searching for something. He shakes his head. Then he tucks the camera into his overcoat. The light isn't quite right— **13** it's getting hot outside as well—so he moves on. Such attention to light defines Kertész's photographic style, resulting in a body of work that makes the most average subject matter seem **14** remarkably extraordinary.

12

A) NO CHANGE
B) courtyard, and having
C) courtyard,
D) courtyard, yet with

13

Which of the following choices provides the most effective support for the author's claim about why Kertész moves on?

A) NO CHANGE
B) the bright sun washes out shadows and details
C) Kertész frowns and fiddles with his camera lens
D) noisy children nearby are distracting as well

14

A) NO CHANGE
B) extraordinary.
C) uniquely remarkable.
D) unusual and unique.

[1] Kertész's artistic gift was a surprise to his family, and not a particularly welcome one. [2] They had hoped that he would become a stockbrocker, but Kertész **15** developed a childhood interest in photography. [3] He once said that while saving to buy his first camera, he spent so much time looking closely at the world that he developed a "composition feeling instinctively" and when he finally bought his first camera in 1912, his compositions were "exact." [4] Unlike later war photographers, **16** Kertész's works never commented on the politics of his images; his belief in simply capturing the subject has earned him credit as the father of photojournalism. [5] Kertész developed as a photo essayist on the front lines of WWI, where he served in the army and shot life in the trenches. **17**

15

A) NO CHANGE
B) develops
C) was developing
D) has developed

16

A) NO CHANGE
B) his photographs
C) the photographs he took
D) he

17

For the sake of the cohesion of this paragraph, sentence 5 should be placed

A) where it is now.
B) before sentence 2.
C) after sentence 2.
D) after sentence 3.

His intriguing compositions frequently rely [18] on the play of [19] shadows; fork tines on a saucer, a worker standing on scaffolding, the patterns of the Eiffel Tower on people below. One particularly famous photograph shows a swimmer, head disappearing in the movement of the water, with bolts of light crossing the water's surface and shadows from nearby trees framing the image. In another, a dancer poses on a couch, mimicking a modernist sculpture behind her. To the art critics and [20] representative public alike, his unique compositions make everyday subjects appear fresh, even in the 21st century.

[21] Robert Doisneau, renowned French photographer and champion of Kertész's work, describes him as someone who "takes a lot of time to love things; he's not at all in a hurry; he really has a sense of time." Since Kertész's death in 1985, the timeless quality of his works [22] has garnered his greater recognition, and museums have taken note. His photographs can now be found in museums across the United States and Europe.

18

A) NO CHANGE
B) under
C) with
D) for

19

A) NO CHANGE
B) shadows: fork
C) shadows, fork
D) shadows, fork;

20

A) NO CHANGE
B) the customary populace
C) laymen
D) everyone

21

Which choice most effectively establishes the main topic of the paragraph and sets up the example that follows?

A) Kertész earned most of his money publishing in magazines, both as a freelance photographer and on commissioned assignment.
B) Kertész's patient, painstaking approach to light and composition earned him the respect of critics and his fellow artists.
C) In 1936, Kertész emigrated to the United States to escape the Nazi persecution of the Jews; he died in 1985 after a long career.
D) Critics divide Kertész's work into four periods: the Hungarian period, the French period, the American period, and the International period.

22

A) NO CHANGE
B) have garnered him
C) have garnered his
D) has garnered him

SUMMIT
EDUCATIONAL
GROUP

Questions 23-33 are based on the following passage.

Deciding What's for Dinner

The public discourse about diet tends to focus on weight loss and greasy fast [23] food, because these are common issues, they dominate our perception of nutrition. However, large sectors of our population—cancer patients, elderly people, those with food allergies or intolerances—have special dietary [24] needs that we don't always think of. Whether an individual wishes to minimize the effects of a gastrointestinal disorder or simply include more fiber in his or her daily diet, education is vital. Educating is where the work of nutritionists and dieticians begins. Not only do these professionals help individuals make healthy choices, but they also frequently educate the public.

While all dieticians are nutritionists, not all nutritionists are dieticians. Dieticians' education requirements are [25] harsher, because they must secure a Registered Dietician Nutritionist (RDN) [26] credential, which requires both a B.A. and a Dietetic Internship Program, and engage in career-long continuing professional education. A nutritionist may have an advanced degree—an M.A. or a Ph.D.—but [27] they won't necessarily have the additional accreditation. Clinical employers tend to prefer candidates with an RDN credential.

23

A) NO CHANGE
B) food, because,
C) food; because,
D) food. Because

24

A) NO CHANGE
B) needs for their meals.
C) needs and requirements.
D) needs.

25

A) NO CHANGE
B) rougher
C) sterner
D) stricter

26

A) NO CHANGE
B) credential which requires, both a B.A. and a Dietetic Internship Program,
C) credential, which requires, both a B.A. and a Dietetic Internship Program
D) credential which requires both a B.A. and a Dietetic Internship Program

27

A) NO CHANGE
B) their
C) those
D) he or she

[1] Their work involves listening with compassion to a client, evaluating the client's needs, and then **28** they must communicate the importance of the plan they devise. [2] **29** Nevertheless, they must be able to interpret scientific research and translate it into practical advice. [3] Dieticians must blend analytical and interpersonal skills. [4] For instance, a dietician in a nursing home might work out a weekly menu by considering the overall population's needs and preferences. [5] He or she would then recommend substitutions according to the medical requirements of individuals. **30**

28

A) NO CHANGE
B) communicating
C) there should be communication of
D) they will communicate

29

A) NO CHANGE
B) Still,
C) At the same time,
D) However,

30

For the sake of the cohesion of this paragraph, sentence 3 should be placed

A) where it is now
B) before sentence 1.
C) after sentence 1.
D) after sentence 4.

Such work would likely be the job of a clinical dietician, which is slightly different from **31** the work of a community dietician, who involves more community outreach. **32** Dieticians can work full-time in a range of settings: hospitals, nursing homes, health clinics, and even spas. Although some work part-time from home or out of a private office, four out of five dieticians are full-time employees.

Dieticians and nutritionists are increasingly important to the health industry. Though they may not be paid as much as some health care professionals, nutritionists on average earn **33** about half of what other health diagnosing and treating practitioners earn. And with an expected increase of 21% in job prospects over the next 20 years, nutrition is not only a viable option for many people interested in helping others, but also a clear growth industry.

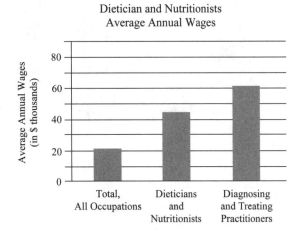

Dietician and Nutritionists
Average Annual Wages

31

A) NO CHANGE
B) the work of a community dietician, which
C) a community dietician, who
D) a community dietician, which

32

The author of this passage is considering adding the following sentence at this point in the essay:

> For instance, a local health department might hire a community dietician to give a presentation on childhood nutrition to groups of new mothers.

Should the author make this addition?

A) Yes, because it offers relevant details that support the statement in the previous sentence.
B) Yes, because it offers a counterargument to the claim made in the previous sentence.
C) No, because it illustrates a point that is already made and does not add new details.
D) No, because it is irrelevant information that distracts from the main purpose of the paragraph.

33

Which choice is an accurate interpretation of the data presented in the chart?

A) NO CHANGE
B) $55,240 more than the average total for all other occupations combined.
C) slightly less than the $34,750 average annual wage of health diagnosing and treating practitioners.
D) about $20,000 a year more than the average total for all occupations.

Questions 34-44 are based on the following passage.

Collision Course

On January 3, 2013, Robert H. McNaught was at work in the Siding Spring Observatory when he noticed something unusual in the Lepus constellation. [34] As a professional astronomer, part of McNaught's work involves searching the sky for signs of comets that could prove hazardous to the Earth. It's a vital but understaffed job; in fact, the Uppsala Southern Schmidt Telescope that McNaught uses is the only professional telescope in the southern hemisphere tasked with [35] the search for dangerous comets. The strange phenomenon McNaught observed in Lepus [36] would be revealed to be a comet, subsequently named the Siding Spring comet, which was headed straight for Mars.

34

A) NO CHANGE
B) As a professional astronomer, the work of McNaught
C) Part of McNaught's work as a professional astronomer
D) A professional astronomer, McNaught's work

35

A) NO CHANGE
B) the job that entails searching for
C) the need to search for
D) DELETE the underlined portion.

36

A) NO CHANGE
B) will be revealed
C) was being revealed
D) is revealing

Once scientists began tracing the comet, they realized that it had come from the Oort Cloud. **37** Oort is a spherical cloud of icy plentiesimals, or solid bits of debris, which are thought to create bodies as large as planets when enough debris comes together. Because the cloud is anywhere from 5 to 100 thousand astronomical **38** units—the average distance between the Earth and Sun) from the center of our solar system, scientists believe that the Siding Spring comet left the cloud millions of years ago.

At first, it appeared as if the comet might strike Mars, but it ultimately passed approximately 82,000 miles from the planet. That might seem like a wide margin, but **39** its actually only about a third of the distance between the Earth and the moon.

37

At this point, the writer is considering adding the following true statement:

> The Oort Cloud was named after the man who discovered it: Dutch astronomer Jan Oort.

Should the writer make this addition?

A) No, because it repeats information that is available later in the paragraph.

B) No, because it distracts from the paragraph's focus on the comet.

C) Yes, because it adds detail to a paragraph that otherwise contains only generalizations.

D) Yes, because it clarifies a confusing term by giving the cloud's name context.

38

A) NO CHANGE

B) units—the average distance between the Earth and Sun—from

C) units the average distance between the Earth and Sun, from

D) units, (the average distance between the Earth and Sun); from

39

A) NO CHANGE

B) they're

C) it's

D) its'

40 Though scientists realized early on that the Siding Spring comet would not strike Mars, they still believed it might pass close enough to create a meteor shower that could damage nearby equipment. In what scientists called a "duck and cover" maneuver, NASA moved its orbiters Mars Reconnaissance, Maven, and Odyssey to the opposite side of Mars from where the comet would pass. **41** Besides, scientists were able to welcome the comet's approach. NASA's Maven Mission to Mars's remote sensing team **42** leader Nick Schneider, asked "What could be more exciting than to have a whopper of an external influence like a

40

Which choice most effectively establishes the main idea of the paragraph?

A) NO CHANGE

B) Because scientists had not anticipated the possible impact of a comet on Mars, they were surprised to hear the analysis developed from McNaught's observations.

C) The Siding Spring comet is just one of over 400 potentially hazardous heavenly bodies passing close to Earth that McNaught has discovered.

D) The NASA Mars missions are more numerous than most people realize and involve multiple orbiting satellites as well as the well-known surface rovers.

41

A) NO CHANGE
B) Conversely,
C) Instead,
D) As a result,

42

A) NO CHANGE
B) leader, Nick Schneider, asked,
C) leader, Nick Schneider asked,
D) leader Nick Schneider, asked,

comet, so we can see how atmospheres do respond?" **43** <u>The Siding Spring comet is one of many celestial bodies discovered by the Uppsala Southern Schmidt Telescope.</u> Because NASA was able to protect the orbiters as the comet shot by at 125,000 mph, scientists now have a **44** <u>giant heap</u> of data to sift through to better understand both Mars and comets.

43

The writer wants to add a sentence that connects the conclusion of the passage to its introduction. Which choice best accomplishes that goal?

A) NO CHANGE
B) It's not yet clear how the Martian atmosphere responded to the comet, or when the next comet will approach.
C) The comet reached remarkable speeds that were recorded by a battery of instruments in the Martian orbiters.
D) McNaught's vigilance preserved the Mars missions and allowed scientists an unprecedented view of his discovery.

44

A) NO CHANGE
B) huge pile
C) wealth
D) ton

Questions 45-55 are based on the following passage.

Opening Up the Office

Google does it. Facebook does it. Even investment bank Goldman Sachs does it. These companies all arrange their workers in an open office layout.

In a large space free of dividing walls, dozens of workers sit at adjacent desks; some even share long tables. At one glance, you can see the entire company's work force. The goal of such an office is not only to allow for an open exchange of ideas 45 but also it fosters company unity.

Designers in Hamburg, Germany, formulated the first open office plan in the late 1950s. This plan represented a departure from workspaces of the past, where employees worked 46 in individual rooms. These designers hoped that an open office—with all the employees seated in one space without walls or cubicles—would inspire creativity and increase productivity.

[1] Nearly 70% of American workers share open-plan offices these days, according to the International Facility Management Association. [2] However, studies are increasingly showing the disadvantages of these systems. [3] The advantages of such designs are clear: shared sense of mission, flexibility of layout, and ease of supervision. [4] While they were intended to enhance the 47 work experience, open offices cause stress, distraction, and decreased productivity. 48

Employees complain first about the noise. Workplace concentration can be adversely affected by 49 poorly planned training for the busy environment. One study, published in the journal "Noise and Health," showed that even employees' ability to do simple arithmetic may be hampered in a noisy office environment.

45

A) NO CHANGE
B) but also to foster
C) but also fostering
D) and to foster

46

A) NO CHANGE
B) around
C) toward
D) between

47

A) NO CHANGE
B) work experience, but open offices
C) work experience, open offices,
D) work experience; open offices

48

To make this paragraph most logical, sentence 2 should be placed

A) where it is now.
B) before sentence 1.
C) after sentence 3.
D) after sentence 4.

49

Which choice provides a supporting example that reinforces the main point of the paragraph?

A) NO CHANGE
B) the many technological distractions in a modern office.
C) a hundred employees talking and typing simultaneously.
D) the stress of always being in the supervisor's line of sight.

The kind of open communication that is the goal of such an office often means unwelcome interruptions. Also, studies have found that a lack of privacy distracts workers from the task at hand. It can be difficult to work when any passerby can see your computer screen or eavesdrop on a conversation.

50 Germs spread more easily without walls to stop them. One Swedish study found that employees in an open office **51** is more likely to take sick days.

50

At this point, the writer is considering adding the following sentence.

> Sharing one large space has health consequences, too.

Should the writer make this addition here?

A) Yes, because it provides an effective transition to a new idea.

B) Yes, because it supplies support for a previous claim.

C) No, because it distracts from the paragraph's main focus on privacy.

D) No, because it does not specify the types of health problems caused.

51

A) NO CHANGE

B) are

C) has been

D) is being

Lost time, dissatisfied employees, and **52** productivity that is lacking are important considerations, and businesses cannot ignore these complaints for long. Collaboration and communication—the hallmarks of an open plan—are **53** pretty good ideas. However, quiet rooms need to be set aside for private phone calls and tasks that require concentration. Meetings (and **54** the loud conversations that noisily accompany them) should be moved into separate areas to foster collaboration. And shared spaces to relax—like break rooms—would help employees recharge and connect with one another. **55**

52

A) NO CHANGE
B) seeing productivity fall
C) when productivity falls
D) decreased productivity

53

A) NO CHANGE
B) huge positives.
C) really good points.
D) worthy goals.

54

A) NO CHANGE
B) the loud conversations that accompany them
C) the loud conversations that accompany them, which can be noisy
D) the noise of the conversations accompanying them, often loudly

55

The writer wants a concluding sentence that restates the main argument of the passage. Which choice best accomplishes this goal?

A) The open plan office was an innovation in 20th-century office environments, but a new era demands new designs.
B) Successfully implementing an open office design requires special workplace strategies to account for the noise and distractions that can occur in these environments.
C) Employees must be responsible for accepting the challenges that come with an open office design.
D) Open office plans have been implemented in some of the most successful companies in the United States.

Questions 56-66 are based on the following passage.

Conserving Ugliness

The wildlife conservation movement has a cuteness problem. Adorable baby pandas and sleek-furred golden lion tamarins—tiny, ridiculously adorable primates— 56 illicit heartfelt cries of "Awww!" and "Where's my checkbook?" 57 They are poster children for habitat loss and human exploitation, furry mammals are unmatched in their ability to open people's hearts and wallets. Yet let the aptly-named purple pig-nosed frog wobble out of its underground burrow, or the Chinese giant salamander—described by one journalist as "a shiny sack of warts"—make the appeal, and those same wildlife-loving supporters will literally look elsewhere, despite the fact that 58 the percentage of critically endangered amphibian species is four times the percentage of critically endangered mammal species.

This inequality is a problem. It's a problem from an ethical standpoint; the admittedly hideous, slime-spewing hagfish has no less right to exist than a sweet-faced, flappy-eared baby elephant, although only one of them will mobilize an army of protestors if it is slaughtered for 59 their meat and skin. It's also a problem from the broader standpoint of real, scientific conservation: the act of maintaining entire ecosystems, which must remain functional in all of their complexity if their inhabitants are to thrive.

56

A) NO CHANGE
B) elicit
C) elicits
D) illicits

57

A) NO CHANGE
B) Poster children, for habitat loss and human exploitation,
C) As poster children for habitat loss and human exploitation,
D) Organizations use them as poster children for habitat loss and human exploitation,

58

Which choice is supported by the data in the chart that follows the passage?

A) NO CHANGE
B) reptiles have the largest total number of vulnerable, endangered, and critically endangered species.
C) invertebrates, like insects, have a much larger percentage of critically endangered species than do mammals.
D) nearly 70% of assessed amphibian species are considered vulnerable, endangered, or critically endangered.

59

A) NO CHANGE
B) it's
C) its
D) there

On that front, the hagfish is at least as important as the elephant. However, the hagfish's table manners are less [60] appealing, rather than plucking leaves and fruits with a fascinatingly sinuous trunk, it burrows into dead animals using double rows of jawless teeth. Yet this distasteful habit is vital to its ocean ecosystem, especially in areas fished by humans. Hagfish clean up large quantities of unwanted fish, called [61] bycatch, discarded by commercial fishers. [62] When hagfish populations drop, so do populations of important food fish like flounder. Fail to protect the repulsive hagfish, and we might just starve the cuddly, soulful-eyed harbor seal. [63]

60

A) NO CHANGE
B) appealing; rather than plucking leaves and fruits. With a fascinatingly sinuous trunk,
C) appealing, rather than plucking leaves and fruits with a fascinatingly sinuous trunk;
D) appealing; rather than plucking leaves and fruits with a fascinatingly sinuous trunk,

---

61

A) NO CHANGE
B) bycatch—
C) bycatch; which is
D) bycatch:

62

At this point, the writer is considering adding the following sentence.

> They are also prey for fish, seabirds, and marine mammals.

Should the writer make this addition?

A) Yes, because it creates a transition to the next paragraph.
B) Yes, because it provides necessary context for the following sentences.
C) No, because it's irrelevant to the purpose of the passage.
D) No, because it would be better placed in the previous paragraph.

63

The writer wants to effectively conclude the paragraph while warning readers of a specific possible consequence of neglecting an "ugly" species. Which choice most effectively achieves this purpose?

A) Our actions often lead to unforeseen consequences.
B) Among fresh-water fish alone, nearly 300 species are critically endangered.
C) The loss of any species can forever damage an entire ecosystem.
D) Seals are more photogenic and more human-looking than hagfish.

[64] You might be concerned about another species that could also be harmed: the human. When we focus our conservation efforts on the cute and lovable, we forget that animals do much more than cater to our desire for beauty. Medical advances, many of the most important of the 20th century, came from the natural world, and they rarely came from cuddly creatures. Pit vipers helped us to develop drugs for high blood pressure, and marine sponges held the keys to treatments for HIV. [65] With reptiles comprising over 70% of the world's endangered species, we must take care that we don't lose a possible cure for cancer. An ugly animal may be unpleasant to look at, but we should not [66] disregard its right to life.

Percentage of Currently Assessed
Species Designated Threatened

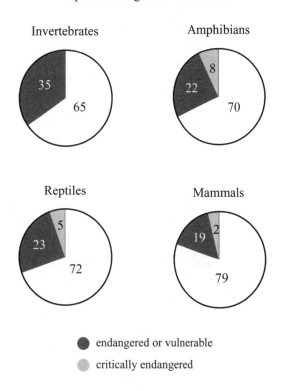

Invertebrates

35 / 65

Amphibians

8 / 22 / 70

Reptiles

5 / 23 / 72

Mammals

19 / 2 / 79

● endangered or vulnerable

○ critically endangered

64

Which choice most smoothly and effectively introduces the writer's discussion of the effect of wildlife conservation on humans?

A) NO CHANGE

B) You might also harm another appealing species.

C) Another appealing species is the human.

D) The human is a species that can be considered appealing and that may be harmed by our actions regarding less appealing species.

65

Which choice offers an accurate interpretation of the data in the chart?

A) NO CHANGE

B) the percentage of vulnerable or endangered reptile species nearly double that of mammal species,

C) the number of vulnerable and endangered invertebrate species exceeding the number of all other vulnerable and endangered species combined,

D) all assessed animal groups having over 20% of their species vulnerable, endangered, or critically endangered,

66

A) NO CHANGE

B) forgo pondering

C) snub

D) sideline

Questions 67-77 are based on the following passage.

The Future is Pearly Bright

Teeth are polished, and their enamel is protected. Decay is repaired, and further damage is prevented. [67] To provide patients with the earliest possible treatment, signs of disease like cancer or lupus are identified. As they oversee these and many other tasks, dentists engage in a wide variety of work.

Dentists do much more than just patch cavities. They compile a dental history for each patient, develop a plan of treatment to address each [68] individual's habits and genetic tendencies, and monitor the health of each patient's teeth, gums, tongue, and mouth. Dentists help with both disease and bad [69] habits, which address diverse issues such as tooth-grinding, bad breath, or rough brushing that erodes enamel.

67

Which choice best maintains the sentence pattern already established in the paragraph?

A) NO CHANGE

B) Identifying signs of diseases like cancer or lupus can help patients to receive the earliest possible treatment.

C) Diseases like cancer or lupus are identified from their signs, allowing patients to receive the earliest possible treatment.

D) Signs of diseases like cancer or lupus are identified, and patients receive the earliest possible treatment.

68

A) NO CHANGE

B) individuals habits

C) individual's habits,

D) individuals habits,

69

A) NO CHANGE

B) habits, addressing

C) habits that address

D) habits, and addressing

Dentists typically work either in individual or in group practices. A 70 dentist, in individual practice must manage staff and plan advertising and pricing, while dentists in group practices may either share these duties or leave them to the care of a business owner or office manager. 71 A private practice must be carefully located to ensure an adequate customer base. Some dentists work from hospitals or clinics, while others operate mobile dentistry businesses.

Many dentists practice general family dentistry, 72 and these practices can often be quite large. Those who focus upon aesthetic dentistry will whiten teeth, add enamel veneers, or even place decorative gold overlays over teeth. Dentists in pediatric practices help children establish good brushing and flossing habits. Other dentists specialize in nervous or anxious patients by offering soothing office atmospheres, gentle care, and 73 even using sedation to help patients overcome their fears.

70

A) NO CHANGE
B) dentist, in individual practice,
C) dentist in individual practice
D) dentist in individual practice,

71

The writer is considering deleting the underlined sentence. Should the sentence be kept or deleted?

A) Kept, because it identifies a potential benefit to starting an individual practice.
B) Kept, because it explains the duties of the business owner.
C) Deleted, because it doesn't explain how to choose an appropriate location.
D) Deleted, because it departs from the paragraph's focus on individual and group dental practices.

72

Which choice results in the most effective transition to the information that follows in the paragraph?

A) NO CHANGE
B) but others specialize in particular types of work.
C) usually finding work as soon as they are licensed.
D) which are needed both in cities and in rural areas.

73

A) NO CHANGE
B) they even use
C) even sedating them
D) even sedation

Dental school is highly competitive, and entry requires excellent grades. Dentists typically complete four-year undergraduate degrees focused on science and then spend four additional years in dental school. **74** However, some schools accept applicants with two or three years of undergraduate work. After each of these students **75** graduate from dental school, he or she must pass a licensing examination and complete one or two years of residency work. A dentist who wishes to specialize in a field like surgery or orthodontics will train for another two to four years.

Dentists pursue rewarding jobs with good pay and a relatively predictable schedule. *U.S. News and World Report* **76** has commonly and consistently ranked the job of dentist as the best in America for those who can meet the stringent entry requirements. In 2012, the United States Department of Labor estimated that there were 5,280 dentists practicing in the United States, with most working in traditional dental practices. The outlook for dental careers in general is positive, **77** and dentists themselves are expected to make up roughly 16% of new jobs in the dental field.

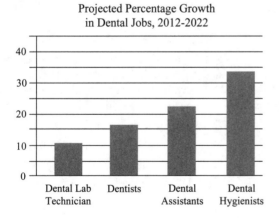

Projected Percentage Growth
in Dental Jobs, 2012-2022

74

A) NO CHANGE
B) In fact,
C) Moreover,
D) Consequently,

75

A) NO CHANGE
B) graduate from dental school, they
C) graduates from dental school, he or she
D) graduates from dental school, they

76

A) NO CHANGE
B) has consistently and with great frequency ranked
C) has consistently ranked
D) has consistently ranked and generally rated

77

Which choice completes the sentence with accurate data based on the graph?

A) NO CHANGE
B) with dentists experiencing a 16% increase in available jobs.
C) although dental laboratory technicians will experience the lowest unemployment at 12%.
D) with only dental hygienists exceeding their impressive 25% job growth.

Questions 78-88 are based on the following passage.

The Sculpture of Edmonia Lewis

The young Edmonia Lewis lived a life suited to her Native American name: "Wildfire." Born to a Haitian father and a mother of Native American and African American descent, Lewis was orphaned at the age of nine in 1853. She was taken in by a series of aunts, a military captain, and finally a boarding school, where Lewis **78** was; "declared to be wild." Accepted to Oberlin College at the age of fifteen, Lewis discovered art and embraced it with a passion. But when Lewis was accused of stealing art supplies, she was refused permission to register for her last semester at Oberlin, even though she was acquitted of charges because of lack of evidence. She subsequently moved to Boston, and then to Rome, to **79** pursue a career as a sculptor.

From Lewis's tumultuous life sprang unexpected artistic **80** elegance. Grace, balance, and restraint shape the lines of her smoothly finished marble busts and statues. Lewis worked in the Neoclassical style, attempting to create contemporary sculptures with the same refined symmetry as **81** the ancient Greeks. For instance, her bust of Minnehaha—a Native American character from Longfellow's poem "Hiawatha"—is draped in classical robes, with **82** a perfectly centered necklace of pearls about her neck and a broad feather curving elegantly over her head in a style more common to medieval Italian courtiers than to Native Americans.

78
A) NO CHANGE
B) was:
C) was,
D) was

79
A) NO CHANGE
B) accompany
C) chase
D) attend

80
A) NO CHANGE
B) elegance, grace,
C) elegance, with grace,
D) elegance, grace, and

81
A) NO CHANGE
B) those of the ancient Greeks.
C) ancient Greek artists.
D) sculptors who worked in ancient Greece.

82
The writer wants to include an example of a detail demonstrating Lewis's symmetrical style. Which choice best accomplishes this goal?

A) NO CHANGE
B) a height of just under a foot
C) her head turned slightly to the right
D) some random cracking across the face

[1] One of Lewis's representative pieces is *Forever Free*, a classically styled depiction of African Americans triumphantly breaking the chains of slavery. [2] She **83** is intent upon perfecting her art, often creating sculptures without buyers in mind. [3] She insisted on performing all of the work herself rather than hiring local sculptors to finish most of the heavy work, as other artists did. [4] This controlled passion was typical in her art and was evident in Lewis's approach to her work, as well. **84**

83

A) NO CHANGE
B) has been
C) was
D) will be

84

To make this paragraph most logical, sentence 4 should be placed

A) where it is now.
B) before sentence 1.
C) after sentence 1.
D) after sentence 2.

[85] Her fame declined as the Neoclassical style became less **[86]** popular. Her work was celebrated in its heyday. *Death of Cleopatra*, a massive 1.5 ton marble statue, was exhibited at the 1876 Centennial Exposition in Philadelphia to considerable acclaim. It was perhaps Lewis's most emblematic piece: calm, **[87]** regal: classically draped, and yet conveying the queen's desperate last agonies. In modern times, Lewis has retained an important place in the artistic canon. The lasting respect for her works and their influence has been kindled by a recent discovery: after being lost for nearly a century, *The Death of Cleopatra* has now been restored and placed in the Smithsonian American Art Museum. **[88]**

85

Which choice most effectively establishes the main topic of the paragraph?

A) The Neoclassical school of art was particularly popular in the early 19th century.

B) Lewis, more than any other artist of her time, left a legacy marked by changing cultural values.

C) Lewis's importance in art history is evident from her lasting importance in the arts.

D) Lewis's major exhibitions in Chicago and Philadelhpia made her studio popular with tourists.

86

Which choice most effectively combines the sentences at the underlined portion?

A) popular; indeed, her work

B) popular, yet before losing popularity it

C) popular, but her work

D) popular; from before this decline, her work

87

A) NO CHANGE

B) regal,

C) regal;

D) regal

88

The writer wants to conclude the passage with a sentence that emphasizes the key characteristics of Lewis's personality and artwork as described in the passage. Which choice would best accomplish this goal?

A) There her work is presented in the company of over 7,000 pieces of the finest American art, both classical and contemporary.

B) Before it was recovered, the statue had been placed over the grave of a racehorse named Cleopatra and later painted by Boy Scouts.

C) It is the perfect tribute to an artist whose burning energy drew passionate, classical works out of cool, white marble.

D) It was once thought that Lewis died in Rome or possibly in California, but scholars have recently concluded that she died in London.

Questions 89-99 are based on the following passage.

Rags and Riches

[89] While recycling has become popular in America only in recent decades, history has plenty to teach us about thrifty re-use of resources. 1840s London, while dark, grimy, and forbidding by modern standards, was a model for urban recycling.

[90] Some consider Victorians to be the first conservationists. Poverty and unemployment drove a flourishing trade in anything that could be re-sold. Candle-ends went to chandlers, who melted them down to make new candles; grease from roasting meat was cooled and sold as cheap cooking fat or for spreading on bread. Even the [91] ashes, from the coal fires used for cooking and heating were carted off to "cinder-yards" where gangs of workers sifted through them for chunks of coal and stray household goods. Scraps of tin were sold to metalworkers; old rags were used to make paper. The dust and cinders became the property of the yard's owner. Nothing slipped past workers paid sixpence per day plus all of the rags, bones, old shoes, and bits of metal they found. [92] Everything in a cinder heap had potential value.

89

A) NO CHANGE
B) If
C) When
D) DELETE the underlined portion and begin the sentence with a capital letter.

90

Which choice most effectively sets up the paragraph?

A) NO CHANGE
B) Most Victorians recycled out of necessity.
C) Modern recyclers could learn a lot from the Victorians.
D) Many unusual items could be recycled in the 1840s.

91

A) NO CHANGE
B) ashes:
C) ashes—
D) ashes

92

The writer wants to conclude the paragraph while also reinforcing the point that some Victorians depended upon recycling for their livings. Which choice best accomplishes this goal?

A) NO CHANGE
B) Even small children helped their parents to work the cinder heaps.
C) What we consider trash formed a major part of these workers' incomes.
D) The cinder yard itself was a monument to recycling.

This intensive recycling was also driven, in part, by the lower standard of technology prevalent in the 1840s. Petroleum fertilizers had not yet been invented; instead, farmers used bone meal to fertilize **93** there fields. **94** As a result, the rag-and-bone shop was a staple of poor neighborhoods. As its name suggest, the rag-and-bone shop was a store selling low-value used goods, including old clothing and bones. These shops were commonly visited by cinder-sifters and by kitchen workers whose right to the household bones was sometimes written into their offers of employment. **95** Industrialization, in the form of industrial factories, had as yet made few inroads into clothing; **96** much of it was still hand-sewn, and the price of such goods was high enough to drive a flourishing trade in old clothes. Buyers would wander the streets trading **97** various tableware for cast-off dresses and linen.

93

A) NO CHANGE
B) they're
C) their
D) these

94

A) NO CHANGE
B) However
C) Meanwhile
D) In contrast

95

A) NO CHANGE
B) Industrialization, with its labor-saving machinery,
C) Industrialization, which would supplant manual labor,
D) Industrialization

96

Which choice best supports the central claim of the paragraph?

A) NO CHANGE
B) both cloth and clothing were expensive.
C) a suit of clothes was often part of a servant's salary.
D) thieves often prowled around drying lines to steal linen.

97

Which choice provides the most specific examples of the types of goods being traded?

A) NO CHANGE
B) their scavenged wares and goods
C) decorative household items
D) pieces of china or cut glassware

This trade in old clothing created another class of eager recyclers: household servants. Traditionally, used clothing was not discarded but rather handed down to the servants who maintained their **98** employers clothes and helped them to dress. Like the cooks and scullery maids who relied upon the sale of fat and bones to supplement their salaries, so too did ladies' maids and men's valets regard old clothing as an expected addition to their income. Most of the poorest laborers counted some sort of cast-away goods—paper, scraps of rope or wood, or even manure—as part of their salaries. In a city **99** to which every garbage-heap was someone's bonus check, recycling was a way of life.

98
A) NO CHANGE
B) employers'
C) employer's
D) employers's

99
A) NO CHANGE
B) in
C) by
D) at

Questions 100-110 are based on the following passage.

The Pursuit of Imperfection

The small ceramic bowl—no more than four inches tall, with an uneven rim and mottled black glaze—doesn't seem like anything special at first glance. **100** First, this bowl is a cherished piece of *raku* pottery made in the late 1600s. This *chawan*, or tea bowl, has had a role in Japanese tea ceremonies for generations. In 2009, it sold for **101** $60,000—at auction.

Raku, meaning "enjoyment," is a method of making ceramics that dates to 16th-century Japan. It is also the honorary title of the first potter to pioneer these techniques, Chojiro. His heirs bear the name Raku to this day.

100
A) NO CHANGE
B) Additionally,
C) However,
D) Also,

101
A) NO CHANGE
B) $60,000 at
C) $60,000, at
D) $60,000: at

102 Both raku and other forms of pottery require care and practice to master. First, the potter shapes and pinches a fat disk of clay into a simple bowl shape. The walls should be of just the right thickness to preserve the heat of the tea but protect the drinker's hands from being scorched. Next, using a delicate pointed tool, the potter carves out a circular foot at the bottom. From there, he glazes the dried bowl in simple earthy tones like black or red. **103** There are no decorations or ornaments added. **104** Yet, he fires the pottery at a low heat, he immediately removes it from the kiln, allowing it to cool in the open air. This rapid temperature change results **105** to unpredictable cracks and discolorations on the surface of the piece. A raku **106** bowls beauty comes from those very imperfections.

102

Which choice most effectively establishes the topic of the paragraph?

A) NO CHANGE
B) The descendants of Chojiro are proud of their craft's tradition.
C) While prized pieces are expensive, raku does not require costly materials.
D) The techniques used in raku involve few steps but result in works of complex beauty.

103

Which choice gives an additional supporting example that emphasizes the simplicity of raku pottery?

A) NO CHANGE
B) The glaze may contain clay, tin, or even copper mixed to traditional recipes.
C) The bottom of the foot remained unfinished so that it does not stick to the kiln.
D) The piece must then rest again until all water from the glaze has dried.

104

A) NO CHANGE
B) After
C) Because
D) DELETE the underlined portion and begin the sentence with a capital letter.

105

A) NO CHANGE
B) with
C) in
D) on

106

A) NO CHANGE
B) bowls'
C) bowl's
D) bowls's

The aesthetics of this style rely on the Japanese ideal of *wabi-sabi*. "Wabi" connotes simplicity and understated beauty, whether in natural or manufactured items. "Sabi" conveys appreciation for the effects of aging, **107** details that give each piece a unique character. These words together highlight the goal of finding beauty in the imperfect, the impermanent, and the incomplete.

Raku pieces are the most revered for use in *chado*, the Japanese tea ceremony. Harmony, respect, purity, and tranquility are the goals of this meditative experience. The movements are highly ritualized, from the ceremonial cleaning of the tea bowl to the drinking of the tea. The simple beauty and craftsmanship of a raku bowl align with the aesthetic ideals embodied in this tradition.

The current Raku master, Raku Kichizaemon XV, still makes pottery in the **108** time-honored method according to historical ways. Although $60,000 may seem a steep price to pay for a small antique bowl, **109** it's value lies in the principles it embodies. It isn't just a unique piece of pottery— it is **110** the product of a master of the Japanese art of raku.

107

Which choice provides the most relevant detail?

A) NO CHANGE
B) like the mellowing of colors over time or a slight chip from years of use.
C) changes that modify the bowl's appearance but do not affect its function.
D) features that connect each piece of raku to cultural traditions.

108

A) NO CHANGE
B) historical method that has stood the test of time.
C) methods of traditional practice.
D) time-honored method.

109

A) NO CHANGE
B) their
C) its
D) its'

110

The writer wants to conclude the passage with a reference to the central tenets of *wabi-sabi*. Which choice best accomplishes this goal?

A) NO CHANGE
B) a hand-made artifact representing Japanese tradition.
C) a reminder that we should embrace the imperfections in life.
D) an essential part of the Japanese tea ceremony.

Questions 111-121 are based on the following passage.

Passenger Pigeon Extinction

The death of 29-year-old Martha in 1914 marked more than the end of a single life. Martha, housed at the Cincinnati Zoo, was the world's last passenger pigeon. Less than a century before her death, passenger pigeons were among the most numerous birds in the **111** world creating dramatic sights as they passed over the land in huge flocks, searching out food and nesting grounds. Naturalist John James Audubon wrote in 1831 that he once attempted to count the flocks passing him near his home in Kentucky but gave up after counting 163 flocks in just over twenty minutes. The pigeons, in great numbers, for three days continued passing by, **112** at times blocking out the sun.

111

A) NO CHANGE
B) world, they created dramatic sights
C) world. Creating dramatic sights
D) world, creating dramatic sights

112

A) NO CHANGE
B) The pigeons continued passing by, both in great numbers and doing so for three days,
C) The pigeons continued passing by in great numbers for three days,
D) In great numbers, the pigeons, continued passing by for three days,

113 An individual passenger pigeon, by traveling with many others, **114** is better protected from predators than if traveling alone. When the birds were nesting, there was little chance a predator would go unnoticed by a large flock, and when attacked in the air, the entire flock could draw tightly together and wheel about like a giant serpent to evade the enemy. Traveling and nesting in large numbers also allowed passenger pigeons to compete effectively for food.

115 Moreover, large flocks were also particularly attractive to hunters. Shooting into a flock of birds was almost guaranteed to bring one down, and throwing a net into a low-flying flock could catch dozens. When the pigeons were migrating over American settlers, families feasted on the pigeons for weeks while barely diminishing the flocks.

113

Which choice most effectively establishes the main topic of the paragraph?

A) The passenger pigeon's unique flocking behavior enabled these birds to avoid some dangers but also made them more vulnerable to others.

B) According to Audubon's estimates, a large flock of passenger pigeons may have contained over a billion birds.

C) Flocking behavior in birds, shoaling behavior in fish, and swarming behavior in insects share a similar purpose and similar movement characteristics.

D) Passenger pigeon flocks attracted a variety of predators, including weasels, raccoons, foxes, owls, hawks, and eagles.

114

A) NO CHANGE
B) are protected
C) were better protected
D) was better protected

115

A) NO CHANGE
B) For instance,
C) Unfortunately,
D) Consequently,

The rapid decline of the passenger pigeon in the late 19th century was due to both a loss of habitat and an increase in hunting efficiency. [116] Deforestation accelerating in the mid-1800s, prevented the birds from traveling and nesting in the large groups that they depended on for survival since the large flocks required city-sized forests to support them. With the widespread use of the telegraph, flock locations could be easily communicated to [117] hunters, they boarded trains to follow [118] the birds' flight paths. These same trains carried freshly killed pigeons to the markets and restaurants of cities throughout the United States, where growing demand encouraged further hunting. By the mid-1890s, the passenger pigeon had almost completely disappeared.

116

A) NO CHANGE
B) Deforestation, which accelerated in the mid-1800s,
C) Accelerating in the mid-1800s, deforestation,
D) Deforestation that accelerated in the mid-1800s,

117

A) NO CHANGE
B) hunters, whom
C) hunters, who
D) hunters, then

118

A) NO CHANGE
B) the birds'.
C) the bird's flight paths.
D) the birds flight paths.

The rapid decline of the passenger pigeon population **119** moved forward the animal conservation movement in the United States. **120** In the late 1890s, several states proposed laws protecting passenger pigeons, but these laws were minimally effective since hunters simply followed the flocks to other states. The first US federal law protecting wildlife across state lines, the Lacey Act, was passed in 1900, but this law came too late to save the passenger pigeon. **121**

119

A) NO CHANGE
B) spurred
C) urged
D) transported

120

The writer is considering deleting the underlined sentence. Should the sentence be kept or deleted?

A) Kept, because it cites a common reason that state laws are ineffective for protecting animals.

B) Kept, because it provides supporting evidence for the author's claim that concern for passenger pigeons motivated animal conservation legislation.

C) Deleted, because it doesn't specify which states passed pigeon protection laws.

D) Deleted, because it blurs the paragraph's focus on how laws, in general, have protected various species of animals from extinction.

121

The writer wants to conclude with a sentence supporting her claim that the Lacey Act came too late to save the passenger pigeon. Which choice would best accomplish this goal?

A) The same year that the Lacey Act was passed, the last wild passenger pigeon was killed, and by 1910 only Martha remained.

B) The numbers of passenger pigeons in the United States had been rapidly declining since the mid-1800s.

C) Seventy-three years later, the United States adopted the Endangered Species Act, which has since saved multiple species of birds, reptiles, fish, and land animals from extinction.

D) Pinpointing an exact year of extinction is difficult since scientists disagree about whether to declare a species extinct when its last member dies or when there are too few members left for successful breeding.

Questions 122-132 are based on the following passage.

Carbohydrates

Since at least the 1950s, popular diets have championed cutting carbohydrates as a way to improve one's health and [122] shrink your waistline. However, before we all race to clear our kitchens of pasta and bread, we should understand how carbohydrates affect our bodies and how they fit into a healthy diet.

Carbohydrates comprise one of three macronutrients, alongside proteins and fats, that provide our bodies with the calories necessary to fuel our activities. In our bodies, carbohydrates are converted to glucose, or blood sugar. [123] Glucose is then transported to our tissues and organs, including our muscles and brains, where it provides an immediate source of energy. Excess glucose is stored in the muscles and liver for later [124] use. It can also be converted [125] to fat for long-term storage.

122

A) NO CHANGE
B) also to shrink your waistline
C) for shrinking one's waistline
D) shrink one's waistline

123

The writer is considering deleting the underlined sentence. Should the sentence be kept or deleted?

A) Kept, because it provides a scientific explanation for the passage's conclusion that some carbohydrates are better for our health than others.
B) Kept, because it provides detail that maintains the paragraph's focus on how the body uses carbohydrates as fuel.
C) Deleted, because it doesn't provide an explanation for how glucose is used as energy.
D) Deleted, because it blurs the paragraph's focus on how carbohydrates are similar to other macronutrients.

124

Which choice most effectively combines the sentences at the underlined portion?

A) use; however, further excess glucose can also be
B) use, being
C) use, also
D) use, or it can be

125

A) NO CHANGE
B) as
C) for
D) like

[1] There are several types of carbohydrates, and our bodies use them differently. [2] Sugars are simple carbohydrates that the body processes for quick energy, a fact that's well known to anyone who has felt a "sugar rush" as blood sugar levels quickly increase. [3] Complex carbohydrates, found in breads, pastas, and whole grains, take a longer time for the body to break down and **126** use, energy is produced more slowly and over a longer period of time. [4] Consequently, complex carbohydrates leave us feeling full and satisfied longer. [5] A third type of carbohydrate, fiber, is found in fruits, vegetables, beans, and whole grains. [6] Fiber provides a slow source of energy, helps us feel full, and **127** commences intestinal health. **128**

126

A) NO CHANGE
B) use, so energy is produced
C) use. Energy production happening
D) use; energy being produced

127

A) NO CHANGE
B) promotes
C) recommends
D) alleviates

128

The writer wants to add the following sentence to the previous paragraph.

> However, since our bodies use simple carbohydrates quickly, we can experience a corresponding crash in our energy level as blood sugar levels decline.

The best placement for this sentence is immediately

A) after sentence 2.
B) after sentence 3.
C) after sentence 4.
D) after sentence 6.

Simple carbohydrates occur in moderate amounts <u>129 in fruits, vegetables, and milk, where they are accompanied by other necessary nutrients.</u> However, large amounts of sugars, unaccompanied by other nutrients, are often added to snacks, candies, sodas, and other prepared foods. Since these foods provide calories but lack the vitamins, minerals, and fiber found in other carbohydrate-rich foods, they are called empty calories. Refined grains like white rice and white flour are also frequently labeled as empty calories since the refining process removes nutrients and changes their chemical structure so that 130 <u>they affect our blood sugar levels faster than fruits and vegetables.</u> 131 <u>Quickly feeling hungry again after eating sugars and refined grains is the reason why it is easy to overeat in an effort to satisfy ourselves, and it also leads to a gain in body fat from overeating.</u>

Furthermore, eating these foods frequently can increase our risk of diabetes if our bodies become less adept at responding to frequent, large glucose spikes. While we need to eat carbohydrates, a diet that favors the carbs found in whole grains, fruits, and vegetables over empty calories will provide steadier energy and a healthier outlook 132 <u>than eating a lot of sugars and refined grains.</u>

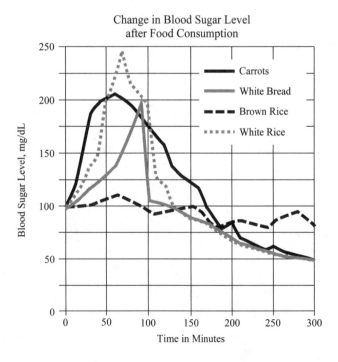

Change in Blood Sugar Level after Food Consumption

Legend:
— Carrots
— White Bread
--- Brown Rice
····· White Rice

Y-axis: Blood Sugar Level, mg/dL (0 to 250)
X-axis: Time in Minutes (0 to 300)

129

A) NO CHANGE
B) in fruits, vegetables, and milk being accompanied by other necessary nutrients.
C) of other necessary nutrients in fruits, vegetables, and milk.
D) along with other necessary nutrients, these being in fruits, vegetables, and milk.

130

Which choice completes the sentence with accurate data based on the graph?

A) NO CHANGE
B) they raise our blood sugar levels for a longer period of time than fruits and vegetables.
C) they produce sharp increases and decreases in our blood sugar levels.
D) they produce little change in our blood sugar levels.

131

A) NO CHANGE
B) Leading to a gain in body fat, overeating to satisfy ourselves is easy since we quickly feel hungry again after eating sugars and refined grains.
C) Overeating sugars and refined grains, which leads to a gain in body fat, since we quickly feel hungry again, is easy.
D) Since we feel hungry again soon after eating sugars and refined grains, it is easy to overeat, leading to a gain in body fat.

132

A) NO CHANGE
B) than sugars and refined grains.
C) than a diet high in sugars and refined grains.
D) than favoring sugars and refined grains.

SUMMIT
EDUCATIONAL
GROUP

Essay

- Essay Format & Scoring

- Working Through the Essay

- Reading the Source Text

- Analysis

  o Evidence

  o Reasoning

  o Stylistic & Persuasive Elements

- Preparing to Write

- Creating Your Outline

- Writing Your Response

  o Writing Your Introduction

  o Quoting the Article

  o Writing Your Conclusion

  o Writing Effectively

  o Proofread

Essay Format

❑ The SAT Essay is an optional test. You are given 50 minutes to complete the essay task, which consists of two parts:

Read a 650-750 word article and consider the author's rhetorical techniques.

Write an essay which analyzes the article and evaluates its persuasiveness.

❑ Learn the instructions before you take the test.

The instructions are the same on every SAT. Memorize the format and instructions before you take the test.

Reading Prompt

As you read the passage below, consider how [*the author*] uses

- evidence, such as facts or examples, to support claims.
- reasoning to develop ideas and to connect claims and evidence.
- stylistic or persuasive elements, such as word choice or appeals to emotion, to add power to the ideas expressed.

A 650-750 word article appears here.

Essay Prompt

Write an essay in which you explain how [*the author*] builds an argument to persuade [*his/her*] audience that [*the article's thesis*]. In your essay, analyze how [*the author*] uses one or more of the features listed in the box above (or features of your own choice) to strengthen the logic and persuasiveness of [*his/her*] argument. Be sure that your analysis focuses on the most relevant features of the passage.

Your essay should not explain whether you agree with [*the author*]'s claims, but rather explain how [*the author*] builds an argument to persuade [*his/her*] audience.

Essay Scoring

❑ Your essay is scored on a 6-24 scale. Your work is evaluated by two essay graders who independently grade on a 1-4 scale in each of three dimensions: Reading, Analysis, and Writing. These grades are then combined to give you your total score.

Essay 6-24					
Reading 2-8		Analysis 2-8		Writing 2-8	
Essay Scorer 1 1-4	Essay Scorer 2 1-4	Essay Scorer 1 1-4	Essay Scorer 2 1-4	Essay Scorer 1 1-4	Essay Scorer 2 1-4

Reading   Comprehension of the source text

Understanding of central ideas, important details, and their interrelationship

Accuracy in representation of the source text (i.e., no errors of fact or interpretation introduced)

Use of textual evidence (quotations, paraphrases, or both) to demonstrate understanding of the source text

Analysis   Analysis of the source text and understanding of the analytical task

Evaluation of the author's use of evidence, reasoning, and/or stylistic and persuasive elements, and/or features chosen by the student

Support for claims or points made in the response

Focus on features of the text most relevant to addressing the task

Writing   Use of a central claim

Use of effective organization and progression of ideas

Use of varied sentence structures

Employment of precise word choice

Maintenance of a consistent, appropriate style and tone

Command of conventions of standard written English

Score	4 – Advanced	3 – Proficient
Reading	The response demonstrates thorough comprehension of the source text. The response shows an understanding of the text's central idea(s) and of most important details and how they interrelate, demonstrating a comprehensive understanding of the text. The response is free of errors of fact or interpretation with regard to the text. The response makes skillful use of textual evidence (quotations, paraphrases, or both), demonstrating a complete understanding of the source text.	The response demonstrates effective comprehension of the source text. The response shows an understanding of the text's central idea(s) and important details. The response is free of substantive errors of fact and interpretation with regard to the text. The response makes appropriate use of textual evidence (quotations, paraphrases, or both), demonstrating an understanding of the source text.
Analysis	The response offers an insightful analysis of the source text and demonstrates a sophisticated understanding of the analytical task. The response offers a thorough, well-considered evaluation of the author's use of evidence, reasoning, and/or stylistic and persuasive elements, and/or feature(s) of the student's own choosing. The response contains relevant, sufficient, and strategically chosen support for claim(s) or point(s) made. The response focuses consistently on those features of the text that are most relevant to addressing the task.	The response offers an effective analysis of the source text and demonstrates an understanding of the analytical task. The response competently evaluates the author's use of evidence, reasoning, and/or stylistic and persuasive elements, and/or feature(s) of the student's own choosing. The response contains relevant and sufficient support for claim(s) or point(s) made. The response focuses primarily on those features of the text that are most relevant to addressing the task.
Writing	The response is cohesive and demonstrates a highly effective use and command of language. The response includes a precise central claim. The response includes a skillful introduction and conclusion. The response demonstrates a deliberate and highly effective progression of ideas both within paragraphs and throughout the essay. The response has wide variety in sentence structures. The response demonstrates a consistent use of precise word choice. The response maintains a formal style and objective tone. The response shows a strong command of the conventions of standard written English and is free or virtually free of errors.	The response is mostly cohesive and demonstrates effective use and control of language. The response includes a central claim or implicit controlling idea. The response includes an effective introduction and conclusion. The response demonstrates a clear progression of ideas both within paragraphs and throughout the essay. The response has variety in sentence structures. The response demonstrates some precise word choice. The response maintains a formal style and objective tone. The response shows good control of the conventions of standard written English and is free of significant errors that detract from the quality of writing.

2 – Partial	1 – Inadequate
The response demonstrates some comprehension of the source text.	The response demonstrates little or no comprehension of the source text.
The response shows an understanding of the text's central idea(s) but not of important details.	The response fails to show an understanding of the text's central idea(s) and may include only details without reference to central idea(s).
The response may contain errors of fact and/or interpretation with regard to the text.	The response may contain numerous errors of fact and/or interpretation with regard to the text.
The response makes limited and/or haphazard use of textual evidence (quotations, paraphrases, or both), demonstrating some understanding of the source text.	The response makes little or no use of textual evidence (quotations, paraphrases, or both), demonstrating little or no understanding of the source text.
The response offers limited analysis of the source text and demonstrates only partial understanding of the analytical task.	The response offers little or no analysis or ineffective analysis of the source text and demonstrates little or no understanding of the analytic task.
The response identifies and attempts to describe the author's use of evidence, reasoning, and/or stylistic and persuasive elements, and/or feature(s) of the student's own choosing, but merely asserts rather than explains their importance.	The response identifies without explanation some aspects of the author's use of evidence, reasoning, and/or stylistic and persuasive elements, and/or feature(s) of the student's choosing.
Or one or more aspects of the response's analysis are unwarranted based on the text.	Or numerous aspects of the response's analysis are unwarranted based on the text.
The response contains little or no support for claim(s) or point(s) made.	The response contains little or no support for claim(s) or point(s) made, or support is largely irrelevant.
The response may lack a clear focus on those features of the text that are most relevant to addressing the task.	The response may not focus on features of the text that are relevant to addressing the task.
	Or the response offers no discernible analysis (e.g. is largely or exclusively summary).
The response demonstrates little or no cohesion and limited skill in the use and control of language.	
The response may lack a clear central claim or controlling idea or may deviate from the claim or idea over the course of the response.	The response demonstrates little or no cohesion and inadequate skill in the use and control of language.
The response may include an ineffective introduction and/or conclusion. The response may demonstrate some progression of ideas within paragraphs but not throughout the response.	The response may lack a clear central claim or controlling idea.
The response has limited variety in sentence structures; sentence structures may be repetitive.	The response lacks a recognizable introduction and conclusion. The response does not have a discernible progression of ideas.
The response demonstrates general or vague word choice; word choice may be repetitive. The response may deviate noticeably from a formal style and objective tone.	The response lacks variety in sentence structures; sentence structures may be repetitive. The response demonstrates general and vague word choice; word choice may be poor or inadequate. The response may lack a formal style and objective tone.
The response shows a limited control of the conventions of standard written English and contains errors that detract from the quality of writing and may impede understanding.	The response shows a weak control of the conventions of standard written English and may contain numerous errors that undermine the quality of writing.

Working Through the Essay

Read and Annotate 1. Read actively and map the passage 2. Note the main ideas of each paragraph	10 minutes
Analyze and Prepare to Write 1. Identify evidence and judge its strength 2. Track the author's line of reasoning 3. Note stylistic techniques and their effects 4. Evaluate the author's overall persuasiveness 5. Write a thesis and outline	10 minutes
Write Your Essay	28 minutes
Review	2 minutes

Read and Annotate

❑ **Do not attempt to start writing before you read the article**. A skilled response to the SAT essay assignment depends on a thorough understanding of the source text, so you must read the article before you attempt to write an essay about it.

❑ Highly skilled readers may be able to read and annotate the article in one pass, but we recommend two passes. During your first pass through the article, you're looking for *what* the author is arguing.

Analyze and Prepare to Write

❑ During your second reading of the article, you're looking for *how* the author makes the argument.

❑ There are three major aspects of the article's rhetoric to consider: evidence, reasoning, and stylistic or persuasive elements.

The article may not contain all three of these in equal measure, or do all of them well. You must identify and judge the author's use (or misuse) of each.

❑ Once you have assessed the effectiveness of the author's arguments, write a thesis based on your judgment. Then expand it to create an outline.

Your central claim should not be your opinion on the issue, but your judgment of the author's overall persuasiveness throughout the source text.

This is your chance to organize your thoughts before you write your introductory paragraph. You don't want to be halfway through your essay when you realize that you could have ordered your writing differently.

Write Your Essay

❑ Using your outline as a guide, spend at least half of the allotted time writing a response to the source text. Refer back to your notes on the article early and often.

Review

❑ Give yourself a couple of minutes to clean up spelling and punctuation errors. Don't erase! It takes too much time. Cross out mistakes and rewrite as necessary.

Reading the Source Text

❑ Before you begin reading the article, find the thesis in the prompt that appears after the article. This will help guide your reading.

> "Write an essay in which you explain how Mark Schoen builds an argument to persuade his audience that noise pollution should be reduced. In your essay, analyze how Schoen uses one or more of the features listed in the box above (or features of your own choice) to strengthen the logic and persuasiveness of his argument. Be sure that your analysis focuses on the most relevant features of the passage."

❑ Actively read the article, just as you would a Reading passage.

- Find the main idea of each paragraph.

- Map the passage.

- Determine how each part of the passage contributes to the thesis.

❑ Label the thesis so that you can refer to it later.

Keep in mind that the articles are not necessarily written in the standard 5-paragraph style, so the thesis may not appear in the first or last paragraphs. Also, the thesis may not appear as a single, direct sentence.

❑ Part of your analytical task is to identify how the author has chosen to structure his or her persuasive argument.

After you're done actively reading and annotating the source text, take a quick look at the main ideas of the paragraphs and consider why the author chose to arrange the ideas in this particular order.

Note the role of each paragraph. Does the paragraph use evidence to support the author's point directly, or does it attack opposing ideas?

❑ Don't be shy with your pencil – mark up the source text with any observations you have! Careful note taking will help you to track ideas across paragraphs.

TRY IT OUT

Read the following source text. Identify the thesis and find the main idea of each paragraph.

This passage is adapted from the 2014 essay "Quiet, Please" by Mark Schoen

1   The Pacific Northwest campgrounds of my childhood are ingrained with memories of deep, patient silence. Days after we parked the car and pitched the tent, the only afternoon sounds to reach our ears were the gurgle of the shoulder-wide brook and the whispers of gently undulating conifers. But in 2013, nearly one-third of all Americans were at risk of noise-induced hearing loss (NIHL), a total number that has scarcely changed in more than three decades. I fear that rather than striving to re-establish crucial quietude, we are simply coming to accept an incessant bombardment of unwanted noise. This spring, as winter fades and the earth comes back to life, we should do our best to sift through the ambiance of the city and appreciate the delicate noises which only silence permits us to hear.

2   As hunter-gatherers, human beings relied on accurate hearing on a background of uncluttered silence to detect our prey and avoid our natural predators. By contrast, many modern urban dwellers wear headphones throughout the day, smothering background noise with additional decibels of music. Such constant elevated sound levels are not just unnatural, but also quite dangerous.

3   Although the Environmental Protection Agency and other health organizations have known since the 1980s that prolonged exposure to traffic noise poses a health risk, most of its concerns focused on NIHL. However, in 2007 the World Health Organization presented new data indicating that noise pollution is a major contributor to heart disease. According to Deepak Prasher, one of the WHO's researchers and a professor of audiology at University College in London, "many people become habituated to noise over time… the biological effects are imperceptible, so that even as you become accustomed to the noise, adverse physiological changes are nevertheless taking place." In Europe alone, long-term exposure to traffic noise may contribute to as many as 210,000 coronary heart disease deaths per year. In countries like the United States, where heart disease is the leading cause of death and public transportation is not as widespread as individual car usage, we cannot simply ignore the public health risks of noise pollution.

SUMMIT
EDUCATIONAL
GROUP

NOTES

4   The adverse effects extend beyond *Homo sapiens* to the greater ecosystem. A 2011 study found that "noise pollution from human traffic networks and industrial activity impacts vast areas of our planets." The data demonstrates that bats, acoustic predators which rely on their sonar to detect and consume insects, have difficulty locating their prey within hearing range of road noise. The study concluded that "the noise impact on the bats' foraging performance will have complex effects on the food web and ultimately on the ecosystem stability." These bats save American farmers billions of dollars in pest control expenses, lowering the quantities of pesticides introduced to our plants and groundwater. If these bats cannot properly maintain their place within our ecosystem, we face the prospect of increased food prices and lowered water quality.

5   There are other qualitative, human costs to high noise levels. Quiet environments help us to reflect, to process the day's labors and discoveries, to create, to plan. Mozart often stayed up late at night, composing until one in the morning; Charles Darwin would often lie awake in bed solving problems until he fell asleep. If either of these monumental figures had lived next to a subway line or busy highway, would they have been able to create in the same way? How many moments of insight have we lost to background noise, and how many will be lost to our children? Even the forest campgrounds I came to know and love are less silent than they used to be: the nearby lake has attracted real estate developers, and now our gurgling brook is interrupted every few minutes by the distant hum of a passing car.

6   Fortunately, several national and global health organizations have begun to measure and address the financial, environmental, and health-related costs of noise pollution. There is now a critical mass of scientific study demonstrating the severity of the issue and suggesting reform measures such as labels for noisy products, informed urban planning, and acoustically-sound construction standards. Perhaps, if public awareness drives well-informed policy, we may yet again be able to pause and appreciate the sound of a gentle wind in the trees.

Write an essay in which you explain how Mark Schoen builds an argument to persuade his audience that noise pollution should be reduced. In your essay, analyze how Schoen uses one or more of the features listed in the box above (or features of your own choice) to strengthen the logic and persuasiveness of his argument. Be sure that your analysis focuses on the most relevant features of the passage.

Your essay should not explain whether you agree with Schoen's claims, but rather explain how Schoen builds an argument to persuade his audience.

1. What is the author's thesis?

2. Where, if ever, does the author state his thesis?

3. What is the main idea of paragraph 1?

4. What is the main idea of paragraph 2?

5. What is the main idea of paragraph 3?

6. What is the main idea of paragraph 4?

7. What is the main idea of paragraph 5?

8. What is the main idea of paragraph 6?

Analysis – Evidence

❑ After you have read through the passage once and developed a strong understanding of its arguments, reread the passage to analyze how effectively the arguments are developed.

❑ Note where the author uses evidence to support arguments.

❑ There are different types of evidence, and not all are equally reliable or persuasive.

❑ **Data-Based Evidence** – Data can take the form of statistics, scientific data, or other numbers. When you see names of people or organizations, check to see if the author uses them as a source for data-based evidence.

> "A study by the Pew Research Center found that 78% of major news organizations get more traffic on mobile devices than they receive on desktop computers."

❑ **Anecdotal Evidence** – An author may use a personal story or tell someone else's story to illustrate a point. These anecdotes can provide support to a claim by showing that is has proven true for someone. However, an anecdote may be weaker evidence than "hard" data because it may not be representative of most people's experiences. A strength of anecdotal evidence is that it can allow the reader to have an emotional connection to the author's argument.

> "As a child, I personally experienced the disparity in educational systems when I transferred to a charter school."

❑ **Hypothetical Examples** – The author may draw upon non-specific examples of events that could happen. A hypothetical example should be supported by an explanation of why the future event is likely to occur, such as by showing a historical precedent. Otherwise, the hypothetical example is a weak rhetorical device.

> "Without doctors, we would be left to diagnose our own illnesses, which would lead to a problematic return to ancient ways of superstition and medical mysticism."

❑ **Generalizations** – An author may make a broad observation about a whole group. This can be used to show similarities that unite individuals. However, a generalization can also oversimplify an issue by assuming that individuals are alike when they might not be.

> "Every culture has its own rituals surrounding the consumption of meals."
> "We all know that the development of cell phones has made driving more dangerous."

TRY IT OUT

Read the following source text. Identify the different types of evidence the author uses.

This passage is adapted from the 2014 essay "Quiet, Please" by Mark Schoen

1   The Pacific Northwest campgrounds of my childhood are ingrained with memories of deep, patient silence. Days after we parked the car and pitched the tent, the only afternoon sounds to reach our ears were the gurgle of the shoulder-wide brook and the whispers of gently undulating conifers. But in 2013, nearly one-third of all Americans were at risk of noise-induced hearing loss (NIHL), a total number that has scarcely changed in more than three decades. I fear that rather than striving to re-establish crucial quietude, we are simply coming to accept an incessant bombardment of unwanted noise. This spring, as winter fades and the earth comes back to life, we should do our best to sift through the ambiance of the city and appreciate the delicate noises which only silence permits us to hear.

2   As hunter-gatherers, human beings relied on accurate hearing on a background of uncluttered silence to detect our prey and avoid our natural predators. By contrast, many modern urban dwellers wear headphones throughout the day, smothering background noise with additional decibels of music. Such constant elevated sound levels are not just unnatural, but also quite dangerous.

3   Although the Environmental Protection Agency and other health organizations have known since the 1980s that prolonged exposure to traffic noise poses a health risk, most of its concerns focused on NIHL. However, in 2007 the World Health Organization presented new data indicating that noise pollution is a major contributor to heart disease. According to Deepak Prasher, one of the WHO's researchers and a professor of audiology at University College in London, "many people become habituated to noise over time… the biological effects are imperceptible, so that even as you become accustomed to the noise, adverse physiological changes are nevertheless taking place." In Europe alone, long-term exposure to traffic noise may contribute to as many as 210,000 coronary heart disease deaths per year. In countries like the United States, where heart disease is the leading cause of death and public transportation is not as widespread as individual car usage, we cannot simply ignore the public health risks of noise pollution.

4   The adverse effects extend beyond *Homo sapiens* to the greater ecosystem. A 2011 study found that "noise pollution from human traffic networks and industrial activity impacts vast areas of our planets." The data demonstrates that bats, acoustic predators which rely on their sonar to detect and consume insects, have difficulty locating their prey within hearing range of road noise. The study concluded that "the noise impact on the bats' foraging performance will have complex effects on the food web and ultimately on the ecosystem stability." These bats save American farmers billions of dollars in pest control expenses, lowering the quantities of pesticides introduced to our plants and groundwater. If these bats cannot properly maintain their place within our ecosystem, we face the prospect of increased food prices and lowered water quality.

5   There are other qualitative, human costs to high noise levels. Quiet environments help us to reflect, to process the day's labors and discoveries, to create, to plan. Mozart often stayed up late at night, composing until one in the morning; Charles Darwin would often lie awake in bed solving problems until he fell asleep. If either of these monumental figures had lived next to a subway line or busy highway, would they have been able to create in the same way? How many moments of insight have we lost to background noise, and how many will be lost to our children? Even the forest campgrounds I came to know and love are less silent than they used to be: the nearby lake has attracted real estate developers, and now our gurgling brook is interrupted every few minutes by the distant hum of a passing car.

6   Fortunately, several national and global health organizations have begun to measure and address the financial, environmental, and health-related costs of noise pollution. There is now a critical mass of scientific study demonstrating the severity of the issue and suggesting reform measures such as labels for noisy products, informed urban planning, and acoustically-sound construction standards. Perhaps, if public awareness drives well-informed policy, we may yet again be able to pause and appreciate the sound of a gentle wind in the trees.

Write an essay in which you explain how Mark Schoen builds an argument to persuade his audience that noise pollution should be reduced. In your essay, analyze how Schoen uses one or more of the features listed in the box above (or features of your own choice) to strengthen the logic and persuasiveness of his argument. Be sure that your analysis focuses on the most relevant features of the passage.

Your essay should not explain whether you agree with Schoen's claims, but rather explain how Schoen builds an argument to persuade his audience.

1. In paragraph 1, the author's details about nature are used as evidence to support what idea?

2. What type of evidence is used in paragraph 2? How effective is this evidence?

3. What type of evidence is used in paragraph 3?

4. How many different pieces of evidence are used in paragraph 4?
   How concrete are they?

5. Within the article as a whole, which pieces of evidence are the most persuasive?

Analysis – Reasoning

❑ A highly persuasive author will clearly present the steps between his or her thesis and the evidence which supports it. *Reasoning* is how the author uses logic to structure arguments.

A **premise** is an assumption upon which an argument depends. The author must prove that the premises within his or her argument are valid, and must then show how logical conclusions may be determined from them.

> Premise 1: All men are mortal.
> Premise 2: Socrates is a man.
> Conclusion: Therefore, Socrates is mortal.

Deductive reasoning involves starting with a generalization and moving to specific details.

Inductive reasoning involves starting with specific details and moving to a larger idea.

❑ There are many different types of unsound reasoning, called *fallacies*. There are too many to list here, but you should learn to identify the common ones. While the SAT will provide you high-quality writing for the essay source document, you may be able to identify weaknesses including, but not limited to, the fallacies below.

Slippery Slope – Claiming that if A happens, then Z will certainly happen, and Z is bad – so therefore A should not happen.

> "If we let students decide what food should be served in the cafeteria, pretty soon the students will be running the whole school and the principal will be out of a job."

Black-or-White – Presenting only two choices or ways to view the situation, typically when one is the author's perspective and the other is undesirable.

> "By not giving money to my election campaign, you're voting to let my opponent win."

Correlation-as-Causation – Claiming that because two things happened at the same time, or one after another, one event caused the other one to occur.

> "Increased sales of pudding occurred during the same time period as a spike in divorce rates. Only by making pudding illegal can we save our society."

Appealing to Emotion – Evoking fear, greed, guilt, shame, anger, or other emotions (rather than reason) to convince an audience.

> "Eat your kale and quinoa casserole! There are starving children in other countries who can only dream of being as fortunate as you are."

Bear in mind that a fallacy doesn't necessarily make an argument wrong or invalid; it just means that the argument is weaker than it could be otherwise.

TRY IT OUT

Read the following source text. Note the reasoning the author uses to relate various pieces of evidence to his central claim.

This passage is adapted from the 2014 essay "Quiet, Please" by Mark Schoen

1   The Pacific Northwest campgrounds of my childhood are ingrained with memories of deep, patient silence. Days after we parked the car and pitched the tent, the only afternoon sounds to reach our ears were the gurgle of the shoulder-wide brook and the whispers of gently undulating conifers. But in 2013, nearly one-third of all Americans were at risk of noise-induced hearing loss (NIHL), a total number that has scarcely changed in more than three decades. I fear that rather than striving to re-establish crucial quietude, we are simply coming to accept an incessant bombardment of unwanted noise. This spring, as winter fades and the earth comes back to life, we should do our best to sift through the ambiance of the city and appreciate the delicate noises which only silence permits us to hear.

2   As hunter-gatherers, human beings relied on accurate hearing on a background of uncluttered silence to detect our prey and avoid our natural predators. By contrast, many modern urban dwellers wear headphones throughout the day, smothering background noise with additional decibels of music. Such constant elevated sound levels are not just unnatural, but also quite dangerous.

3   Although the Environmental Protection Agency and other health organizations have known since the 1980s that prolonged exposure to traffic noise poses a health risk, most of its concerns focused on NIHL. However, in 2007 the World Health Organization presented new data indicating that noise pollution is a major contributor to heart disease. According to Deepak Prasher, one of the WHO's researchers and a professor of audiology at University College in London, "many people become habituated to noise over time… the biological effects are imperceptible, so that even as you become accustomed to the noise, adverse physiological changes are nevertheless taking place." In Europe alone, long-term exposure to traffic noise may contribute to as many as 210,000 coronary heart disease deaths per year. In countries like the United States, where heart disease is the leading cause of death and public transportation is not as widespread as individual car usage, we cannot simply ignore the public health risks of noise pollution.

4   The adverse effects extend beyond *Homo sapiens* to the greater ecosystem. A 2011 study found that "noise pollution from human traffic networks and industrial activity impacts vast areas of our planets." The data demonstrates that bats, acoustic predators which rely on their sonar to detect and consume insects, have difficulty locating their prey within hearing range of road noise. The study concluded that "the noise impact on the bats' foraging performance will have complex effects on the food web and ultimately on the ecosystem stability." These bats save American farmers billions of dollars in pest control expenses, lowering the quantities of pesticides introduced to our plants and groundwater. If these bats cannot properly maintain their place within our ecosystem, we face the prospect of increased food prices and lowered water quality.

5   There are other qualitative, human costs to high noise levels. Quiet environments help us to reflect, to process the day's labors and discoveries, to create, to plan. Mozart often stayed up late at night, composing until one in the morning; Charles Darwin would often lie awake in bed solving problems until he fell asleep. If either of these monumental figures had lived next to a subway line or busy highway, would they have been able to create in the same way? How many moments of insight have we lost to background noise, and how many will be lost to our children? Even the forest campgrounds I came to know and love are less silent than they used to be: the nearby lake has attracted real estate developers, and now our gurgling brook is interrupted every few minutes by the distant hum of a passing car.

6   Fortunately, several national and global health organizations have begun to measure and address the financial, environmental, and health-related costs of noise pollution. There is now a critical mass of scientific study demonstrating the severity of the issue and suggesting reform measures such as labels for noisy products, informed urban planning, and acoustically-sound construction standards. Perhaps, if public awareness drives well-informed policy, we may yet again be able to pause and appreciate the sound of a gentle wind in the trees.

Write an essay in which you explain how Mark Schoen builds an argument to persuade his audience that noise pollution should be reduced. In your essay, analyze how Schoen uses one or more of the features listed in the box above (or features of your own choice) to strengthen the logic and persuasiveness of his argument. Be sure that your analysis focuses on the most relevant features of the passage.

Your essay should not explain whether you agree with Schoen's claims, but rather explain how Schoen builds an argument to persuade his audience.

1. What are the premises and conclusion of the author's argument in paragraph 4?

2. What logical fallacies, if any, does the author deploy in paragraph 4?

3. What reasoning connects the anecdotal examples in paragraph 5 to the author's thesis?

4. What logical fallacies, if any, does the author deploy in paragraph 5?

5. What is the pattern, if any, to the flow of ideas from one paragraph to the next? Why might the author want to structure his article according to this particular flow of ideas?

SUMMIT
EDUCATIONAL
GROUP

Analysis – Stylistic & Persuasive Elements

❑ A stylistic element is the author's way of influencing the feelings of the reader. When you come across powerful words in the source text, ask yourself: Why did the author choose this word instead of a milder version of the word, and what is the overall effect on the audience?

❑ Strong words can be used to emphasize ideas and judgments. Look for positive or negative words that illustrate how the author is portraying topics.

> Compare the following pairs of sentences:
>
> "Without reinforcements, our army's defeat is probable."
> "Without reinforcements, our army's defeat is inevitable."
>
> "Public support does provide some benefit to a politician's efforts."
> "Public support certainly provides a tremendous boost to a politician's efforts."

❑ It's important to note that this type of subtle change can have a powerful dramatic effect, even if the dramatic language is being used to describe data-based evidence.

❑ When the author poses a question to the reader, consider what is implied by the question. Rhetorical questions can be used to criticize, suggest a course of action, or indicate that a point of view is obvious.

> "Why not embrace these new changes as an opportunity to broaden our horizons?"
>
> "Who knows how terribly our carelessness could affect future generations?"

TRY IT OUT

Read the following source text. Identify any stylistic choices or persuasive elements.

This passage is adapted from the 2014 essay "Quiet, Please" by Mark Schoen

NOTES

1   The Pacific Northwest campgrounds of my childhood are ingrained with memories of deep, patient silence. Days after we parked the car and pitched the tent, the only afternoon sounds to reach our ears were the gurgle of the shoulder-wide brook and the whispers of gently undulating conifers. But in 2013, nearly one-third of all Americans were at risk of noise-induced hearing loss (NIHL), a total number that has scarcely changed in more than three decades. I fear that rather than striving to re-establish crucial quietude, we are simply coming to accept an incessant bombardment of unwanted noise. This spring, as winter fades and the earth comes back to life, we should do our best to sift through the ambiance of the city and appreciate the delicate noises which only silence permits us to hear.

2   As hunter-gatherers, human beings relied on accurate hearing on a background of uncluttered silence to detect our prey and avoid our natural predators. By contrast, many modern urban dwellers wear headphones throughout the day, smothering background noise with additional decibels of music. Such constant elevated sound levels are not just unnatural, but also quite dangerous.

3   Although the Environmental Protection Agency and other health organizations have known since the 1980s that prolonged exposure to traffic noise poses a health risk, most of its concerns focused on NIHL. However, in 2007 the World Health Organization presented new data indicating that noise pollution is a major contributor to heart disease. According to Deepak Prasher, one of the WHO's researchers and a professor of audiology at University College in London, "many people become habituated to noise over time… the biological effects are imperceptible, so that even as you become accustomed to the noise, adverse physiological changes are nevertheless taking place." In Europe alone, long-term exposure to traffic noise may contribute to as many as 210,000 coronary heart disease deaths per year. In countries like the United States, where heart disease is the leading cause of death and public transportation is not as widespread as individual car usage, we cannot simply ignore the public health risks of noise pollution.

SUMMIT
EDUCATIONAL
GROUP

4   The adverse effects extend beyond *Homo sapiens* to the greater ecosystem. A 2011 study found that "noise pollution from human traffic networks and industrial activity impacts vast areas of our planets." The data demonstrates that bats, acoustic predators which rely on their sonar to detect and consume insects, have difficulty locating their prey within hearing range of road noise. The study concluded that "the noise impact on the bats' foraging performance will have complex effects on the food web and ultimately on the ecosystem stability." These bats save American farmers billions of dollars in pest control expenses, lowering the quantities of pesticides introduced to our plants and groundwater. If these bats cannot properly maintain their place within our ecosystem, we face the prospect of increased food prices and lowered water quality.

5   There are other qualitative, human costs to high noise levels. Quiet environments help us to reflect, to process the day's labors and discoveries, to create, to plan. Mozart often stayed up late at night, composing until one in the morning; Charles Darwin would often lie awake in bed solving problems until he fell asleep. If either of these monumental figures had lived next to a subway line or busy highway, would they have been able to create in the same way? How many moments of insight have we lost to background noise, and how many will be lost to our children? Even the forest campgrounds I came to know and love are less silent than they used to be: the nearby lake has attracted real estate developers, and now our gurgling brook is interrupted every few minutes by the distant hum of a passing car.

6   Fortunately, several national and global health organizations have begun to measure and address the financial, environmental, and health-related costs of noise pollution. There is now a critical mass of scientific study demonstrating the severity of the issue and suggesting reform measures such as labels for noisy products, informed urban planning, and acoustically-sound construction standards. Perhaps, if public awareness drives well-informed policy, we may yet again be able to pause and appreciate the sound of a gentle wind in the trees.

Write an essay in which you explain how Mark Schoen builds an argument to persuade his audience that noise pollution should be reduced. In your essay, analyze how Schoen uses one or more of the features listed in the box above (or features of your own choice) to strengthen the logic and persuasiveness of his argument. Be sure that your analysis focuses on the most relevant features of the passage.

Your essay should not explain whether you agree with Schoen's claims, but rather explain how Schoen builds an argument to persuade his audience.

1. What dramatic imagery does the author use in the first paragraph? Does this imagery appear anywhere else? What is the overall effect?

2. How does the author choose words in paragraph 1 to emphasize his point?

3. What stylistic choices does the author use in paragraphs 3 and 4 to frame data-based evidence?

4. From the reader's perspective, what is the effect of the rhetorical questions in paragraph 5?

Checkpoint Review

Read the following source text. Map the passage and annotate appropriately for Evidence, Reasoning, and Stylistic/Persuasive elements.

As you read the passage below, consider how Jennifer Dewey uses

- evidence, such as facts or examples, to support claims.
- reasoning to develop ideas and to connect claims and evidence.
- stylistic or persuasive elements, such as word choice or appeals to emotion, to add power to the ideas expressed.

This passage is adapted from the 2013 article "Class Dismissed" by Jennifer Dewey

1   A puzzling shift has occurred in the American education system in the last two decades. While funding for schools has more than doubled, the tutoring industry has expanded exponentially, and free online learning resources have blossomed, teachers – especially young teachers – are actually leaving their profession in droves.

2   According to a 2008 study published by the American Educational Research Association titled *Teacher Attrition and Retention*, teaching has developed a turnover rate much higher than those of other demographically-comparable professions. The rates of attrition are steepest among younger teachers, ages 25 to 29. According to the data, an estimated 45% of young teachers leave their jobs within the first 5 years.

3   That so many young teachers now conclude that this foundational role is not for them bears disturbing implications for future generations. If the high reported rates of attrition were mostly the result of teachers shifting from school to school, this might not be such a worrisome statistic. But those 45% leave the profession altogether –and the loss of so many initially-motivated young teachers is of no insignificance.

4   The systemic loss of so many teachers creates ripple effects beyond the classroom. Not only do students pay the metaphorical price, but taxpayers, too, pay the literal price. In his 2011 New York Times opinion piece *The High Cost of Teacher Salaries*, publisher and author Dave Eggers points out that "[teacher] turnover costs the United States $7.34 billion yearly." This money comes out of public coffers – and therefore comes out of each of our paychecks. Ironically, reinvesting these lost funds into teacher salaries would likely lower turnover and budgetary shortfalls in the first place. When polled, 68% of undergraduates at top-tier colleges affirmed that they would consider teaching if salaries started at $65,000. The average starting salary for a first-year teacher currently stands at around $36,000.

5   It is precisely these top-tier, well-educated undergraduates who wind up quitting their teaching posts within 5 years. *Teacher Attrition and Retention* found that but that teachers under the age of 30 are 5.32 times more likely to attrite out of the profession than those just 5 years older. Furthermore, high-demand math and science teachers tend to leave at higher rates than teachers of other subjects. This is not a healthy attrition, characterized by the shedding of deadwood or the honorable pensioning-off of retirees. These numbers reflect the ominous truth that our most talented and energetic teachers elect to leave our education system for the private sector.

6   There is also a civic price to pay for under-educating our children. According to data from the Department of Justice and the National Education Administration, our country spends far more money per incarcerated criminal than it does per enrolled student. New York, for instance, spends $60,000 per inmate per year, more than half of which is paid by taxpayers. By contrast, New York spends less than $20,000 per student per year. This is not only a Northeastern or urban problem. According to Tim Callahan, spokesperson for the Professional Association of Georgia Educators, "if we don't have well-educated students who later in life may turn to crime, they'll end up costing us twice as much as it would to educate a student." Callahan's observation appeals to the bottom line, but there's more to it than just dollars and cents. Given the choice, wouldn't you and most people you know rather improve the education system than maintain an extensive prison-industrial complex?

7   The data clearly indicates that under-funding our public education system has severe long-term effects on our country's social structure. The high numbers of young educators who regularly decide to quit teaching strongly indicate a bleak trend away from quality careers for recent college graduates, consistent education for our children, and appropriately low rates of incarceration. We are long overdue for a serious policy-level discussion about structural reform, rather than patchwork repairs, of our education system. The longer we defer the injection of much-needed capital at the ground level, the more costly it will become down the line – perhaps at a time when we can no longer afford it.

Write an essay in which you explain how Jennifer Dewey builds an argument to persuade her audience that under-funding our schools is harmful. In your essay, analyze how Dewey uses one or more of the features listed in the box above (or features of your own choice) to strengthen the logic and persuasiveness of her argument. Be sure that your analysis focuses on the most relevant features of the passage.

Your essay should not explain whether you agree with Dewey's claims, but rather explain how Dewey builds an argument to persuade her audience.

Preparing to Write

Once you've critically read and mapped the source text, annotated the pieces of evidence and stylistic pieces, and tracked the author's reasoning, you're ready to form the thesis for your response essay.

❑ **Your central claim should not be your own opinion on the topic of the article**. Do not write about whether you agree or disagree with the author's thesis. Instead, your essay should be your judgment of the author's persuasiveness.

Incorrect: "I disagree with the author's central claim about social media."

Incorrect: "The author's claim about social media is correct, as he says."

Correct: "The author uses economic data and strong reasoning to craft a strong, if dry, argument against the War on Drugs."

Correct: "The author uses well-crafted stylistic elements and poignant personal anecdotes to persuade his audience that social media can bring us together as never before."

❑ The SAT uses professional-grade source texts for essay prompts. However, if you have assessed the text and are prepared to show how the source text is not very persuasive, it is also possible to write a high-scoring response that criticizes the text.

Nevertheless, this is still not an opinion piece. If you do write a critical response, your response must be based only on rhetorical shortfalls within the source text. You cannot insert your own opinion on the issue.

"The author's central claim about central media is unconvincing, primarily because it over-relies on rhetorical appeals to emotion and lacks supporting evidence."

"The author cites many studies and statistics, but fails to tie these facts together in a logical and persuasive manner."

❑ Keep your analysis focused. It is better to write a narrow, precise, defensible thesis than to write a broad, impressive-sounding claim for which you have no evidence.

Creating Your Outline

❑ After you have formed your thesis, you should plan the order in which you want to present your ideas and your evidence. Your outline needs to incorporate an introduction, conclusion, and evidence-based support for your judgment of the source text's persuasiveness.

❑ Use the template below as a general guide for the purpose of each part of your essay.

Introduction:

  Address the issue and restate the author's central claim.

  Make your thesis statement about the effectiveness of the author's arguments.

  Foreshadow the pieces of evidence you will use to support your thesis.

Supporting Paragraph 1:

  Write a topic sentence addressing one of the aspects of the source text.

  Support your point by quoting the source text.

  Explain the overall significance of the quoted text.

Supporting Paragraph 2:

  Write a topic sentence addressing one of the aspects of the source text.

  Support your point by quoting the source text.

  Explain the overall significance of the quoted text.

Supporting Paragraph 3:

  Write a topic sentence addressing one of the aspects of the source text.

  Support your point by quoting the source text.

  Explain the overall significance of the quote text.

Conclusion:

  Conclude by restating the author's central claim, and your overall assessment of the author's persuasiveness (or lack thereof). You will already have evaluated this within your body paragraphs in more specific ways.

  Summarize how the quoted text proved your thesis about the source text.

SUMMIT
EDUCATIONAL
GROUP

TRY IT OUT

Refer back to your annotations on "Class Dismissed" by Jennifer Dewey. Use your notes to form your thesis and an outline based on that thesis.

Introduction

The author's central claim: _____

_____

_____

Your thesis: _____

_____

_____

Foreshadow Evidence: _____

_____

_____

Supporting Paragraph 1

Topic sentence: _____

_____

Supporting Quotations: _____

_____

_____

_____

Supporting Paragraph 2

    Topic sentence: _____

    _____

    Supporting Quotations: _____

    _____

    _____

    _____

Supporting Paragraph 3

    Topic sentence: _____

    _____

    Supporting Quotations: _____

    _____

    _____

    _____

Conclusion

    Restate thesis: _____

    _____

    _____

    Summarize Quotations: _____

    _____

Writing Your Introduction

❑ The purpose of the introduction is to address the central point of the source text and to state your assessment of the author's persuasiveness. You can also use the introductory paragraph to mention your supporting points or to summarize your main arguments.

❑ The introductory paragraph states your main idea and establishes what you will be discussing in your essay. This helps your reader understand what your focus is and know what to expect in your essay.

❑ There are three essential elements to an introduction:

- A strong **opening** that relates to the source text and grabs the attention of the reader.

- Your **thesis statement**, which states your assessment of the author's persuasiveness.

- **Foreshadowing** of the types of textual evidence you will use to support your thesis.

These pieces of textual evidence will be quoted and analyzed in your supporting paragraphs. You can mention these examples in your thesis statement or in a sentence that relates them back to your thesis.

opening statement

foreshadowing

thesis statement

In their New York Times article "Why US Women Are Leaving Jobs Behind," Claire Cain Miller and Liz Alderman argue that many American women are being driven from the workplace by a combination of company policies and cultural attitudes. Readers of their article may find themselves not only convinced by their arguments and evidence, but also personally moved by the individual anecdotes incorporated into the article. This combination of data-based evidence from a wide variety of research studies and personal experiences which reflect the studies' results creates a highly persuasive argument.

TRY IT OUT

Refer back to your annotations on "Class Dismissed" by Jennifer Dewey and to your outline. Use your notes to write an introductory paragraph to your response essay.

_____

_____

_____

_____

_____

_____

_____

_____

_____

_____

Quoting the Article

❑ In order to properly support your claims about the author's persuasiveness (or lack thereof), you must quote from the source text. It is not enough to simply talk about what the author does and presume that your essay grader will find the sentences to which you refer.

❑ You must quote the article accurately. Since the source text is right there in front of you, there's no excuse for copying the text incorrectly.

❑ Don't quote out of context. Twisting the meaning of the text, or interpreting it in a way that the author clearly didn't intend, does not create a clever argument. Rather, your readers will presume that you simply don't understand the author's point, and you will lose points for Analysis.

❑ Remember that the purpose of this Essay test is to explain how the author uses various writing elements to strengthen logic and persuasiveness. Persuasiveness does not exist in a vacuum; it is something that the author directs towards an audience.

Therefore, it is your responsibility to not only present quotations in the proper context, but also to **explain the effect on the audience**.

❑ You don't have to quote entire sentences at once and separate them from your own writing. It's fine to select words, phrases, or even strings of phrases from the article and work them into your own essay.

When you incorporate quotations into your own writing, maintain appropriate tense, person, and number. You're allowed to alter the quoted text for the sake of grammatical consistency and context, as long as you mark changes with brackets and omitted text with ellipses.

Source Text:

> It is now easier than ever before for those with physical disabilities to participate fully in society. In a recent study conducted through the Architectural College of Worthington (ACW), 68% of recent graduates say that they consider accessibility options such as ramps, elevators, and automatic doors to be necessities within their initial designs. An identical study conducted almost a decade before indicated that only 15% of fledgling architects from the school were concerned with accessibility. This is a testament to the ACW's recent initiative to promote both aesthetic and practical purposes in all its students' designs.

Quoting the source text:

> The author refers to two identical studies in order to demonstrate that accessible design choices in architecture are a growing concern. He writes that "68% of recent graduates consider accessibility options… [while a decade ago] only 15% of fledgling architects" from the ACW did the same.

TRY IT OUT

Refer back to your annotations on "Class Dismissed" by Jennifer Dewey and to your outline. Use your notes to write two supporting paragraphs for your response essay.

Supporting paragraph 1

_____

_____

_____

_____

_____

_____

_____

Supporting paragraph 2

_____

_____

_____

_____

_____

_____

_____

Supporting paragraph 3

_____

_____

_____

_____

_____

_____

_____

Writing Your Conclusion

❑ The conclusion of an essay summarizes the arguments of the essay, giving your reader a sense of what is most important in your essay.

Think of the conclusion as a restatement of your essay's introductory paragraph. Just as the introduction establishes the essay's central argument and what examples will be used to support it, the conclusion reaffirms the essay's argument and reviews how the examples proved it.

restatement ⎨ In these ways, Miller and alderman demonstrated that American women in particular have a wide variety of incentives to depart the workplace, and there is no obvious policy solution to luring this demographic back into the office. Readers of all stripes will

summary of citations ⎨ be convinced: social scientists will appreciate the comprehensive presentation of studies, moms will sympathize with the multiple personal narratives throughout, and non-Americans can learn from Miller and Alderman's comparison of European and American policies and outcomes. Whoever reads this piece will

final statement ⎨ find something to agree with.

❑ The conclusion should not introduce new material or new ideas. Your conclusion should tie everything together, not bring up new topics that would need further discussion.

❑ Effective conclusions show how the text you quoted proved your thesis. You should summarize the textual evidence you cited, briefly explaining how they proved your point.

❑ If you are low on time, try to quickly summarize any unfinished supporting paragraphs and get at least two sentences written for the conclusion. This summary can be easily done by taking phrases from the introduction's thesis statement or supporting paragraphs' topic sentences and using synonyms for key words.

Make sure you end with a strong, definitive statement about your essay's argument.

TRY IT OUT

Refer back to your annotations on "Class Dismissed" by Jennifer Dewey and to your outline. Use your notes to write an introductory paragraph to your response essay.

_____

_____

_____

_____

_____

_____

_____

_____

_____

_____

Writing Effectively

❏ In general, you will improve your writing by paying attention to the grammar and usage skills covered in the English Test. Additionally, you can improve your writing by making sure that your language is efficient and precise and that every sentence is relevant and advances your arguments.

❏ Make sure each sentence is necessary. Do not try to stuff your essay with irrelevant facts. Your writing will have more impact if it is focused.

❏ Avoid wordiness. Do not try to sound more intelligent by making your sentences overly complex. Your writing will have a stronger effect if it is concise.

> Rewrite:
>
> He expressed his own personal thoughts in a certain way that truly may have seemed to be unnatural.
>
> _____
>
> _____

❏ Use appropriate language. Avoid the use of clichés and slang.

> Rewrite:
>
> You should take his opinion with a grain of salt.
>
> _____

Proofread

☐ Take time during the last two minutes to read through your essay. You won't have time to make major changes, but you can make some minor improvements. It's easy to skip or misspell words when you're trying to write quickly, so this step is very important.

☐ Reread your thesis statement and topic sentences for each paragraph. Make sure that they are clear. Rewrite them, if necessary.

Since the graders won't spend a long time reading your essay, it's important that the structure and organization are clear. A strong, well-written thesis statement and topic sentences that stay focused will help the graders, and your essay, stay on track.

☐ Read through your essay looking for spelling and grammar errors.

Catching glaring errors will pay off. It's important that careless mistakes don't distract the readers from the content of your essay.

☐ You can save time by crossing out and rewriting words rather than erasing. Your essay does not need to look perfect; it's more important that you have time to develop strong arguments. That said, your writing must still be legible and clear.

TRY IT OUT

Proofread the following essays, which are responses to "Class Dismissed" by Jennifer Dewey. Underline or circle any errors. Use the space provided to explain what corrections need to be made.

Student Response 1

Dewey does a good job of making the point that young teachers are leaving the profession early and our education is suffering because of this. She gets her point across using evidence and facts. Too many young teachers are leaving their jobs and we as taxpayers are paying for this loss. Also, without consistent education, kids might not get the teaching they deserve and might end up in jail later on in life. Dewey makes it clear that this isn't a good situation and something must be done about it.

A lot of sources are used in this article. The American Educational Research Association gives us data on teacher turnover rate and how it is much higher for young teachers and is higher than other professions. It was surprising to ready that "45% of young teachers leave their jobs within the first 5 years" because that's almost half of all young teachers. Hearing this makes the reader wonder about what's so bad that the teachers aren't staying at their jobs when they are young and full of energy. Dave Eggers opinion piece says that the cost of teacher turnover in the U.S. is $7.34 billion per year. That is a lot of money! That means we are paying a price for this high rate of attrition. Dewey continues Eggers' point by saying that putting back this lost money into teacher salaries "would likely lower turnover and budgetary shortfalls in the first place." It seems like a no-brainer to do this, but instead, initial teacher salaries continue to be low and many college graduates would not even consider getting into the teaching profession at this rate.

Another source from the article – *Teacher Attrition and Retention* – says that "teachers under the age of 30 are 5.32 times more likely to attrite out of the profession than those just 5 years older." This is an interesting fact and highlights the issue even more. Even math and science where there is a high demand for teachers can't seem to hold on to their young educators for very long. If these teachers only stay a year or two, what effect does this have on the students? They suffer, too. The Department of Justice and the National Education Administration says we spend more than 50% more on inmates in prison per year than on students in schools. Does this make sense? No. If teachers aren't invested in their profession, education, then we can't expect kids to be, either. With no role model to look up to, a kid might be led into a life of drugs and crime and end up in jail.

Dewey gives a lot of facts on young teacher turnover rate and she also speaks to us who are reading by using intense words and language that causes us to be concerned about the issue. She says things like "disturbing implications for future generations" and "worrisome statistic" to make us squirm and think about the issue and how it relates to our own lives. Telling us "this is not a healthy attrition" causes us to side with her and want to make a change. Nobody wants to have "severe long-term effects" on the social structure of our society. If we don't do something about it now, who is to say those turnover percentages won't be higher in the future?

Everyone knows teachers work hard and are not always paid accordingly. What some people might not realize is that lots of young teachers are not sticking around for the long-term and are leaving the schools and the students after only a couple of years. Dewey addresses this issue in this article and gives a lot of good facts, statistics, and evidence to get her point across. She uses some emotional language with her word choice, but she mostly focuses on the facts. Because these statistics are so startling, the facts are a good way to get us to see how big of an issue this is and to get us to want to make a change. As a society, we should want to put a lot of effort, time, and money into the future generation- the kids. To do that, we must focus on education and the educators who teach the kids.

Student Response 2

Besides parents and family, no one has a greater impact on a child's life than his or her teacher. Teachers are the backbone of our education system and we, as taxpayers, parents, and citizens, should have concern for the state of their profession. In her passage, "Class Dismissed", Jennifer Dewey presents an analysis on a startling trend in the teaching profession: many young teachers are leaving their jobs within the first five years of being employed. Her focus isn't primarily on the cause of this attrition rate; instead, she focuses her argument on the effect of the high teacher turnover rate on students and society. With a multitude of credible sources, supporting evidence, and persuasive appeals to both logos and pathos, Dewey is able to convince the reader that the high percentage of talented young teachers leaving the profession is a serious issue and a cause for action.

Evidence plays a key role in Dewey's argument. She cites several credible, compelling sources that reflect the gravity of the situation and alert the reader to the consequences for him or her if this trend continues. Using data from the American Educational Research Association, Dewey provides an estimated percentage of young teachers who quit teaching within the first five years. Since this percentage is close to half, 45 percent, it is easy for the reader to understand the significance of this attrition rate. To further highlight this significance, Dewey cites the same source later in the passage, finding that "…teachers under the age of 30 are 5.32 times more likely to attrite out of their profession than those just 5 years older." These numbers are relative to her argument and help to solidify her main point about teacher turnover rate being an issue for young teachers.

Appealing to logos, Dewey provides evidence from reliable sources on the effect of teacher attrition in society. She cites an opinion piece by Dave Eggers in the New York Times that gives the astonishing amount that teacher turnover costs the United States yearly, "7.34 billion." If this number isn't disturbing enough for the reader, Dewey makes sure to include the fact that this money comes from taxpayers' dollars. She proposes that "reinvesting these lost funds into teacher salaries would likely lower turnover and budgetary shortfalls in the first place." By providing a solution to this issue, she doesn't leave the reader in a depressed state; instead, she gives the reader a reason to listen and take action.

The comparison in the passage of the amount of money spent on incarcerated criminals and the amount spent on students appeals to the reader's regard to finances and to his or her role as a citizen. It also connects the issue of teacher retention with the higher rate of students ending up in jail. Data from the Department of Justice and the National Education Administration shows a problem that all citizens should be concerned about: we are paying much more for incarcerated criminals than we are for our students in public school systems. By providing this evidence, Dewey is able to make the connection that with higher teacher turnover, more students end up in jail later on in life. Furthermore, we are paying more for those students once they are in jail than we are when they are in school.

Although the amount of credible evidence in the passage strongly and fully supports the argument, the use of diction and emotional appeal provide another persuasive element. Dewey uses dramatic words and phrases, such as "disturbing implications", "worrisome statistic", "ominous truth", and "severe long-term effects" to appeal to the reader's emotions and instill a sense of urgency in the passage. Certain words and phrases that are used, "foundational role", "future generations", "ripple effects beyond the classroom", and "civic price to pay for under-educating our children" relate to all citizens. She uses an analogy of the characterization of "the shedding of deadwood" to show that the high teacher attrition rate is not a natural or healthy process. With regards to the high cost to taxpayers of incarcerating criminals to the lesser cost of paying for students, she asks a rhetorical question that plays on the role of the reader as a "good citizen." She knows that a good citizen would not agree on maintaining a prison system over improving an educational system.

In the passage, Dewey provides a multitude of valid sources with evidence to justify her argument that young teachers are leaving their professions at a high rate and this attrition is having an effect on both students and citizens as taxpayers. Through her use of sources and her use of diction, her argument is compelling and persuasive. Teachers have an important role in society and if we as citizens don't protect and promote their satisfaction in their profession, we are as much to blame for the attrition rate and lower quality of education as those who write the policies and enforce the laws.

Essay Summary

- ❑ **Do not attempt to start writing before you read the article**. A skilled response to the SAT essay assignment depends on a thorough understanding of the source text, so you must read the article before you attempt to write an essay about it.

- ❑ During your second reading of the article, you're looking for *how* the author makes the argument.

- ❑ Once you have assessed the effectiveness of the author's arguments, write a thesis based on your judgment, and expand it to create an outline.

   Your central claim should not be your opinion on the issue, but your judgment of the author's overall persuasiveness throughout the source text.

- ❑ Using your outline as a guide, spend at least half of the allotted time to write a response to the source text. Refer back to your notes on the article early and often.

- ❑ Give yourself a couple minutes to clean up spelling and punctuation errors. Don't erase! It takes too much time. Cross out mistakes and rewrite as necessary.

Essay Practice

As you read the passage below, consider how David Roberts uses

- evidence, such as facts or examples, to support claims.

- reasoning to develop ideas and to connect claims and evidence.

- stylistic or persuasive elements, such as word choice or appeals to emotion, to add power to the ideas expressed.

Adapted from David Roberts, "Climate Change is Already Happening."

Used with permission of Popular Science Copyright© 2015. All rights reserved. Originally published July 2012

1   There is no longer any question of preventing climate change. Some 98 percent of working climate scientists agree that the atmosphere is already warming in response to human greenhouse-gas emissions, and the most recent research suggests that we are on a path toward what were once considered "worst case" scenarios.

2   How much warmer must it get before things really go to hell? "Climate sensitivity" remains a subject of intense investigation, and what counts as hellish is a matter of judgment, but United Nations climate negotiators have settled on a goal to limit atmospheric carbon dioxide to 450 parts per million, which would cause the global mean temperature to peak no more than 3.6°F above preindustrial levels. If it gets much hotter than that, we will most likely be confronted by levels of drought and severe storms for which humanity has no precedent. That sounds bad enough—and indeed, postindustrial temperatures have already risen by as much as 1.6°—but there's increasing reason to believe, as James Hansen and many other climate scientists do, that severe effects will arrive well below 450 ppm, and possibly below today's level of 396 ppm. Danger is much closer than we thought.

3   We will almost certainly blow past 3.6° in any case. One recent study found that the average global temperature would rise another 3.2° by the end of the century even if human carbon emissions dropped to zero tomorrow, a scenario that is, of course, extremely unlikely. Simply limiting the temperature rise to twice the "safe" level would require heroic, sustained global effort, a level of ambition that appears nowhere in evidence. And if humanity does nothing to restrain climate pollution, the trajectory it's on right now could carry the rise to as much as 10° within the century.

4   In 2009, researchers from the University of Oxford, the Tyndall Center for Climate Change Research and the U.K. Met Office Hadley Center organized a conference on what a change of 7.2° or greater might look like—oddly, one of the first concerted scientific examinations of the impacts of temperatures that high. Here are some of the results: 7.2°, which could conceivably arrive as early as 2060, would mean a planet that was hotter than at any time in the past 10 million years. By 2100, sea levels would rise by as much as six feet, leaving hundreds of millions of the world's coast-dwellers homeless, even as huge swaths of the ocean itself became "dead zones." Glaciers and coral reefs

would largely vanish from the planet.

5   We no longer have a choice about whether to confront major changes already in the works. By the end of this century, sea levels will rise, drought will spread, and millions of animals, human and otherwise, will be driven from their homes. Scientists call the process of preparing for these changes "adaptation," but a more apt term can be found in the tech world: ruggedizing. Greater extremes require tougher, more resilient societies.

6   It may be possible to weather this onslaught if we begin preparing now, by building low-carbon, high-density cities away from the coasts, radically improving the efficiency of water and energy systems, boosting local and global emergency-response capacities, and adjusting to a less consumption- and waste- oriented lifestyle. But although humans are an ingenious species, some changes simply exceed any realistic capacity for adaptation. The real threat, the existential threat, is that climate change will gain so much momentum that humanity loses what remaining power it has to slow or stop it, even by reducing carbon emissions to zero. If change becomes self-sustaining, our children and grandchildren will inherit an atmosphere irreversibly out of control, with inexorably rising temperatures that could, according to one recent study, render half of Earth's currently occupied land uninhabitable—literally too hot to bear—by 2300.

7   These are stark and discomforting findings. Above all, they suggest that global temperature should be held as low as is still possible, at virtually any cost. But they also make clear that some changes are inevitable. We no longer have a choice between mitigating climate change and adapting to climate change. We must do both.

Write an essay in which you explain how David Roberts builds an argument to persuade his audience that urgent responses to climate change are necessary. In your essay, analyze how Roberts uses one or more of the features listed in the box above (or features of your own choice) to strengthen the logic and persuasiveness of his argument. Be sure that your analysis focuses on the most relevant features of the passage.

Your essay should not explain whether you agree with Roberts' claims, but rather explain how Roberts builds an argument to persuade his audience.

PLANNING PAGE   You may plan your essay in the unlined planning space below, but only use the lined pages following this one to write your essay. Any work on this planning page will not be scored.

Use the next 4 pages for your ESSAY ⟶

FOR PLANNING ONLY

Use the next 4 pages for your ESSAY ⟶

As you read the passage below, consider how Rolf Sander uses

- evidence, such as facts or examples, to support claims.

- reasoning to develop ideas and to connect claims and evidence.

- stylistic or persuasive elements, such as word choice or appeals to emotion, to add power to the ideas expressed.

Adapted from Rolf Sander, "The Vicious Circle of Recycling."

1   Last week, when the North Carolina House of Representatives spent 30 minutes considering House Bill 430, taxpayers came very close to footing another type of bill: high fees for an unwanted program. The proposed legislation, which was postponed for further amendments, would permit county commissioners to create recycling collection programs and charge fees that reflect the costs of this service. There are several problems with this, not the least of which is that under the proposal, all households would pay the same fee regardless of how much they recycle.

2   Of course, it's not fair to charge people for something they don't need, didn't ask for, and may not use even if they required to pay for it. Both environmentalists and the recycling industry itself would have you believe that recycling is a no-brainer. But before our government forces us to pay for the enormous amount of infrastructure that recycling requires, we owe it to ourselves to ask a few reasonable questions: How does the recycling process work, exactly? How much good does it do us, and is it worth the high costs?

3   Most people who recycle honestly have no idea why they do it, besides the general idea that it somehow saves the planet. If we don't put plastics and paper into landfills, the argument goes, then we'll save the earth and money, too – because we'll transform the garbage into new products. However, this presumption isn't very well-grounded in reality. The truth is that recycling common consumer goods is not only very expensive, but it also does quite a bit of damage to the environment.

4   The recycling process is so expensive due to the sheer number of steps required to transform waste into new consumer goods. Recycled paper, for instance, isn't just made from mashed-up bits of old paper; it's also treated with bleach and other toxic chemicals, and the many processing stages of cleaning and rinsing use tremendous amounts of water. In places like the Southwest, where land is cheap but fresh water is precious, recycling really only serves to alleviate human guilt – it certainly doesn't help thirsty local plants.

5   For this sense of environmental consciousness, the taxpayer foots quite a high bill. According to Professor Daniel K. Benjamin of the Property and Environmental Resource Center (PERC), the current models of government-subsidized recycling programs simply aren't cost-effective. When Benjamin compared the prices of landfill disposal, standard recycling systems, and state-of-the-art recycling programs, he found that landfill disposal averaged $119 per ton. State-of-the-art recycling programs averaged costs of $199 per ton, even after factoring in government subsidies and revenues from resold recycled material.

6   Increased water usage and high monetary costs aren't even the worst of it: recent studies for the National Institute of Health indicate that the "organic" chemicals used to recycle plastics may in fact be harmful to children. A 2014 study found both flame retardants and plasticizers in a variety of children's toys made from recycled plastics. Inexplicably, the content levels of plasticizer were not high enough to significantly increase flexibility or durability, and the levels of flame retardant were not high enough to significantly reduce flammability. However, the levels of both chemicals were high enough to cause health concerns. And yet, many parents are still attracted to packaging which bears the "made from recycled material" logo. It's only the environmentally-conscious thing to do, right? Wrong.

7   Although many householders think that they're helping to do their part, many are actually inadvertently raising the costs and slowing the effectiveness of recycling programs through sheer ignorance. For instance, many don't know that containers have to be washed and stripped of labels before they can be recycled – and some types can't be recycled at all, including cardboard pizza boxes and other paper food containers. If the consumer doesn't sort, strip, and clean at home, it has to be done at the facility, where the volume to sort is simply enormous. If improper materials get through, they could contaminate an entire batch of raw plastic and generate even more waste. What's the solution – public awareness campaigns? Those, of course, would come out of the taxpayer's pocket, and it wouldn't necessarily solve the problem.

8   Although noble intent drives our desire to recycle, we should be pragmatic about any taxpayer-funded infrastructure. It's not enough to simply want to save the environment; we have to ask whether the systems we've built are actually helping. If we've done our best to make recycling viable but have failed nevertheless, it's time to put our hard-earned money into other programs that actually make a difference.

Write an essay in which you explain how Rolf Sander builds an argument to persuade his audience that recycling causes more harm than good. In your essay, analyze how Sander uses one or more of the features listed in the box above (or features of your own choice) to strengthen the logic and persuasiveness of his argument. Be sure that your analysis focuses on the most relevant features of the passage.

Your essay should not explain whether you agree with Sander's claims, but rather explain how Sander builds an argument to persuade his audience.

PLANNING PAGE   You may plan your essay in the unlined planning space below, but only use the lined pages following this one to write your essay. Any work on this planning page will not be scored.

Use the next 4 pages for your ESSAY ⟶

FOR
PLANNING
ONLY

Use the next 4 pages for your ESSAY ⟶

As you read the passage below, consider how Elie Wiesel uses

- evidence, such as facts or examples, to support claims.

- reasoning to develop ideas and to connect claims and evidence.

- stylistic or persuasive elements, such as word choice or appeals to emotion, to add power to the ideas expressed.

Adapted from Elie Wiesel, "The Perils of Indifference: Lessons Learned from a Violent Century." The speech was delivered at the White House in Washington, D.C. on April 12, 1999.

1   Fifty-four years ago to the day, a young Jewish boy from a small town in the Carpathian Mountains woke up in a place of eternal infamy called Buchenwald[1]. Liberated a day earlier by American soldiers, he remembers their rage at what they saw. Though he did not understand their language, their eyes told him what he needed to know – that they, too, would remember, and bear witness.

2   We are on the threshold of a new century, a new millennium. What will the legacy of this vanishing century be? How will it be remembered in the new millennium? Surely it will be judged, and judged severely, in both moral and metaphysical terms. These failures have cast a dark shadow over humanity: two World Wars, countless civil wars, the senseless chain of assassinations (Gandhi, the Kennedys, Martin Luther King, Sadat, Rabin), bloodbaths in Cambodia and Algeria, India and Pakistan, Ireland and Rwanda, Eritrea and Ethiopia, Sarajevo and Kosovo; the inhumanity in the gulag and the tragedy of Hiroshima. And, on a different level, of course, Auschwitz and Treblinka. So much violence; so much indifference.

3   What is indifference? Etymologically, the word means "no difference." A strange and unnatural state in which the lines blur between light and darkness, dusk and dawn, crime and punishment, cruelty and compassion, good and evil. What are its courses and inescapable consequences? Is it a philosophy? Is ta philosophy of indifference conceivable? Can one possibly view indifference as a virtue? Is it necessary at times to practice it simply to keep one's sanity, live normally, enjoy a fine meal and a glass of wine, as the world around us experiences harrowing upheavals?

4   Of course, indifference can be tempting – more than that, seductive. It is so much easier to look away from victims. It is so much easier to avoid such rude interruptions to our work, our dreams, our hopes. It is, after all, awkward, troublesome, to be involved in another person's pain and despair. Yet, for the person who is indifferent, his or her neighbor are of no consequence. And, therefore, their lives are meaningless. Their hidden or even visible anguish is of no interest. Indifference reduces the Other to an abstraction.

5   Over there, behind the black gates of Auschwitz[2], the most tragic of all prisoners were the "Muselmanner," as they were called. Wrapped in their torn blankets, they would sit or lie

---

[1] One of the first and largest Nazi concentration camps
[2] A Polish town which was the site of several Nazi concentration and death camps

on the ground, staring vacantly into space, unaware of who or where they were – strangers to their surroundings. They no longer felt pain, hunger, thirst. They feared nothing. They felt nothing. They were dead and did not know it.

6   In a way, to be indifferent to that suffering is what makes the human being inhuman. Indifference, after all, is more dangerous than anger and hatred. Anger can at times be creative. One writes a great poem, a great symphony. One does something special for the sake of humanity because one is angry at the injustice that one witnesses. But indifference is never creative. Even hatred at times may elicit a response. You fight it. You denounce it. You disarm it.

7   Indifference elicits no response. Indifference is not a response. Indifference is not a beginning; it is an end. And, therefore, indifference is always the friend of the enemy, for it benefits the aggressor – never his victim, whose pain is magnified when he or she feels forgotten. The political prisoner in his cell, the hungry children, the homeless refugees – not to respond to their plight, not to relieve their solitude by offering them a spark of hope is to exile them from human memory. And in denying their humanity, we betray our own.

8   Indifference, then, is not only a sin, it is a punishment. And this is one of the most important lessons of this outgoing century's wide-ranging experiments in good and evil. When adults wage war, children perish. Oh, we see them on television, we read about them in the papers, and we do so with a broken heart. We see their faces, their eyes. Do we hear their pleas? Do we feel their pain, their agony? Every minute one of them dies of disease, violence, famine. Some of them – so many of them – could be saved.

9   And so, once again, I think of the young Jewish boy from the Carpathian Mountains. He has accompanied the old man I have become throughout these years of quest and struggle. And together we walk towards the new millennium, carried by profound fear and extraordinary hope.

Write an essay in which you explain how Elie Wiesel builds an argument to persuade his audience that indifference presents a grave danger. In your essay, analyze how Wiesel uses one or more of the features listed in the box above (or features of your own choice) to strengthen the logic and persuasiveness of his argument. Be sure that your analysis focuses on the most relevant features of the passage.

Your essay should not explain whether you agree with Wiesel's claims, but rather explain how Wiesel builds an argument to persuade his audience.

PLANNING PAGE   You may plan your essay in the unlined planning space below, but only use the lined pages following this one to write your essay. Any work on this planning page will not be scored.

Use the next 4 pages for your ESSAY ⟶

FOR
PLANNING
ONLY

Use the next 4 pages for your ESSAY ⟶

SUMMIT
EDUCATIONAL
GROUP

Answer Key

READING

Reading at a Higher Level

p. 19 Put It Together

1. D
2. B
3. C
4. B

Active Reading

p. 21 Try It Out

1. Biologists and weather researchers are teaming up to study bats, which are facing various threats.
2. Radar stations gather a lot of data, including data on bats.
3. Radar data archives include vast amounts of information on bats.
4. Radar data is useful, but more research needs to be done to better interpret this data.
5. The study of bats is important and radar imagery offers an unlikely but useful source of data.

Anticipating the Answer

p. 23

As it is used in context, the phrase "they are not technically alive" means that viruses cannot reproduce like other living creatures can.

A

p. 26 Put It Together

1. B
2. A
3. B
4. D
5. A
6. C
7. A
8. C
9. C
10. A
11. C

Process of Elimination

p. 29

A – No evidence

B – Yes, he is driving at night, but not being kept up by cars

C – He does not talk about the daytime

D - CORRECT

p. 30 Put It Together

1. A
2. A
3. C
4. D
5. D
6. A
7. A
8. D

Checkpoint Review – p. 32

1. C
2. A
3. B
4. A
5. D
6. B
7. D
8. D
9. D
10. D

Detail

p. 35 Put It Together

1. B
2. C

Main Idea

p. 37 Put It Together

1. C
2. C

Words in Context

p. 39 Put It Together

1. B
2. D

Inference and Analogous Reading

p. 41 Put It Together

1. A
2. C

Evidence

p. 43 Put It Together

1. D
2. D

Point of View

p. 45 Put It Together

1. C

Purpose
p. 47 Put It Together
1. C
2. C

Structure
p. 49 Put It Together
1. A

Word Choice
p. 51 Put It Together
1. B
2. A

Data Graphics
p. 53 Put It Together
1. C
2. C

Paired Passages
p. 55 Put It Together
1. D
2. C
3. B
4. A
5. A
6. A
7. C
8. D
9. B
10. A
11. A

Reading Practice
p. 62

Passage 1
1. she finds her mother's feeling difficult to read.
2. ties the mother and daughter together.
3. she disapproves of her daughter's decision.
4. lines 33-35
5. A
6. B
7. C
8. C
9. D
10. D
11. D

Passage 2
12. C
13. B
14. preserved a record of hitherto unsuspected species.
15. the fossils did not belong in the groups to which Walcott assigned them.
16. A
17. D
18. C
19. A
20. D
21. A
22. D

Passage 3
23. C
24. B
25. indicate the Henshawes' wealth.
26. favors.
27. A
28. B
29. C
30. he would relieve her from her anxious encounter with Myra.
31. D
32. B

Passage 4
33. D
34. B
35. A
36. D
37. D
38. A
39. C
40. A
41. C
42. B
43. A

Passage 5
44. A
45. D
46. B
47. D
48. C
49. B
50. A
51. D
52. C
53. C
54. B

Passage 6
55. A
56. C
57. D
58. C
59. B
60. A
61. D
62. B
63. D
64. D
65. B

Passage 7
66. B
67. C
68. D
69. A
70. A
71. D
72. C
73. C
74. C
75. C
76. B

Passage 8
77. D
78. C
79. D
80. C
81. D
82. C
83. B
84. C
85. C
86. C
87. D

Passage 9
88. B
89. C
90. C
91. B
92. A
93. A
94. A
95. B
96. C
97. C
98. A

Passage 10
99. B
100. A
101. C
102. A
103. D
104. A
105. B
106. D
107. B
108. A

Passage 11
109. C
110. C
111. D
112. A
113. A
114. A
115. C
116. D
117. D
118. A

WRITING

General Tips
p. 104
> D
> D
> D
> "attitude of genuine interest"

Pronouns
p. 108
> its
> ...as the captains.
> the governor had not...
> me
> me
> who
> who
> its
> you

p. 111 Put It Together
1. A
2. B
3. C
4. D
5. D

Subject-Verb Agreement
p. 112
> was
> cause
> are
> are
> wants

p. 113 Put It Together
1. B
2. B
3. C
4. B
5. A

Comparisons
p. 114
> the stories of most children.
> any other boy in his class
> least
> quicker

p. 115 Put It Together
1. A
2. D
3. A

Idioms
p. 116
> in
> of

p. 117 Put It Together
1. A
2. B
3. D

Diction
p. 118
> except
> accept
> affect
> effect
> than
> then
> loose
> lose
> lay
> lie
> lead
> led
> principle
> principal
> number
> amount
> fewer
> less
> between
> among

p. 119 Put It Together
1. C
2. C
3. A
4. B
5. A

Fragments

p. 120

...decided to acquire...

Severe drought conditions caused...

p. 121 Put It Together
1. C
2. C
3. D

Run-Ons

p. 122

... and I've learned a lot from her

...Eurotunnel, which was close...

p. 123 Put It Together
1. D
2. D
3. A

Conjunctions

p. 124

but

Because

but also

P. 125 Put It Together
1. A
2. B
3. B
4. D

Parallelism

p. 126

shared responsibilities

supervision of two employees

assistance in food preparation

to betray your country

p. 127 Put It Together
1. D
2. B
3. D

Modifiers

p. 128

Lyme disease is often difficult for doctors to diagnose.

smashed flat

hamburger

Big Dog sniffed at what was left of the half-eaten hamburger, which had been smashed flat by a passing truck.

p. 129 Put It Together
1. B
2. B

Verb Tense

p. 130

has stood

p. 131 Put It Together
1. B
2. B
3. A

Semicolons and Colons

p. 132

; it made...

...deployed, but...

...innovations in many...

p. 133 Put It Together
1. C
2. D
3. D

Commas

p. 134

After the heavy rain, frogs...

...originated in Italy, but the fruit...

...cake recipes, my parents, and Ben Franklin.

p. 135 Put It Together
1. C
2. D
3. C
4. C
5. B

Apostrophes
p. 136
Children's
hers
theirs

p. 137 Put It Together
1. B
2. A
3. C

Main Idea
p. 138
The English language does not have a word for every idea.
Each language is largely a product of the culture from which it originates.
The information about online databases can be removed.

p. 139 Put It Together
1. B
2. D

Addition
p. 140
After 2nd sentence

p. 141 Put It Together
1. D
2. B

Deletion
p. 142
6

p. 143 Put It Together
1. A
2. B

Organization
p. 144
2, 3, 1

p. 145 Put It Together
1. C
2. A
3. D

Transitions
p. 146
Therefore
indeed
however
nevertheless

p. 147 Put It Together
1. A
2. A
3. A
4. A

Wordiness
p. 148
...he is the most popular.
...makes an analysis...
...as greedy, people rush...

p. 149 Put It Together
1. D
2. D
3. D

Style
p. 150
established
develop
formidable

p. 151 Put It Together
1. B
2. A
3. B
4. A
5. B

Data Graphics
p. 153 Put It Together
1. B
2. A

Writing and Language Practice – p. 162

PASSAGE 1

1.	B
2.	D
3.	A
4.	B
5.	D
6.	C
7.	D
8.	A
9.	C
10.	D
11.	D

PASSAGE 2

12.	C
13.	B
14.	B
15.	A
16.	D
17.	D
18.	A
19.	B
20.	C
21.	B
22.	D

PASSAGE 3

23.	D
24.	D
25.	D
26.	A
27.	D
28.	B
29.	C
30.	B
31.	B
32.	A
33.	D

PASSAGE 4

34.	C
35.	A
36.	A
37.	B
38.	B
39.	C
40.	A
41.	D
42.	B
43.	D
44.	C

PASSAGE 5

45.	B
46.	A
47.	A
48.	C
49.	C
50.	A
51.	B
52.	D
53.	D
54.	B
55.	B

PASSAGE 6

56.	B
57.	C
58.	A
59.	C
60.	D
61.	A
62.	B
63.	C
64.	A
65.	D
66.	A

PASSAGE 7

67.	D
68.	A
69.	B
70.	C
71.	D
72.	B
73.	D
74.	A
75.	C
76.	C
77.	B

PASSAGE 8

78.	D
79.	A
80.	A
81.	B
82.	A
83.	C
84.	C
85.	C
86.	C
87.	B
88.	C

PASSAGE 9

89.	A
90.	B
91.	D
92.	C
93.	C
94.	A
95.	D
96.	A
97.	D
98.	B
99.	B

PASSAGE 10

100.	C
101.	B
102.	D
103.	A
104.	B
105.	C
106.	C
107.	B
108.	D
109.	C
110.	C

PASSAGE 11

111.	D
112.	C
113.	A
114.	D
115.	C
116.	B
117.	C
118.	A
119.	B
120.	B
121.	A

PASSAGE 12

122.	D
123.	B
124.	D
125.	A
126.	B
127.	B
128.	A
129.	A
130.	C
131.	D
132.	C

ESSAY

Reading the Source Text
p. 213 Try It Out
1. Noise pollution should be reduced.
2. Paragraph 3: "We cannot simply ignore the public health risks of noise pollution."
3. We are coming to accept noise pollution as normal, but we should not do so.
4. Elevated noise levels are unnatural and dangerous.
5. Health organizations agree that noise pollution poses long-term health risks.
6. Noise pollution also hurts bats, which in turn hurts the agricultural industry and the environment.
7. Natural quiet helps human beings think and create.
8. If we structure government policy correctly, we can reduce noise pollution.

Analysis - Evidence
p. 217 Try It Out
1. We can only appreciate beautiful natural sounds if we reduce noise pollution.
2. The claims about "hunter-gatherers" and "modern urban dwellers" are generalizations. This is weak, non-specific evidence.
3. There are multiple pieces of data-based evidence. The EPA evidence is summarized, the WHO's researcher is quoted directly, and the statistic about coronary heart disease is unattributed.
4. 3 types: data-based evidence is quoted, but the source is unnamed. The author then makes an uncited generalization about bats' positive economic influence, and poses a hypothetical negative scenario.
5. The data-based evidence is the strongest, but there is more weak and non-specific evidence in the article than strong and specific evidence.

Analysis - Reasoning
p. 221 Try It Out
1. Premise 1: "bats… have difficulty locating [food] within hearing range of road noise. Premise 2: bats save farmers money by preying upon pests.
   Conclusion: "[as the result of these bats' difficulty], we face the prospect of increased food prices and lowered water quality."
2. This is a slippery slope argument: If bats cannot hunt prey, then farmers must use more pesticides; if farmers use more pesticides, then water quality and food costs suffer. This reasoning is weak: how much of America's farmland is inhabited by bats? How much of it is within hearing range of road noise? Do farmers use pesticides regardless, to combat pests that bats do not consume?
3. The author implies that Mozart would not have been able to compose music, and Darwin would not have been able to develop the theory of evolution, if they had been subject to noise pollution.
   The author then poses a hypothetical question which implies that current levels of noise pollution has prevented us, and will prevent our children, from attaining Mozart's and Darwin's levels of genius.
4. This is an appeal to fear: if we do not reduce noise pollution, then we will prevent ourselves and our children from developing potential genius.
5. The author appeals to fear in every paragraph except the last:
   • fear of "[accepting] an incessant bombardment of unwanted noise,"
   • fear of "dangerous" sound levels,
   • fear of "public health risks,"
   • fear of "increased food prices and lowered water quality," and
   • fear of stunting our potential genius.
   Each specific fear is framed with some type of evidence; some are concrete but most are non-specific.
   However, this organization is powerful because it allows the author to lead up to a final paragraph in which there is hope – and that hope is in the author's proposed "well-informed policy."

Analysis – Stylistic & Persuasive Elements

p. 225 Try It Out

1. The author uses romantic and nostalgic language to describe his childhood camping memories. He returns to this imagery in the final two paragraphs, first to evoke fear that the beauty of the campgrounds is disappearing and then to evoke hope that it can be maintained. This creates the overall impression that we have been losing something valuable over time and we must fight to save it.

2. The author anthropomorphizes his childhood campground: silence is "patient," the conifers "whisper," and "the earth comes back to life".
   By contrast, noise is a "bombardment" destroying "crucial quietude".

3. In paragraph 3, the author chooses words that make non-conclusive data sound more threatening than is necessary: "In Europe <u>alone</u>, long-term exposure to traffic noise <u>may contribute to</u> <u>as many as</u> 210,000 coronary heart disease deaths per year." Although the cause of the deaths is not clear, the author uses words that allow him to draw a correlation and use the highest number possible. Then the author calls to action: "we cannot simply ignore the public health risks."
   In paragraph 4, the author provides evidence only about bats, yet introduces the paragraph by implying risk to "the greater ecosystem." The study which the author cites does not explicitly say what the effects will be, calling them only "complex" – and yet the author cautions us that the cost of food will rise and the quality of water will drop.

4. In paragraph 5, the author appeals to both fear and vanity. First, he leads urban dwellers to wonder if they could have been geniuses like Mozart or Darwin if we hadn't been bothered by noise pollution. Second, he leads parents to fear that they are holding their children back from potential brilliance. This primes the reader to accept his proposals for change in the final paragraph.

Writing Effectively

p. 240 Try It Out

He expressed his thoughts in an unnatural way.
You should be skeptical of his opinions.

Proofread

p. 242 Try It Out

Student Response 1

makes

Dewey does a good job of making the point that young teachers are leaving the profession early and our education is suffering because of this. She ~~gets~~ her point ~~across using~~ evidence and facts~~:~~ ~~too many young teachers are leaving their jobs,~~ and we as taxpayers are paying for this loss~~,~~ ~~Also, without consistent education,~~ **and** kids might not get the teaching they deserve ~~and might end up in jail later on in life~~. Dewey makes it clear that this isn't a good situation and something must be done about it.

(margin right: with)

Many

they are

why

informal

obvious

~~A lot of~~ sources are used in this article. The American Educational Research Association gives us data on teacher turnover ~~rate~~**s** and how ~~it~~ ~~is~~ **both** much higher for young teachers and is **also** higher than **in** other professions. It was surprising to read~~y~~ that "45% of young teachers leave their jobs within the first 5 years~~,~~" because that's almost half of all young teachers. Hearing this makes the reader wonder ~~about what's so bad that the~~ teachers aren't staying at their jobs when they are young and full of energy. Dave Eggers~~'~~ opinion piece says that the cost of teacher turnover in the U.S. is $7.34 billion per year. *~~That is a lot of money!~~* That means we are paying a price for this high rate of attrition. Dewey continues Eggers' point by saying that putting back this lost money into teacher salaries "would likely lower turnover and budgetary shortfalls in the first place." It seems ~~like a no-brainer~~ to do this, but instead, initial teacher salaries continue to be low and many college graduates would not even consider getting into the teaching profession at this rate.

which have

According to

provides

many

statistics

Another source from the article – *Teacher Attrition and Retention* – says that "teachers under the age of 30 are 5.32 times more likely to attrite out of the profession than those just 5 years older." ~~This is an interesting fact and highlights the issue even more.~~ Even math and science ~~programs,~~ **where there is a** high demand**s** for teachers~~,~~ can't seem to hold on to their young educators for very long. If these teachers only stay a year or two, what **affect** does this have on the students? They suffer, too. ~~The~~-Department of Justice and the National Education Administration **data,** ~~we~~ spend**s** more than twice as much on inmates in prison per year than on students in its schools. Does this make sense? No. If teachers aren't invested in their profession, ~~education,~~ then we can't expect kids to be **invested**, either. With no role model to look up to, a kid might be led into a life of drugs and crime and end up in jail.

Dewey ~~gives a lot of facts~~ on young teacher turnover ~~rate~~**s** and she also speaks to ~~us who are reading~~ by using intense words and

(margin right: New York)

(margin right: the reader)

language that causes ~~us to be~~ concerned ~~about the issue~~. She ~~says things~~ like "disturbing implications for future generations" and "worrisome statistic" to make us squirm and think about ~~the issue and~~ how ~~it~~ relates to our own lives. Telling us **that** "this is not a healthy attrition" causes us to ~~side with her and~~ want to make a change. Nobody wants ~~to have~~ "severe long-term effects" ~~on the social structure of our society~~. If we don't do something about it now, who is to say those turnover percentages won't be higher in the future? ~~Everyone knows~~ <u>T</u>eachers work hard and are not always paid accordingly. What some people might not realize is that lots of young teachers are ~~not sticking around for the long-term and are~~ leaving ~~the schools and the students~~ after only a couple of years. Dewey addresses this issue in this article, ~~and gives a lot of good facts, statistics, and~~ evidence to get her point across. She uses some emotional language with her word choice, but she mostly focuses on the facts. Because these statistics are so startling, the facts are a good way to ~~get us to see how big of an issue this is and to get us to want~~ to make a change. As a society, we should want to put a lot of effort, time, and money into ~~the~~ future generation**s** ~~–the kids~~. To do that, we must focus on ~~education and~~ the educators ~~who teach the kids~~.

Margin annotations:
- the issue
- uses phrases
- to this social problem
- providing
- persuade her audience

Student Response 2

Besides parents and family, no one has a greater impact on a child's life than his or her teacher. Teachers are the backbone of our education system and we, as taxpayers, parents, and citizens, should have concern for the state of their profession. In ~~her passage,~~ "Class Dismissed", Jennifer Dewey ~~presents an analysis on~~ a startling trend in the **analyzes** teaching profession: many young teachers are leaving their jobs within the first five years of being employed. Her focus isn't primarily on the cause of this attrition rate; instead, she focuses her argument on the effect of the high teacher turnover rate on students and society. With a multitude of credible sources, supporting evidence, and persuasive appeals to both logos and pathos, Dewey ~~is able to~~ convince<u>s</u> the reader that the high percentage of talented young teachers leaving the profession is a serious issue and a cause for action.

Evidence plays a key role in Dewey's argument. She cites several credible, compelling sources that reflect the gravity of the situation and alert the reader to the consequences ~~for him or her~~ if this trend continues. Using data from the American Educational Research Association, Dewey provides an estimated percentage of young teachers who quit teaching within the first five years. Since this percentage is **45%,** close to half, ~~45 percent,~~ it is easy for the reader to understand the significance of this attrition rate. To further highlight this significance, Dewey cites the same source later in the passage, finding that "...teachers under the age of 30 are 5.32 times more likely to attrite out of their profession than those just 5 years older." These numbers ~~are relative to her argument and~~ help to solidify her main point about teacher turnover rate being an issue for young teachers.

Appealing to logos, Dewey provides evidence from reliable sources on the effect of teacher attrition in society. She cites an opinion piece by Dave Eggers in the New York Times that gives the astonishing **statistic** ~~amount~~ that <u>"[teacher] turnover costs the United States ~~yearly~~ $7.34 billion **yearly**</u>." If this number isn't disturbing enough for the reader, Dewey makes sure to include the fact that this money comes from taxpayers' dollars. She proposes that "reinvesting these lost funds into teacher salaries would likely lower turnover and budgetary shortfalls in the first place." By providing a solution to this issue, she ~~doesn't leave the reader in a depressed state; instead, she~~ gives the reader a reason to listen and take action.

Dewey's ~~The~~ comparison ~~in the passage~~ of the amount of money spent on incarcerated criminals **~~and~~** the amount spent on students appeals to the **to** reader's ~~regard to finances and to his or her~~ role as a citizen. It also connects the issue of teacher retention with the higher rate of students ending up in jail. Data from the Department of Justice and the National Education Administration shows a problem that all citizens should be concerned about: we are paying much more for incarcerated criminals than we are for our students in public school systems. By providing this evidence, Dewey is able to make the connection that with higher teacher turnover, more students end up in jail later on in life. Furthermore, we are paying more for those students once they are in jail than we are when they are in school.

Although the amount of credible evidence in the passage strongly and fully supports the argument, the use of diction and emotional appeal provide another persuasive element. Dewey uses dramatic words and phrases, such as "disturbing implications", "worrisome statistic", "ominous truth", and "severe long-term effects" to appeal to the reader's emotions and instill a sense of urgency in the passage. ~~Certain~~ ~~words~~ **Other**

such as ~~and~~ phrases**,** ~~that are used,~~ "foundational role", "future generations", "ripple effects beyond the classroom", and "civic price to pay for under-educating our children," relate to all citizens. She uses ~~an~~ analogy of ~~the~~ **the** ~~characterization of~~ "the shedding of deadwood" to show that the high teacher attrition rate is not a natural or healthy process. ~~With regards~~ **By comparing**

~~to~~ the high cost ~~to taxpayers~~ of incarcerating criminals to the lesser cost

education of ~~paying for students~~, she asks a rhetorical question that plays on the role of the reader as a "good citizen." She knows that a good citizen

prefer to would not ~~agree on~~ maintaining a prison system ~~over improving~~ **rather than** an educational system. **improve**

~~In the passage,~~ Dewey provides a multitude ~~of valid sources with~~ evidence to justify her argument that young teachers are leaving their professions at a high rate and **that** this attrition is having an effect on both students and ~~citizens as~~ taxpayers. Through her use of sources and

She crafts a ~~her use of~~ diction, ~~her argument is~~ compelling and persuasive **argument**. Teachers have an important role in society**,** and if we as citizens don't protect and promote their **professional** satisfaction ~~in~~ ~~their profession~~, we are as much to blame for the attrition rate and lower quality of education as those who write the policies and enforce the laws.

Test Week Checklist

Week of the Test

❑ You worked hard. Feel confident that you are prepared for the test. If you want to study more, review the Chapter Summaries, but do not try to cram at the last minute. By now, you know what you know.

❑ Take it easy, and get good sleep throughout the week. You want to be well rested for test day.

❑ If you are not testing at your own school, make sure you know where you're going. Don't rely on an online mapping program the morning of the test. If you need to, take a test run the weekend before.

Friday night

❑ Again, you know what you know. Do something relaxing and fun.

❑ Lay out everything you need to bring with you:

- Your admission ticket

- Official photo ID

- 3 or 4 sharpened No. 2 pencils with erasers

- Approved calculator with new batteries (check the College Board website for a list of approved calculator models)

- Watch

- Water (the College Board allows you to bring a clear bottle with the label removed)

- A small snack that won't get your hands sticky

❑ Visualize success. See yourself solving question after question. Envision completing the last question, putting your pencil down, and closing the test booklet. Let yourself feel the good feeling of a job well done.

❑ Go to sleep at the same time you've been going to sleep all week. Otherwise, you'll just toss and turn. Don't worry if you have trouble sleeping. You'll have plenty of adrenaline to keep your brain going during the test.

Test Week Checklist

Morning of the Test

❏ Have a backup alarm – either another clock or a parent.

❏ Eat a good breakfast. Make sure to avoid heavy, fatty foods.

❏ Do something easy that you enjoy (take a walk or listen to music). You want to go into the test awake and upbeat.

At the Test

❏ Arrive early to the test center to find your room and settle in.

❏ Make sure to use the bathroom before you start the test. You only have a few short breaks during the test; you don't want to have to worry about a line at the restroom.

❏ Find your seat and sit for a minute. Continue to visualize yourself working successfully through the test, using all of the skills and strategies you've learned. You're ready!

❏ During breaks, stand up and walk around. It helps you to stay focused.

❏ Pace yourself and keep your eye on the clock.

❏ If you start losing focus, try this concentration exercise: Every five questions, put down your pencil, stare at the ceiling, blink a few times, take several deep, slow breaths and then continue with the next five questions.

After the Test

❏ Plan to do something positive and fun. You deserve it!